Christ Is My Life

Christ
Is My Life

(Philippians 1:21)

Jesús Colina

Director of Zenit News Agency

interviews

Marcial Maciel

Founder of Regnum Christi
and the Legionaries of Christ

SOPHIA INSTITUTE PRESS®

Manchester, New Hampshire

Sophia Institute Press®
Box 5284, Manchester, NH 03108
1-800-888-9344
www.sophiainstitute.com

Library of Congress Cataloging-in-Publication Data

Maciel, Marcial, 1920-
    Christ is my life.
        p. cm.
    "Interview with the founder of the Legionaries of Christ
and the Regnum Christi Movement".
    Includes index.
    ISBN 1-928832-97-0 (pbk. : alk. paper)
    1. Maciel, Marcial, 1920 — Interviews. 2. Catholic
Church — Clergy — Interviews. 3. Regnum Christi
(Organization) 4. Legion of Christ. I. Title.

BX4705.M1276 A5 2003
271'.79 — dc21   2003009918

03 04 05 06 07 08 09 10 9 8 7 6 5 4 3 2 1

Love for our Church:
  love that keeps watch,
  fights,
  forgives,
  extols,
  love that senses our Mother's heartbeats,
  meditates on her in faith,
  accepts her in obedience,
  expands her in apostolate,
  and makes her holy in our lives.

Marcial Maciel, LC

Contents

Foreword

In recent decades the Catholic Church has witnessed an utterly unexpected phenomenon: the birth and extraordinary growth, especially since Vatican II, of new movements and religious communities. No sociologist or theologian foretold them, and in them millions of people from all social and cultural origins, from every continent and all states of life, have embarked on the thrilling path of the gospel.

As the Rome correspondent for a number of journals since 1992 I have come into contact with a good percentage of these movements, and I have met several of the men and women who founded or initiated them. I have often asked myself what has caused the Church's "new springtime," to use John Paul II's words. How do you explain it? What enables so many young men and women with promising careers, full of dreams, to lay aside the seductive offers of our consumer society and consecrate their lives in poverty, chastity, and obedience, or face the difficult challenge of "living in the world without being of the world"? The explanations my colleagues sometimes gave in their articles did not always satisfy me.

For this reason, I thought it would be much more effective to go directly for answers to one of the founders. Father Marcial Maciel was only twenty years old when, in a basement in Mexico

City, at the height of World War II, he began founding the Legion of Christ and Regnum Christi, two of these new Catholic realities. The first is among the religious congregations nowadays with the most priestly vocations; the second, a commitment to a way of life and apostolate that has transformed the lives of tens of thousands of laymen and laywomen — both consecrated and not — and diocesan priests.

It was not easy to convince him to grant the interviews that made this book possible. But once he committed to it, he rose to the task. As you will see, he answers with disarming sincerity and spontaneity all my questions about his life, his call, the founding of the congregation and the movement, and his vision of the Church and the future.

Over the long hours of conversation with Father Maciel at his residence on Via Aurelia in Rome, I gradually discovered and outlined the fundamental answer I was searching for. For Father Maciel, Christianity is not an idea, a moral or philosophical system, or a set of abstract principles. As this book shows, Christ is the person he discovered in the early years of his youth, and he was captivated by him forever. Without this personal, unique, and unrepeatable "encounter," as he calls it, the Legion of Christ and Regnum Christi would likewise lose all their meaning and purpose.

I have grouped the questions under eight main topics. The first three are historical in nature, with Father Maciel describing the milestones of his life: his childhood in the town of Cotija, Mexico; the unexpected call to be a priest when he was fourteen; the first steps in founding, full of surprises. The next two chapters contain my questions about the Legion of Christ and Regnum Christi, which he still directs personally. The last three topics center on his more personal experiences in the spiritual life and the priesthood, and they present his vision, full of hope, for the future of the world and the Church.

On rereading them, I think the word that best sums up these pages is *hope*. In our final conversation, Father Maciel told me, "Yes, the world is a valley of tears; but it is also the theater of divine action. In it we can meet the eyes of God-with-us and feel his helping hand grasp ours and invite us, as Jesus did to Peter, 'Put out into the deep. Walk. Do not be afraid. I am with you.' "

Jesús Colina

Christ Is My Life

I

Childhood

1. Father Maciel, you were born into a very Catholic family, and your early life coincided with a harsh religious persecution. What are some of your memories from those childhood years in your hometown, Cotija?

As you say, my family was very Catholic, but that was not unique. In Mexico there were and still are families deeply rooted in their faith. Our life was centered on the truths of the Christian faith in a very simple but also very deep way. My father[1] owned large tracts of pasture and farmland. He was often away from home, doing the rounds of the ranches. He always tried to take care of the needs of his workers and their families. My memories are of an honest man, faithful to his personal and Christian commitments, very much a man of conscience. In this regard, I remember a man with whom my father had a handshake deal to buy his ranch came to our house once. The government had expropriated his property in the meantime, and it no longer legally belonged to him, but since my father had made the deal before this happened and had given his word to buy, he paid the man for the land even though it had been confiscated.

---

[1] Mr. Francisco Maciel Farías (1880-1950).

3

Christ Is My Life

My mother[2] spent all her time with us children; she was totally dedicated to us. Of her many pregnancies, eleven of us survived infancy, seven boys and four girls. Two of my brothers died in childhood, one at five and the other at six. Two others died later on: Alfonso as a young man, and the eldest, Francisco, in middle age, in a traffic accident in 1973. My mother was a very devout woman, truly holy. When she was young she wanted to be a Teresian nun, but she chose to marry in obedience to her father (as was still customary in those days) and resolved to seek her complete holiness in the married life and raising her children. I remember going with her to visit two lepers who lived in our town, the Tolento sisters. She took care of the sick personally, with great love, gentleness, and respect, because in them she saw the image of Christ. Though I was very little, I asked myself why she did this. Over time, I learned that she did it because she was a Christian. There was no other reason.

I believe I was a child like any other. I liked to play, explore the countryside, get into mischief like everyone else. The parish church wasn't far from my house, so I used to go there often, quite spontaneously, for Sunday Mass, daily family rosary — especially in May — confession and adoration of the Eucharist every first Friday of the month. For our family it was very normal and spontaneous to practice our faith. It was part of life itself. There was no separation whatever between our daily life and our contact with God. My mother taught us to see God's hand in everything that happened in our lives, the pleasant and the painful. A loving hand that led us to him by the most unexpected of paths. What we could never question was God or his love. She also taught us to discover his creating power in nature, which he made out of love

[2] Mrs. Maura Degollado Guízar (1895-1977). The Legionaries and Regnum Christi members call her "*Mamá Maurita*," out of affection.

for us. Sometimes when we were out with her, she would stop in front of a simple wildflower and say, "Look, children, how much God loves us." And she would teach us how to recognize the flower's beauty in its color, its shape, its perfume. . . . It all spoke to her of God's love and power and wisdom.

Mexico first saw religious persecution under president Plutarco Elías Calles, and many of Mexico's Catholics, especially from the states of Guanajuato, Michoacán, and Jalisco, rose up in arms between 1926 and 1929 to defend their rights. It was a popular movement. There were no political motives whatsoever, nor were they seeking any other interest. All they wanted was for the government to allow Christians to practice their faith freely and let the priests carry out their ministry. They weren't looking for special privileges, only respect for the basic right of religious freedom. Many people I knew went into the hills to fight this war, which was called the "Cristero War" because the men lived and died to the shout of "Long live Christ the King!"

I was still very young, but I must say I envied the ones who went out to fight for Christ. That's how I saw it. I lived it from the age of six to nine. Once my family had to abandon our home and the town of Cotija, and take refuge in Jamay and Zamora, which were safer for us, especially because my mother, Maura Degollado, was the sister of the Cristero army's last commander-in-chief, Jesús Degollado Guízar. I sometimes saw my mother with a rifle in her hands to defend us in case of an attack on the house. I saw many dead Cristeros hanging from the lampposts, strung up by government troops. We used to help the dying to die well, and would treat the wounds of those who had taken bullets. We saw our friends and neighbors hanged or shot in the town square. In my simple logic of a child I would tell myself that they had given their lives for Christ and were now with him in heaven. I, too, wanted to give my life for him, though at the time I didn't know that God had another kind of battle in mind for me.

2. To your mind, is there a connection between these experiences — seeing your friends and acquaintances die for the faith — and the founding of the Legion of Christ?

Now, many years later, I sincerely think there is. From the beginning of Christianity, Christians understood the value of the martyrs. Tertullian, towards the close of the second century, said that the blood of martyrs is the seed of new Christians. The Church's history has shown this to be true, and this is why many local churches that seemed totally destroyed and razed by persecution have witnessed great fires arise from the few embers that remained on the pyre. There is no direct, demonstrable relation between the religious persecution in Mexico and the Legion of Christ, but my faith tells me that the Legion is in a certain sense the fruit of those martyrs' blood, because blood shed for love of Christ always bears fruit. I do believe that in his wisdom and providence God has wished that blood to bear fruit through the apostolate of the Legion of Christ and Regnum Christi.

3. What was your life in Cotija like?

As I mentioned earlier, my life was absolutely normal. I went to school, I played with my friends, I visited the poor with my mother. I must confess, though, that quite early on, in my adolescence — I must have been about twelve or thirteen — I began to ask myself very serious questions that didn't seem to be of much concern to my friends who were the same age as I was. I liked to climb a small hill, Calabazo Hill, where you could see the town, and I would be there reflecting and conversing with God. From up there I could see the red roofs, the people coming and going, busy with their daily chores, the cemetery nearby, the bell tower of the parish church, mountains on the horizon that suggested distant lands and other unknown men and women busy also with all the cares that life entails. Spontaneously, the basic questions of every human person opening up to existence came into my mind:

"Where does life come from? Where are we going? What is the point of all this bustle if it all ends in a grave? What is the meaning of my life and of human life?" I didn't have an answer for everything, but one thing I did have clear: only God could give me a satisfactory answer to those questions, only with him and for him was life worth living, and only he could ransom time and give it the value of eternity. I felt a great longing for eternity. I wanted to hold on to God and not pass away like so many other things, without a trace. I wanted to walk with him. I also wanted to spend the time God gave me to live doing something for him and for my neighbor.

In these simple conversations God gradually prepared me for the mission and vocation that would come later. At that time the vocation was not yet a factor. I was very certain, though, that success in life comes from God. Not wealth, vanity, pleasure, or glory. What I wanted was God, to have him for my friend, never lose his friendship or his grace. Now as I look back on it, my faith shows me God's loving hand preparing me, like a skillful teacher, for what would later become the great task of my life: to shape and forge the Legion and Regnum Christi.

I particularly want to mention our visits to the poor. At home we had everything. We were in need of nothing. We lived in discipline, austerity, and daily work, but we also had everything we needed. But many other people in the town suffered from real want. My parents were very sensitive to Christian charity. They couldn't imagine a Christianity that separated faith from love for your brothers and sisters. So from our earliest years they taught us to help the poorest, the sick, the elderly, the weakest, and the neediest. A lot of needy people knocked on our door, and there was always something in the pantry for them. My mother listened to and helped one and all. They never left without receiving a smile, a word of consolation and encouragement, and something to ease their hunger and material needs. Our parents "assigned" each of us children a poor person in the area to help, using our wits and imagination. My mother's example with her visits to the two leper women and so many other sick people moved me to imitate her, and from quite a young age I tried to emulate her charity.

I was very much at home with the poor. I was able to give them a few little things — really not worth much, but important to them. They would welcome me warmly into their homes, and after school I often dropped in on them, to visit with them and spend time there. I liked to be with them and help them in whatever way I could. Sometimes I found clothing or food to bring them, and I was really happy I had a few coins I could put towards solving one or another of their needs.

When the Lord called me to found the Legion I understood that I would have to live any calling to serve the poor in a different way, and that meant a great sacrifice for me. I would have to spend most of my time not working directly with the poor but forming other people to do the work I myself liked to do, and which I found so rewarding from a human and spiritual point of view. But I wasn't going to do this directly, but through the priests and laypeople I would form. Humanly speaking, I would have preferred to be a parish priest in a small town, among the very poor. I felt especially attracted to that kind of ministry, which also would have been more directly rewarding, but that was not what God wanted for me.

4. Any particular story you remember from the Cristero War?

Many things happened that remained etched on my young heart, instances of people who gave their lives for Christ, but I would have to mention especially the martyrdom of my friend José Sánchez del Río. At that time I was away from Cotija with my family because of the persecution. This time we had gone to the town of Sahuayo. José, who was fourteen, asked me to go into the mountains with him and fight with the Cristeros, but I was very young (about seven). He took off to the mountains. A few days later he was caught by government troops, who decided to teach the civilian population, who supported the Cristeros, a lesson to remember. They asked him to renounce his faith in Christ, under pain of death. José refused to apostatize. His mother, too, was pierced with sorrow and grief, but, like the mother of the seven sons in the book of Maccabees, she encouraged her son to be true to his faith. So they skinned the soles of his feet and forced him to walk through the town towards the cemetery. He cried and moaned in pain. But he would not give in. Every so often they stopped and said to him, "If you shout 'Death to Christ the King,' we will spare your life. Say 'Death to Christ the King.' " But he would answer, "Long live Christ the King." Once they got to the cemetery, before shooting him, they asked him for the last time if he would give up his faith. He didn't, and they killed him right there. Like many other Mexican martyrs, he died shouting "Long live Christ the King!" These are pictures that can't be erased from my memory and the memory of the Mexican people, although they are often not mentioned in the official version of history. As you can understand, all of this was leaving its mark on me, the desire to give my life for Christ and the faith. I believe that God made use of all this to shape my soul and prepare it for the mission of founding the Legion of Christ.

5. When you were a child, did you have any inkling of what your mission and vocation in life were to be later on?

Truly, I didn't. As I said, my life was absolutely normal. It's true that God gave me the grace to be especially intimate with him — in the sense that I used to tell God, quite simply, about everything that happened to me, my worries, what I had done, what I wanted to do, other people's needs. Thanks to what we learned at home God was someone very close for my siblings and me, and we connected with him quite spontaneously. My mother had taught us to do it like that, and for us it was entirely normal to live in an atmosphere of simple and spontaneous relations with God.

6. Can you say a little more about your mother?

My mother married my father when she was very young, and there was quite a difference in age between them. She was seventeen and he thirty-two. Though she had wanted to be a Teresian, as I mentioned, she saw that God's will was the marriage that her father suggested to her, and she undertook the commitments of mother and wife as the expression of her love for God.

She came from a very Catholic family, although some of its members had been of liberal political leanings, such as General Santos Degollado, who was a friend and comrade of Benito Juárez, collaborated with him in drafting and applying the laws of the Reform, and held several cabinet positions in the Reform government. My grandmother on my mother's side was Maura Guízar Valencia; her brothers were Blessed Rafael Guízar Valencia, bishop of Veracruz, and Antonio Guízar Valencia, bishop of Chihuahua. Other close relatives of my mother included Francisco González Arias, bishop of Campeche and Cuernavaca, Luis Guízar Barragán, bishop of Campeche and Saltillo, José María González Valencia, bishop of Durango, and Mother María de Jesús Guízar Barragán, foundress of the Guadalupan Servants of Christ the Priest. All were from Cotija.

My mother received a thorough Christian education from the Teresian nuns whom her uncle, Blessed Rafael Guízar, had brought to Zamora. Her relationship with God was very deep yet very simple. As I mentioned earlier, my mother saw God everywhere — her relationship with him seemed second nature to her. Out of love for God she would visit the poor, the sick, the marginalized, and the dying as often as she could, and she often asked one of us to go with her. She practiced charity in word and deed. It was second nature in her to speak well of others; neither she nor my father would let us say a bad word about anyone in front of them.

She told me that when I was an adolescent and she couldn't make out what would become of me, she entrusted me to the Blessed Virgin. The very day she told Mary to take care of me — she was by then almost at wits end with my adolescent mischief — I came to her that night to tell her I wanted to go and become a priest. My mother always supported me in my life as a priest and founder with her prayers and unobtrusive concern. She really loved the Legionaries and Regnum Christi members, and they loved her. She offered many of her prayers and sacrifices to God for the holiness and apostolic fruit of the Legionaries and Regnum Christi members, and later as a widow she herself consecrated her life to God in the Regnum Christi Movement.

II

The Call

7. What age were you when you perceived the call to be a priest, and how did you perceive it? In other words, why did you decide to be a priest?

I felt God's call when I was fourteen. It was May. On May afternoons we used to pray the rosary at the parish, as an act of devotion to Mary. We also used to make a beautiful floral offering. That day I was on my way home from praying the rosary at the parish when I met two nuns who were in Cotija, away from their communities for reasons of health and because of the religious persecution. They stopped to chat and asked me where I had been. I said, in Mexico City with the bishop of Veracruz, Rafael Guízar. Since the religious persecution was still going on in his diocese, he lived in the capital and ran a clandestine seminary there. "And why didn't you stay with him?" they asked. It was the first time anyone had ever mentioned to me the possibility of going to the seminary to be a priest. I asked them if I could be a priest. They said yes, if God had given me the gift of a vocation.

After that brief conversation with the two sisters, I was firmly convinced that God was calling me to serve him as a priest. Each vocation is particular and unique. Mine came unforeseen, without my ever having thought of it or looked for it. In that seconds-long conversation with the nuns I had the moral certainty that God's will for me was the life of a priest. I really don't have any more details to give you. It was all very simple, but I must admit that I didn't harbor any doubt that my call was authentic. Later there would be many difficulties and setbacks, but I have never doubted my call. I consider this a very special grace from God, and I thank him for it every day.

I remember that on that May afternoon in my fourteenth year, I returned to the parish church I had just come from after praying the rosary. I was absolutely sure God wanted the priesthood for me. At the time I didn't know the particular circumstances in which it would happen, but I couldn't doubt that it was God's will for me. I know this is hard to explain, especially when you haven't had that kind of experience. I thanked God for this immense gift and asked him to help me be faithful to him on this path as long as I lived.

8. How did your relatives take your decision to go to the seminary?

At the time I was very young, and my father and some of my brothers thought it would be better if I waited and matured my vocation. My mother, on the other hand, supported me right from the start. Mothers have a sixth sense for perceiving their children's interior situation. As a good mother, she told me not to say anything about it to my father and told me not to worry about it in the least; she assured me she would work everything out. My father was not quick to understand a vocation at fourteen years old. I'm sure he thought it was just a whim since I was an adolescent. But I thank God that over time all of my family came to support and understand my vocation to be a priest as a gift for them too.

After so many years of working with priestly vocations, I've realized that parents who live by faith see their son's vocation to priesthood or their daughter's vocation to consecrated life as an enormous gift from God to the family. It's true that humanly speaking the increased physical distance is a suffering that they must all offer up. But over time a special spiritual unity among all the family members develops around the son's or daughter's vocation. That family might, like any other, go through all kinds of trials. But thanks to the vocation of one of the children, they seem to have a special strength that enables them to live it all with new peace. It's something unique, but you see it right away in families that are blessed with the gift of a vocation to the priesthood or consecrated life.

9. Once you discovered your call to be a priest, did you go to the seminary right away?

I began writing to various seminaries asking for information. One of my older brothers knew I had asked for information, but he thought I was too young, and so the answers I got from the seminaries never reached me. At long last I did receive a letter from the Carmelite priests in Puebla accepting me, but I would have to pay thirty pesos a month. So I talked to my father and he told me he didn't have the money, and to wait a year to mature my decision.

So I had to wait a whole year. I kept going to school every morning, and in the afternoon I worked to pay for my future priestly studies. I sold eggs and did odd jobs. With the money I earned, I bought the clothes I needed for the seminary. And so I had everything together to leave home on January 3, 1936. My father eventually gave me his blessing before I left, as is customary in Mexico. I remember that it was a First Friday and the Blessed Sacrament was exposed in the parish church. I went to entrust myself to Christ in the Eucharist before going to take the bus. I left home bound for an unknown adventure. I had a little suitcase with my clothes, twenty-five pesos that my brother José had gotten for me at the last minute, and I was ready and eager to serve Christ. That was all I wanted, and it had my heart on fire. I knew hardly anything about the Puebla Carmelites, where I was headed. Really, the only thing I wanted was to put myself totally at Christ's disposal, following God's call. I had plenty of time to reflect on the mystery of God's call that night spent under the stars, lying on a bench at the train station in a town called Tingüindín, where I was to catch the train for Mexico City. Truth to tell, everything was filled with the mystery of God that fills your heart with peace, and the sensation that I was embarking on an adventure, God's style. In all vocations, the person called gradually discovers God's will, step by step. Each instant you have to correspond to the graces of the moment, without worrying about the past or the future, abandoning yourself entirely to God's hands.

10. So you began your novitiate with the Carmelites?

In the end I didn't. Before going to join the Carmelites in Puebla, I stopped in Mexico City to see my uncle, the now-beatified Rafael Guízar Valencia, bishop of Veracruz. My mother had strongly insisted that I call on him. He gave me a very warm welcome, and when I told him that I was off to the Carmelite novitiate, he answered with a very Mexican expression: "¡Qué carmelitas ni qué carmelitas! — "The Carmelites? Forget it!" — you're staying here with me in my seminary to see what God wants of you." Two days later the seminary's rector, Father Jerónimo Ugalde, came by to see the bishop, and he took me to the seminary. So that's why I didn't go to the Carmelites as planned, but to the Veracruz seminary, which was in the Atzcapotzalco section of Mexico City.

The seminary was clandestine since the government didn't allow seminaries at the time. We lived as in the catacombs — with all the accompanying graces. We couldn't disturb the neighbors or draw attention to ourselves at all because someone might report us. If word reached the government, they would seize the house, close the seminary, and scatter the seminarians. Materially it was very poor: our refectory was a small room, our dormitory was wooden planks, a kind of large room, but it was beautiful to live with these limitations for love of God. I tried to live our seminary life to the full as regards the prayer life, studies, community life with the other seminarians. That's how I spent my first few months in the seminary.

11. When did you get the idea to found a religious congregation?

It was on a First Friday, the nineteenth of June 1936. It was a special day for the seminary, the feast of the Sacred Heart. During the morning recess I went to our little chapel to visit the Blessed Sacrament. During that short time of personal conversation with Christ, I had a very clear spiritual perception: God wanted me to gather together a group of priests who would dedicate their lives wholeheartedly to preaching the Gospel — missionary priests who would live the Gospel thoroughly, love Christ with all their strength, be missionaries of that love, and preach Christ's new commandment of love among all people. It was something very simple, but very clear. It wasn't just an idea of mine that popped into my head. I saw and felt that it was not only an inspiration, but a powerful motion of the Holy Spirit regarding what God wanted of me. I experienced it very strongly in my soul.

Naturally I felt small, unworthy and unprepared for this task, and I didn't know where to begin or what to do. But my spirit could not doubt that God truly wanted me to do this. To be sure that it wasn't merely subjective, I mentioned it right away to my spiritual director, and he told me to write down any insights I received about it.

12. After this experience, how did your life at the seminary change?

Outwardly, in nothing. I kept the pace of formation along with the other formators and seminarians, and it progressively educated my mind, matured my personality, and shaped my character. But from now on I approached it all from the perspective of how I was going to fulfill what God wanted me to do. Naturally, I had no idea at the time as to the exact difference between diocesan and religious clergy, and the various religious orders. Nor did it matter much to me at the time. What I wanted was to find ways to achieve what I saw was God's will.

As I said, all this developed in the context of seminary life and some enriching apostolic experiences, since they used to send the seminarians to help priests in their parishes so we could see up close what a priest's life was like.

13. What kind of apostolic experiences did you have?

I was sent to help Father Antonio Maldonado, the parish priest of Jesús María, a village near Orizaba, in the State of Veracruz. Two of us seminarians spent our vacation time with him. In the morning we studied Latin, Spanish, and some other subject, and in the afternoon we often went out with him to visit the villages that were part of his parish. We taught catechism, led the rosary, and visited people in their homes to find out firsthand their religious situation and help them insofar as we could.

I have especially fond memories of the times when he let us carry the Blessed Sacrament from one ranch to another, since in those days not only was there a lack of priests, but also a persecution against the Church, especially in the State of Veracruz. I remember once I had the grace to take the Blessed Eucharist to a little rural community (then called San Isidro, now Chilapa) in the foothills of Orizaba Peak, crossing by night the magnificent mountainous terrain full of forests and ravines. The whole journey was a conversation with Christ, a spontaneous and simple conversation, friend to friend, that lifted up my heart. Those experiences fanned the flame of my desire to receive the gift of priesthood some day, and thus give my life to Christ and work with him helping him to save many souls.

14. I heard that as a seminarian you also participated in the campaign to open the churches in the State of Veracruz, and that you even played the leading role in the case of Orizaba. Is that true?

Yes, it's true that I did participate in the opening of the churches in Veracruz State. But if I remember correctly, it wasn't in my vacations after my first year as a seminarian but my second year. The governor had decreed that all the Catholic churches be closed. The Catholics had submitted to this unjust decree, but they helped the priests organize clandestine Masses in private homes. In February of 1937, while Father Flores, the parish priest of Orizaba, was celebrating Mass at someone's house, the police showed up to arrest him. He managed to escape, but a row broke out between the police and the faithful participating in the Eucharist. A bullet struck a young worker, a woman called Leonor Sánchez, and she died.

This episode was the straw that broke the camel's back. The workers and the Catholics began to hold massive, peaceful demonstrations for the churches to be reopened. While this was going on, I was helping Father Maldonado with the parish work, but we got wind of what was happening in Orizaba and how the Catholic workers and the Catholics in general had planned a large-scale peaceful demonstration to press for the opening of the churches. The parish priest asked me to go to the demonstration with him. On the appointed day, the Catholics gathered in large numbers. Many of them came from the outlying ranches and towns near Orizaba. They were simple folk, but willing to defend the Church. The peaceful crowd ran into the government troops that had been sent to control and disperse them. The demonstration was held in front of the city hall, and the people wanted to enter and demand that the civil authorities return them their churches. I was a young seminarian, barely seventeen, but I saw that the situation was growing too tense on both sides and somehow, I don't know how, I found myself talking to the commanding officer of the troops. He took me inside City Hall and told me to address the crowd from the balcony so as to calm them down and get them to break up. Since I saw that a massacre was likely I asked the Catholics not to force their way in and told them that the possibility of opening the churches was being addressed with the governor. On that occasion the crowd held itself back and the demonstration disbanded peacefully.

Days later, however, the workers and the Catholics arranged another meeting, and their numbers had swollen considerably. The demonstration lasted the whole day and by evening the air was charged with anger. The soldiers pulled out their rifles and fixed bayonets. I remember being struck by a bayonet and I still have the scar on my leg. Some of the demonstrators, infuriated, began drawing their pistols and firing them in the air. It was getting dark and both sides were ready for action. The officer who had called me earlier to talk to the crowds asked me to do so again, since he saw a bloodbath coming. I got up on the roof of an army truck and began to talk to the Catholics, shouting "Long live Christ the King!" and "Long live Our Lady of Guadalupe!" Some people started calling me a traitor, since that day there were a lot of new people and not everyone knew me. At the moment the only thing I could think of was to tell them not to worry, that permission had been given to open the churches. I told them we would all head for the church, that we could go in.

Actually the government hadn't issued any permission, but I knew where the keys to the church were kept. So I went and got them, we opened the church, and all the people went in, singing and cheering Christ the King and Our Lady of Guadalupe. The priests entered the church triumphantly and we held Adoration of the Blessed Sacrament. We left pickets to guard the church so that they wouldn't come and close it, and then we went ahead and opened the other churches in Orizaba and the nearby towns.

This episode is like a symbol of what my life has been. Not knowing how, without looking for it, I was caught up in a series of events that humanly speaking were too much for me. Yet through it all a mysterious, provident hand seemed to be with me and to guide me at every moment.

15. How did Providence show itself later in your seminary formation years?

Sometimes it showed itself in setbacks and surprises as well. One such surprise was my expulsion from the Veracruz seminary in Mexico City. While my uncle Bishop Rafael Guízar Valencia was alive, the seminary staff respected me, but they did not look kindly on my desire to form a new congregation. They most likely thought it was all madness, an illusion, a dream. My uncle died in June 1938. A month or two later I was told that I could no longer study at the Veracruz seminary. I was only eighteen. This decision seemed to cut off, at least in part, my great desire to be a priest. I didn't have any money and I didn't know what to do, but I still clearly perceived inside that God wanted me to be a priest and to gather a group that would work for his Kingdom. Of course, it was a hard blow for me. However, as always, Providence crossed my path: an uncle of mine, Bishop Rafael Guízar's brother Emiliano, encouraged me and told me not to worry, because the bishop of Chihuahua, Antonio Guízar Valencia (his brother and also brother of the bishop of Veracruz), could accept me as a seminarian in his diocese.

Sure enough, I spoke with His Excellency Antonio Guízar, and he sent me to the seminary in Montezuma, New Mexico, USA, run by the Jesuits. The Mexican bishops had opened an interdiocesan seminary there, since they couldn't do so in Mexico because of the religious persecution. So when I was eighteen I left Mexico City for the United States to continue studying for the priesthood.

16. Several times you have mentioned Bishop Rafael Guízar Valencia, beatified by John Paul II in 1995. What do you remember about this holy bishop?

Rafael Guízar was my mother's uncle. He too was born in Cotija. He was an exemplary priest and bishop. His life was pretty hectic, since he lived through the stormy years of the revolution and the religious persecution. When he was a priest his bishop once suspended him from the ministry (*a divinis*), an unjust punishment motivated by slander and envy, and he submitted in a spirit of heroic obedience.

He had to live amid the turmoil of the Mexican Revolution, ministering spiritually to the troops on both sides. Twice he was sentenced to be shot, but he escaped miraculously on both occasions — on one of them he was actually in front of the firing squad, their fingers on the trigger. He had to go into exile because of the anticlerical laws, and worked with admirable zeal as a missionary in Guatemala, Colombia, the United States, and Cuba. While he was in Cuba he received word of his nomination as bishop of Veracruz in Mexico, which at that time covered a vast area. Though he was bishop of Veracruz for eighteen years he was only able to reside in the diocese for eight since the anticlerical laws were still in force in that state. He traveled the length of his enormous diocese several times, often by mule or on horseback. Each pastoral visit was a true mission that renewed the Christian life of the parishes.

What he liked most was to go on missions, to preach Christ. I remember him inviting me once to go to the Promenade in Mexico City with him. He brought an accordion with him — he played very well — but I had no idea what it was for. When we got to the place it was crowded; he pulled out the accordion and began to play popular tunes. The people gathered in a circle around him. When there were enough of them he put the accordion down and began to preach Christ. I don't know if he did it to teach me. I think it just came straight from his soul, you could see that he really enjoyed when he had the chance to talk about Christ to others.

He was a man to whom God gave many supernatural gifts, a great fighter for the cause of religious freedom, he feared no one, watched over his seminary like the apple of his eye, was obedient to a heroic degree during his early years as a priest, and lived the utmost spirit of poverty. When he fell very ill towards the end of his life I remember him asking to be laid on the ground because he wanted to die poor, without comforts. And that's how he died. On the floor, in extreme poverty, in exile, away from his diocese, in a little house in Mexico City.

17. What was your life like at the Montezuma seminary?

There were quite a few seminarians from all the dioceses of Mexico there. Many future bishops of Mexico received their training there. The standard of discipline, prayer, and study was high. It was there that I began my philosophy studies. It was a life typical of a seminary. We were freer to move around than we had been at the seminary in Mexico City, since we were not under pressure from the religious persecution. The formators and the professors were very capable.

I still had the idea of forming a group of zealous priests who would be willing to pour out their energy spreading Christ's Kingdom, even if that meant that their lives would be short, but lived to the full defending the rights of Christ and his Church. I put special emphasis on living authentic Christianity, which means living Christ's charity. I shared this idea with a group of seminarians of all ages from among those studying Latin, philosophy, and even theology. I used to get together with them to see how I would start this foundation, for the idea wouldn't go away; actually it got clearer and more precise. With this group I tried to help the level of discipline, prayer life, and study in the seminary so that all of us being formed there would want to be holy priests and true apostles for Christ's Kingdom. I did this spontaneously, trying myself to be the first to fulfill a seminarian's commitments, and I kept in touch with the formators about it all.

18. Why did you drop your studies at the Montezuma seminary?

A year after entering, they sent me to Mexico City during the summer to raise money for some seminary scholarships. Before Christmas 1939 the bishop of Chihuahua, Antonio Guízar, told me that he would not send me to Montezuma if I still held onto my ideas about founding a congregation. The superiors there had written him about the problems that my idea of founding a congregation caused in the seminary. The bishop told me that either I gave up the idea of founding — in which case he would continue to sponsor me at the seminary — or he would retract his support. I answered that I would have to reflect on that in God's presence and consult my spiritual director.

It would have been easier to say I would drop the idea so as to go back to the seminary in Montezuma. But my conscience wouldn't let me. I couldn't drop the idea because I felt deep inside that it didn't come from me, it was God's will and not my notion. So I told him I was going to Mexico City and there I would figure out what I was going to do, whether that was to go home or see if I would be able to continue in another seminary. It was a time of darkness, humanly speaking. People thought I was a fool, a dreamer, mad, willful, bent on building castles in the air. Nevertheless, in my conscience I saw that I had to go through with the foundation because that was God's will for me.

I came to Mexico City from Chihuahua with no money and not knowing where to go. A friend offered to put me up while I worked things out. I remember that I spent those days in prayer to find God's will for me. While I was working through all of this, the thought came to look up His Excellency Francisco González

Arias, Bishop of Cuernavaca. He was also related to us, though more distantly than the Guízar Valencia family. I didn't know him personally, but had heard his name mentioned at home. I went to Cuernavaca to meet him and explain my situation.

Bishop González Arias accepted me for his diocese right away, and so I returned to the seminary in Montezuma to continue studying philosophy, but now as a seminarian for the Cuernavaca diocese. A few months later, coming up to the summer vacation, the rector hinted to me that I most likely would not be able to continue studying in the seminary. Over the holidays he wrote to the bishop of Cuernavaca telling him that I should not return, but the bishop asked me to go back anyway and discuss the reason for my expulsion with the rector.

In September 1940 I had not been back long when a lay brother sent by the rector came to my room and told me I had to pack my bags and leave the seminary immediately; he himself would take me to the train station. I asked him if I could speak with the rector or one of the formators but he said that I couldn't, that his instructions were precise and I had to be on the next train out of Albuquerque for Mexico. I knew why I was being expelled; the rector had explained it to me before I left for summer break: the superiors were afraid that the Mexican bishops would object to the fact that some seminarians had joined a religious congregation, and they feared the foundation would cause problems for the seminary. In spite of this I had hoped to talk to the rector again and at least propose that I continue my studies and not talk about the foundation again until I was ordained a priest.

That is why I was very surprised and deeply saddened when I received this news. It's not easy to know you're being expelled, especially for a second time — and, besides, without the chance to discuss matters with the seminary authorities as my bishop had told me to, and without being able to ask anyone for an explanation. Humanly speaking it was a long, sad trip. The final view of the Montezuma seminary is deeply imbedded in my memory: the view from the curve in the road of the building where I had studied, prayed, and shared joyful times with my fellow seminarians. The whole way to Albuquerque I wept in silence; I wept and prayed. I reached Ciudad Juarez. There, the parish priest paid for my train ticket to Chihuahua. But my hope never left me. Though I didn't know how I was going to go on I was firmly convinced that God would find a way, one that I could not foretell at the time but which he in his wisdom already had in mind.

The bishop of Cuernavaca, a man of great virtue and an exceptional gift of counsel, took me back as his seminarian with the utmost kindness. He originally planned to send me to one of the national seminaries as a seminarian for the Cuernavaca diocese. He also tried to send me to the Franciscan school of theology, but the superiors there said that it was only for their own religious and they normally did not accept outside seminarians. When all these efforts failed the bishop came up with another solution: he assigned several theology professors to teach me under the direction of professor Manuel González Rojas, who had obtained several doctorates in Rome. I lived in Mexico City and as I finished each subject I went to Cuernavaca. The bishop had a room for me at his residence and I stayed a few days with him and took oral exams before a panel of several professors. Bishop González told me to finish my theology studies this way, and he assured me that once I was ordained a priest I could go through with the foundation.

III

Founding the Congregation

19. But I was of the idea that you founded the congregation when you were still a seminarian, before finishing your priestly studies.

The bishop's plan was for me to finish studying for priesthood and then found the congregation as a priest. However, with the bishop's permission in October 1940 I had to go to Cotija because my brother Alfonso had come down with typhoid and was dying. While in my hometown, besides being with my brother in his final days and consoling my parents and brothers and sisters, I took the opportunity to gather together a group of eight boys who wanted to become priests. I found them a house and professors to ensure their formation, and entrusted the spiritual care of the group to a priest-friend. When I told the bishop about it, I asked his permission to visit the school from time to time so as to keep abreast of its progress. He thought for a while and then told me he would offer me a house in the diocese of Cuernavaca instead, so that I wouldn't have to commute all the way to Cotija. His proposal seemed very good to me, but I thought it would be hard to find financial support and vocations in Cuernavaca. I figured it would be easier to find financial support, professors and priests in Mexico City. I told the bishop what I was thinking; at first it didn't seem to him the right thing to do, but since he was a man of God, he left the door open to see what God's will was for the project.

Some time later he agreed to my proposal and personally asked permission from the archbishop of Mexico City, Luis María Martínez, to open an extension of the Cuernavaca minor seminary there; this was to become the vocational center of the Missionaries of the Sacred Heart, as I called the group before using the name Legionaries of Christ.

20. You were only twenty and still a seminarian. How did you manage to get together the first group of students for the vocational center and raise the funds to keep it going?

Really, it wasn't I who did it. I was only the tool of God's providence, and day after day I tried to carry out his will for my life and for the project of the foundation. I didn't exactly have well-defined plans — actually, quite the opposite. My idea was to do my best not to get in the way of God's grace, and to offer myself as an instrument for him to do as he saw fit with me.

Once it had been decided that the vocational center would open in Mexico City I moved there with the bishop's permission. I continued studying and taking my exams with Professor González, but I also spent time looking for possible vocations and financial aid for the foundation. This was in the final months of 1940. I spent several hours a day studying so as not to fall behind the schedule of exams I had set myself, and the rest of my time went in looking for donations so as to have funds enough to guarantee that the school would open and then stay open.

On weekends I made trips to look for vocations. I went to Querétaro, some cities in Michoacán, and Mexico City itself. I still can't fathom how I managed to convince the parents and the boys themselves about going to Mexico City to begin the vocational center. When I think about it now, so many years later, I see clearly through it all God's powerful hand on an inexperienced young man. A twenty-year-old youth, a seminarian proposing a priestly formation program — something absolutely new, something with rather shaky guarantees from a human point of view — could not have accomplished anything on his own. Truth to tell, at the time I never wondered about these things. I only knew that I had to take the steps, and so I did. That's how I managed to get about thirty boys together who were willing to begin this adventure, though only thirteen came to begin the vocational center.

To fund the project I had to go door to door and ask for donations. Some friends gave me the addresses of people who might help. I visited them and they helped me with a few pesos or a few centavos, which I carefully collected. Someone gave me five hundred pesos, and I used them to buy a beautiful altar, chalices, and some liturgical items for the future vocational center. By December 1940, I still had hardly any money to open the school. Hearing this, the Retes family offered me part of their house and enough money to begin. With this news, I spoke to the bishop of Cuernavaca again — it was December 12, 1940, the feast of Our Lady of Guadalupe — to see if we could begin the vocational center. The bishop invited me to go to the chapel and pray with him. I thought it was going to be a brief moment of prayer, but we stayed there two hours begging the Lord to give us light and to show us his will. At the end the bishop said to me, "Look, Marcial, I believe God wants us to start, and since we have that financial backing, we also have a good human starting point." Then he asked me to suggest a good date to found.

21. But for the foundation you also needed a house and a priest for a chaplain.

True. I had the bishop's permission, and to me this guaranteed that God's blessing was upon what I was doing. I had committed with a number of families whose sons were interested in the vocation and who were willing to let them go. We had financial backing of sorts. But there were still many problems to solve, such as the ones you mention — the house and the chaplain. For each of these problems, which in my inexperience I discovered day by day, the Lord in his wonderful providence came out to meet me, as if to get the message across — to me first of all — that what was being born there was not the doing of Marcial Maciel or Bishop González Arias, but of God. I can say that my whole experience as a founder has been like that; it has always been like that, always surprising and amazing me.

I approached the bishop of Cuernavaca to ask for a chaplain, and he assigned a holy Salesian priest who for health reasons was forced to retire from his ministry in South America. He was Father Daniel Santana, about fifty years old, and he would function as rector and chaplain. My official position was dean of discipline, but the bishop had given me complete freedom to begin inspiring those first students with the spirit of the congregation. I was only twenty years old.

As for the house, as I mentioned, the Retes family lent us part of theirs, the whole half-basement area. I bought fifteen small desks for study, fifteen chairs, some notebooks and pens, and that's all the equipment we had to start with. I didn't have money for beds so we made do with the floor, putting down newspaper to keep out the damp, until we had enough money to buy beds.

22. The official day of the founding was January 3, 1941. Is there anything special about the date, or was it just coincidence?

I had suggested to the bishop to found the vocational center of the Missionaries of the Sacred Heart on January 1, but Father Santana, who was supposed to come and celebrate Mass for the founding, wasn't feeling well, and we had to postpone it.

At the end of December 1940, I traveled around the states of Querétaro, Jalisco, and Michoacán to pick up the boys who had shown interest and received permission from their families. As I mentioned, I ended up with only thirteen, even though there were about thirty on the list. While we were waiting for Father Santana to come I took the boys to the Shrine of Guadalupe to put the foundation in Mary's hands. Father Santana finally arrived on January 2, and on January 3 he celebrated the first Mass in our house on the altar I had bought for this purpose. That year January 3 was also a First Friday, just as the day I first left home for the seminary had also been January 3 and a First Friday. As I said, this might look like mere coincidence humanly speaking, but under the light of faith I discovered a message from the Heart of Christ for us, a sign of his love and special favor.

23. What can you tell me about the early stages of the founding? Normally there are all kinds of obstacles to overcome, but also very special graces.

The first few months were quite peaceful and calm. Materially we were very poor, but we were utterly unaware of what we didn't have. I remember constantly thanking God for helping us so clearly and manifestly. The boys at the vocational center were very happy and content as well, with their Latin, math, Spanish, and other classes. I did what I could to inspire in them the spirit God wanted for us, as I perceived it in prayer. I kept up my studies, though I had to invest a lot of time asking for donations so that the project wouldn't fall through for lack of funds. For me, those years were very beautiful but at the same time very draining. Taking care of and educating the brothers and looking for money to support them kept me extremely busy the better part of the day. Someone gave us a cow named *Mariposa* ["Butterfly"], and then we were given another one. I would get up early to milk them, then I would go out and sell the milk, and also eggs and vegetables; I would buy breakfast for the brothers and be back to wake up the community. Educating them meant organizing many activities: giving them conferences on spiritual formation, teaching them the basic habits of prayer and even how to be neat and tidy. I also had to look for financial support. This meant going door to door almost every day in search of benefactors. When the day was over and the brothers had gone to bed, professor González Rojas came to give me classes. The good man always adjusted to my nocturnal schedules and thanks to that I was able to finish my studies. After the classes I studied late into the night and as a result in those years I never got more than two or three hours of sleep a night. God always strengthened me and held me up.

After just a few months someone threatened to report us to the police (seminaries were forbidden in those days unless they had the government's express permission). The owners of the house were worried because it could be confiscated, and all of us would be homeless. So I saw that we had to look for somewhere else where we could be more undisturbed.

In April of 1941 I found a little house with a large garden in Tlalpan, a town south of Mexico City. Thanks to the money that came from selling the Retes family's house in Mazatlán and a loan of four thousand pesos from the bishop of Cuernavaca, we were able to buy it and move in by the second week in May.

As you were saying, there was no shortage of hurdles but also countless blessings. I remember those times with true spiritual enjoyment. From an outward point of view, it wasn't as if life was easy for me, but certainly there were numerous blessings. I had the same experience over and over again, under varying circumstances, when founding all of the first houses, especially during those early years.

We have to thank God that we never once went without food — well, there was one day when I had nothing at all to give them. I made a sort of tea by brewing lemon-tree leaves, mixing in some sugar, and that was all we had that day. By nighttime, looking at their faces I felt so bad that I went to a store and got a big can of sardines and a roll of bread for each one on credit so they wouldn't have to go to bed on an empty stomach. However, thank God, with the exception of that day we always had what we needed though certainly it was all very poor, but everyone was happy because we knew we were starting something important for the Church and in doing so we were pleasing God.

24. What kinds of motivations did you give the boys to keep their spirits up and help them bear with these hardships?

I think the main motivation you can give a young man who wants to be a priest is to live entirely focused on the ideal of loving Christ. I gave them this basic motivation in talks and meditations, adjusting it to their age. I am firmly convinced that not only can adolescents understand this type of supernatural motivation, but that they are also very receptive to it and give themselves to it heart and soul, within the characteristics of their age.

I remember telling them, even then, that they would study at the best universities and have a first-rate human, spiritual, and intellectual preparation, because that was what their mission as missionary priests in a more and more estranged and secularized world required. They understood these ideas perfectly and strove for a high ideal of perfection. Naturally they were still adolescents with all their mischief, innocence, and fickleness. But they understood the spiritual motivations perfectly, even though you had constantly to repeat them and be behind the boys to fulfill their duties as a concrete way to show their love for God.

Some people might have thought that all of the things I promised the boys were no more than a dream or a fantasy, but I said them because I was convinced of them. I didn't know when it would all happen, but I knew someday it would. I wanted those teens, priests-to-be, to have a meticulously complete training, if the congregation was to fulfill its apostolic mission to serve the Church.

25. What happened in the years between the founding and your ordination as a priest?

As I have mentioned, they were very hard years for me humanly speaking because of the regimen I had to keep, with all the work I had to take upon myself educating the students, looking for funds, and studying on my own. There were also hardships due to misunderstanding, envy, and slander. I soon understood that this is all part of a founder's life. At first it can startle you, especially if it comes from good people, even priests, but then you realize that's human nature and God allows it all to purify us and lead us on a path like Christ's, the path he took to save us.

There were also some problems with the rectors who were assigned to me while I was not yet a priest. Doubtless they were good men, but not all of them understood the spirit that I wanted to impart in the Legionaries' formation. This brought me no little grief, and there was the potential for clashes of authority in the seminary: the rector on one side and I on the other. When this occurred I asked the Holy Spirit to help me, I sought consolation in the Eucharist, and I sought advice from the bishop of Cuernavaca, who always followed our first steps closely and gave me his unconditional support and fatherly advice.

Apart from that the brothers' life gradually grew more regular and stable. The groups grew steadily, which meant I regularly had to travel through the country to look for vocations, obliging me to be away from the vocational center. In a humanly inexplicable way God kept blessing us with new vocations: great boys who wanted to be priests, from very Christian families who placed no obstacle to their sons' studying for priesthood.

26. You were ordained a priest on November 26, 1944, in the Basilica of Guadalupe. How did you prepare for priesthood, and what did this new step mean for you? At any time before your ordination did it occur to you to doubt the authenticity of your vocation?

Time went by. I worked through my theology studies and took the remaining exams. Finally His Excellency told me that I would begin to receive the preparatory orders that led up to priestly ordination. This was in 1944. I had to keep up the pace of my external work training the first Legionaries, but as the great day of my ordination drew near I tried to unite myself spiritually more and more to Christ, because I knew that priesthood means fully identifying yourself with him and implies accompanying him and climbing Calvary with him. I prayed to the Holy Spirit for his seven gifts so that I would not be a mediocre priest but greatly glorify God and effectively help the Church extend Christ's Kingdom.

I didn't have what people usually call vocational crises, by the grace of God. The night before receiving the gift of priesthood, though, I couldn't sleep because I started wondering if it really would be better not to take the step for fear of being a lukewarm priest and not living the priesthood radically. I remember waking up my spiritual director to tell him my doubt. He calmed me down and invited me to trust in God, putting everything in his hands. He reminded me that the priesthood is so great a gift that no one is worthy of it; if God gives it to you, it's not for you, but for you to put at the service of others and the Church, placing your trust in the one who calls.

It was deeply comforting for me to receive this boundless gift at the feet of Our Lady of Guadalupe in her Basilica at Tepeyac.[3] Mary had been constantly at my side ever since the first moment of my call. Hers was an unobtrusive but strong presence throughout all the adventures of the founding. It was a tremendous consolation to feel her by me as I received the anointing of the Holy Spirit to be able to consecrate the bread and wine into Christ's Body and Blood, to increase the numbers of the children of the Church by baptism, to forgive sins, to bring God's consolation and strength to the gravely ill and dying, to help Christian spouses be witnesses of Christ's love for the Church, and to preach the word

[3] Tepeyac is the name of the hill on which Our Lady of Guadalupe appeared to St. Juan Diego.

of God. In fact, I entrusted to her care not only my priesthood but also the foundation, for her to protect it with her motherly care.

After my ordination our life changed in one sense, and in another it didn't. We no longer needed a rector on loan; I was named rector by the bishop, and I could put a stronger seal on the charism that the Lord was giving us, celebrate the Eucharist for the community, and above all present myself to families and benefactors as a priest and no longer as a mere seminarian.

As for the more external aspects, by then we had moved to another house in Tlalpan on Madero Street, since the archbishop of Mexico City asked us for our house on 21 Victoria Street to build the diocesan seminary there.

27. In 1946 you took your first trip to Rome. Why did you get this idea, and how did it come about?

Several reasons moved me to make the trip. First of all, I wanted to submit my petition for the approval of the congregation to the Pope. Naïve as I was, I thought it would be easy to get to Rome, set up an interview with His Holiness, explain all our plans, and ask him for his blessing. I wanted to present him with the Constitutions. I had been drafting them on and off since 1936, retouching and perfecting them with the help of others. The Constitutions contain the essence of a religious congregation's charism; in them a religious finds what God and the Church want of him in every aspect of life, from the apostolic to the formative to the spiritual. That's why I had always given great importance to writing the Constitutions, so that the religious of the future would find in them the genuine spirit of the congregation.

The first canonical step in founding a religious congregation is diocesan approval, but even this requires a *nihil obstat* from the Holy See. I spoke with the bishop, and he wrote a letter asking the Holy See for permission to erect the congregation. He also suggested that I ask for letters of support from other Mexican bishops. This meant traveling the length and breadth of the country, calling on bishops and asking them for letters of support. It took a lot of work, but I was able to garner the support of the great majority of the bishops.

In addition to the approval of the Constitutions, I traveled to Europe for the purpose of transferring my students there to continue their studies to become priests. In Mexico I had met Father Francisco Javier Baeza, SJ, rector of Comillas University in Santander, Spain, one of the best ecclesiastical universities in Europe at the time. He promised me some scholarships for my students. I went to Europe in May 1946 to address the question of the scholarships and to present the Constitutions of our congregation to the Holy Father.

28. Why did you want your students to study in Europe? Couldn't they do so in Mexico?

From the very beginning of the foundation I believed that our religious had to receive a painstakingly complete training if they really wanted to fulfill their mission and evangelize a secularized society such as the one taking shape at the time. As you have seen from the various steps I took to found the congregation, the process put me in contact with a wide variety of situations, and I had perceived how necessary it was to offer the world priests who were both faithful to the Church and her Magisterium and also capable of meeting the challenges of the times; their thorough intellectual formation would enable them to dialogue with contemporary men and women, and thus lead them to God more easily.

There were good seminaries in Mexico, but as you can understand, with the long, hard religious persecution the country had suffered, our good professors and educators were scattered and it wasn't easy to gather them in one place to help us. There was no doubt that Europe at the time had the best formation centers for priests, and hence my determination to have our men trained there. My meeting the rector of the Comillas Pontifical University seemed providential in this regard.

29. What were the results of the trip?

It was a somewhat eventful and long trip, with many stopovers. Before reaching Madrid I had to stop in Brownsville, Houston, Temple, New Orleans, Atlanta, Washington, and New York. I switched planes, stopped over in Gander [Newfoundland], and finally landed on the other side of the Atlantic in Shannon, Ireland. Then from Shannon to Lisbon and from Lisbon to Madrid. Airplanes back then didn't have the conveniences they do now, and in Europe you felt the effects of World War II, which had ended the year before. As well, the trip ended up being so expensive for me that I had only twenty dollars left for personal expenses. The Paulist Fathers very kindly offered me free lodging in New York, Lisbon, and Madrid.

When I got to Madrid I met with the rector of Comillas University, Father Baeza, and he informed me that for various reasons the scholarships he had promised were unfortunately no longer available. This first setback did not discourage me. I told myself I hadn't come to Europe for nothing, just to return empty-handed to Mexico, so I decided to go house-to-house begging for donations to pay for our students' tuition. Looking back on that decision it might seem like folly, but at the time I didn't see any other way, and since I was convinced that God would help us by whatever means, I decided to go begging. The results were not very flattering but the families did donate, however little it was. As I was looking for a street in Madrid where I was told a certain person lived who could help us, I asked a man standing on the corner for directions. When he replied, I could tell from his accent he was Mexican and right away we struck up a conversation. It turned out that he was a historian from the Yucatán, Jorge Rubio Mañé, finishing a research project in Spain. I told him why I was there, and he said,

"Father, tonight I have an appointment with Mr. Alberto Martín Artajo, the Spanish Minister for Foreign Affairs. I will mention your case to him and see if he can help you." Sure enough, that night he got an appointment for me with Mr. Artajo for the next day. The minister was very considerate and promised to help me on condition that I back up my request with a letter of recommendation from a cardinal of the Roman Curia. This promise from the minister made me move forward my planned trip to Rome.

30. What was your impression of the Eternal City and your first contact with the Vatican?

I was very much struck by the post-war atmosphere: allied forces had commandeered all the hotels; there were absolutely no means of communication, markets, food, et cetera. I intended to stay with the Missionaries of the Holy Spirit, but it was impossible, as there were still quite a few allied soldiers scattered through the hotels and religious houses of Rome and suspicion and insecurity was in the air everywhere. I had no money and no idea where to go, so I thought of making for the Tiber to sleep under a bridge. On my way there a young Belgian, seeing me a little lost, came up and suggested that I ask for a room at the Latin-American College. To my surprise, there I was received by a priest I knew from the Montezuma seminary, Father Maina. He very kindly offered me lodging and shared a frugal supper with me — a little mozzarella — since food was still scarce in Rome.

The eternal city had been completely devastated by the war. Many public services didn't work. The city was semi-paralyzed. But I had come to Rome very eager to see and especially to speak personally with the Pope, explain my plan for the congregation and offer him the little handful of seminarians being formed in Mexico.

Since I had no one to recommend me and arrange an audience with the Holy Father, I looked for some way to get near him.

During a ceremony at St. Peter's I went with my surplice on and stood beside Cardinal Giuseppe Pizzardo as if I were one of his secretaries. When the ceremony was over, the cardinals went to greet the Holy Father before he took the elevator out of the basilica. I kept close to Cardinal Pizzardo and took advantage of the situation to go up to His Holiness: "Holy Father, I am a Mexican priest and have something important to tell you, but I don't have anyone to introduce me."

Pius XII turned to Monsignor Callori di Vignale, his secretary at the time, and said, "Tomorrow at twelve."

The next day I went to the audience, and the Pope showed a lot of interest for the foundation. He greatly encouraged me, offered me his advice, and invited me to submit to the Sacred Congregation for Religious the request for canonical approval that Bishop Francisco González Arias of Cuernavaca had signed weeks earlier, and I had with me. During the interview, when I touched on our apostolic charism, the Pope insisted that we emphasize the thorough formation of Catholic leaders, especially for South America. I took this to prayer and tried to understand better in God's presence what he was asking of us through the mouth of his Vicar on earth.

The person and presence of Pius XII impressed me deeply. He was truly a *Pastor Angelicus*; his bearing radiated something of the supernatural. But beyond his personal qualities I saw in him the successor of St. Peter, Christ's Vicar on earth, the one to whom Christ had entrusted the keys of the Kingdom of heaven.

During my visit to Rome I submitted our Constitutions to the Sacred Congregation for Religious, for their approval. After a while they answered, telling me that the approval was not yet possible because we needed more members, and they would write to the bishop of Cuernavaca to inform him of this decision. In my naïveté, I had thought I would return to Mexico with the approval given by the Pope himself. I was unaware that canonical processes take time and it was prudent and normal to wait. At the Roman Curia I met truly exceptional men selflessly serving the Church, although logically there were also the limitations you find in every human group.

I visited the Coliseum with the heart of a pilgrim, and I recalled so many martyrs who had shed their blood for Christ during the early years of Christianity. Later as I visited the many churches throughout the city, I was deeply saddened to find them so empty. They were beautiful, a dazzling testimony to the faith of our forebears, but it grieved me to find Jesus so alone in so many tabernacles. I decided I had to dedicate my life to preaching God's love to all people. Many others had given their lives for him because they believed in love, Christ's mad love for us, dying to save us all. I understood that I must try to live this love, teach it, spread it to others so that they in turn would become its witnesses wherever they went.

Cardinal Nicola Canali set up an appointment for me with Cardinal Giuseppe Pizzardo, Prefect of the Sacred Congregation for Seminaries and Universities. I asked him for the letter of recommendation that the Spanish Minister of Foreign Affairs had requested, and he agreed to this with pleasure. With this at least achieved, though I didn't have the approval I had hoped for, I took a boat from Genoa to Spain.

31. So, how did you manage to transfer the seminarians to Europe if you didn't have the scholarships you had originally been promised?

The Lord kept opening doors that seemed closed. All I had to do was keep up with him. I returned to Spain and with the note that Cardinal Pizzardo had written for me, Mr. Alberto Martín Artajo, the Minister of Foreign Affairs, gave me thirty-six scholarships for our students to study at Comillas University. While speaking with the minister, I realized that I had no money to bring the young men from Mexico to Spain, and the minister himself put me in contact with Juan Claudio Güell y Churruca, the Count of Ruiseñada, the eldest son of the third *Marquis of Comillas*, who was the president of a maritime transportation company then operating between Spain and the Americas. Not only did he give me free transport from Havana to Bilbao, but he even offered to house our students in the summer residence of the Marquis of Comillas, the Sobrellano palace. God helped me brazenly each step of the way, placing in my path the people who could give me everything I needed so our students could come to Europe to study.

On July 8, 1946, I returned to Mexico to make the necessary preparations for the trip and to let the bishop of Cuernavaca know about it. I found him very ill and in the hospital. Since our flight left Mexico City for Havana on September 2, I had to spend the remaining month and a half preparing everything that we needed. It wasn't easy to convince the students' families to let them go to Europe. I had to do the rounds, talking to them and explaining why. Those who were not totally convinced later spoke to Bishop González Arias, who was a hundred percent in support of me. I also had to find money for the preparatory expenses: clothing, suitcases, passports, plane tickets from Mexico City to Havana. And I had to find as well financial support, a rector, and formators for the vocational center that would continue to operate in Mexico City. I found strong financial support in the Spanish community of Mexico City, and after all these expenses were covered, I had fifty dollars left. With this sum we left for Spain: thirty-six students and I. From a human point of view it might seem crazy, but I trusted totally that Providence would help us step by step, as indeed happened.

So we were able to leave Mexico City for Havana on September 2. There we stayed at the Bethlehem School, run by the Jesuits, thanks to a recommendation from Archbishop Manuel Arteaga Betancourt of Havana, who welcomed me because he had known

Bishop Rafael Guízar when, in his days of exile, he did missionary work in Cuba. There in Havana we boarded the Marquis of Comillas bound for New York. We were in what's called the orlop, the lowest deck, where you feel the roll of the boat more. Though there were many people and a lot of noise during the trip, we still fulfilled all our religious commitments. In New York we received a very warm welcome from Cardinal Francis Joseph Spellman, who gave each of the students a Coke and some money to buy candy. We left New York for Spain, and by nightfall on September 27 we reached the port of Bilbao. Since we didn't have enough money, I rented a few rooms at a boarding-house and put one group there for the night. The rest of us slept out in Plaza del Arenal, though things didn't go too well for us and a strong downpour forced us to take shelter in the bandstand. We aroused the suspicion of the patrolling Guardia Civil (the national police) who wanted us out of there, but we finally convinced them that we weren't going to do any harm and we stayed there for the remainder of the night. I spent the fifty dollars I had on food: lots of grapes for everyone. Thankfully, someone on the boat had taken to the seminarians and given us a donation, and with that we were able to survive for the first few days in Spain.

32. What were your students' initial experiences at Comillas University?

Everyone — the rector, formators, faculty, and students — made us very welcome. The brothers would take their classes at the university and then return to the house that the Marquis of Comillas had lent us. But we by no means had the use of the palace rooms. They had lent us the attic, which was a big open space with a wooden floor, four walls, and a roof — enough room for the thirty-six seminarians. There we organized our life. We had to leave the palace a few weeks later, and I rented another two small houses. Since we couldn't afford beds or furniture, we slept on the floor, and each one came up with his own way to set up his books and study. For a dormitory we had no choice but to use the cowshed attached to one of the houses. We tried to fix it up as best as possible so that it would be sanitary, and, to remind us all of Christ's poverty, I put a statue of the Baby Jesus in the middle of our cowshed-dormitory, and this encouraged and motivated us spiritually amid our privations.

A group of students began studying classical humanities. The novices continued their formative activities at home. Some of the seminarians at the university took interest in the congregation, without our ever promoting this; rather, seeing the lifestyle of the brothers, especially their charity towards one another, they felt attracted by our spirituality. And so, as time went on, some of the seminarians, philosophers, and theologians joined the congregation and were ordained with the first groups of priests.

33. I understand that around that time you received the *nihil obstat* from the Holy See and carried out the canonical establishment of the congregation, by which you obtained canonical recognition at a diocesan level.

The *nihil obstat* and the canonical establishment came a little later, in 1948. I really wanted this, since until then, juridically speaking, we were an extension of the minor seminary of the Cuernavaca diocese, with no other juridical standing. I now know that this process is somewhat slow; the Church with her two millennia's worth of wisdom and experience studies each case minutely and then gives her definitive verdict on whether or not a certain form of religious life can receive her official stamp of approval. In my inexperience, which God used successfully to carry out his plans, I thought it would be enough to submit the Constitutions and the bishop's request in order for the establishment to take place. Seen in perspective, two years is objectively a very short time to receive the Church's juridical approval for a diocesan establishment.

Here, too, as with every step the young congregation took, you can detect the special protection of divine providence — I could sense it for myself. In May 1948 I returned to Rome to see if I could speed up the process of the Congregation's approval. At first they really got my hopes up, telling me that the Congregation of the Holy Office had given its acceptance and it would be a matter of days before we were approved in the Congregation's plenary meeting. A few days later, however, they told me that in the meeting they decided it would be better to wait *sine die* until our congregation had more members and was economically more stable. *Sine die* — that could mean never. Disconsolate, I left the house where Monsignor Arcadio Larraona Navarro lived; he was the sub-secretary for the Congregation for Religious. First, I stopped to visit the Blessed Sacrament in the church of St. John of the Florentines. Then I headed for St. Peter's to pray before the altar of Our Lady, called the Gregorian Altar. There Mary gave me special graces of consolation and support. In gratitude, the Legionaries in Rome visit the altar once a year to thank Mary for all the graces we have received from God through her intercession.

Providentially, in a goodbye visit to the offices of the Congregation for Religious on May 25, 1948 before leaving Rome, thanks to the help of a friendly prelate I received to my great surprise the news the *nihil obstat* had been granted.

Overjoyed, I returned to Spain and from there traveled to Mexico to speak with the new bishop of Cuernavaca, Alfonso Espino y Silva, the successor to Bishop Francisco González Arias, who had passed away on August 20, 1946. His Excellency and I decided to go ahead with the canonical establishment and scheduled it for June 29, the feast of St. Peter and St. Paul. On Sunday, June 13, while celebrating the Eucharist, I received a strong motion from God to do the canonical establishment that very day. I spoke with His Excellency, who agreed on condition we had an official Latin version of the Document of Establishment. The apostolic protonotary of the Archdiocese of Mexico City, Monsignor Gregorio Araiza, very kindly helped me write out the Latin document even though he was in bed with a fever. Once we had fulfilled this requirement, that evening [Sunday, June 13, 1948] the Congregation of the Legionaries of Christ was juridically born. Up to then we were nothing in the Church. Then and there a new religious congregation was born in the Church. I made my religious vows in the presence of Bishop Espino y Silva. He then named me general superior of the congregation, and gave me authority to name the general council and receive the vows of the members.

The next day I received an urgent phone call from the bishop asking me to go and see him immediately. When I got to Cuernavaca, he explained that he had received an urgent letter from the Vatican asking us not to proceed with the establishment of the congregation. The letter had reached Cuernavaca the Saturday before, but the priest in charge of the mail had not been able to pick it up because of pastoral commitments. The bishop told me that he could not annul the establishment, which had already taken place, and that he would send a detailed explanation of what happened to Rome. Then if the people in Rome wanted to annul the establishment, they would send us a request to that effect. The reason for the annulment was, according to the letter from Rome, a series of very serious accusations against me which branded me as a liar and a drunkard and a thief, and declared that I was practically holding the seminarians prisoner, not letting them go to confession with anyone except me. The bishop gathered testimonies and proved to the Holy See the falsehood of the accusations, exposing the lies with documented proofs and testimonies from the individuals alluded to in the accusations, from the Cistercian confessor, Father Luis Yagüe of the abbey in Cóbreces, who heard the confessions of my seminarians weekly, and from others.

In all these adventures I see and admire God's hand upon this work, which at the time was like a mustard seed, but which already was inexplicably a sign of contradiction. "Inexplicably," because, objectively speaking, we were nothing more than a handful of young men, novices, and humanities students.

34. How did you react to all these accusations? Did they discourage or embitter you? Did they make you think about the part of the Church that is often full of grave human errors, sins, and misery?

I remember the first grave accusations did affect me a lot. I don't mean the accusations against me in the Veracruz and Montezuma seminaries — because really what they were accusing me of was my desire to found a congregation — but rather the accusations that were leveled against me when I was a young priest. Above all, what was hardest for me to understand was the fact that the accusations came from good people who thought they were acting in the interests of God's glory by accusing me in that fashion. Under such circumstances, with the help of God's grace I tried never to judge people's intentions, which may have been good. I have also tried sincerely never to harbor the least grudge. Whenever the case called for it, I simply took steps to make the real facts known. When this wasn't necessary, I preferred to let it pass and not waste time defending myself, because I believe we ought to dedicate our lives to positive things, working for the Church and for God's Kingdom in souls.

With the passing of time such accusations against our congregation or me personally shock me less. I view them as something normal in — I would say almost inherent to — the discipleship of Christ. John's gospel tells us very clearly: "If they persecuted me, they will persecute you too; if they kept my word, they will keep yours as well" (John 15:20). The Lord chose to dedicate a Beatitude to persecution so that we, his disciples, would not be dismayed or scandalized by all of this. Trials help us draw closer to

God, they purify us, and above all they enable us to obey to its utmost consequences the commandment to love those who persecute or slander us.

That is not to say that human nature doesn't feel the weight of these hard blows, because, humanly speaking, they are very difficult to take. But all of this reminds us that the Church is made up of men, and men will have their errors and limitations, their failings and sins; in spite of this the Church is the universal sacrament of salvation. That is why, quite simply, I can acknowledge that these calumnies and persecutions never made me bitter, or did the least damage to my faith in the Church. On the contrary, they have helped me to be more deeply united to the mystery of Christ. We must never forget that Christ on the Cross is the Lamb of God who takes upon himself the sin of the world, and was condemned as an evildoer, slandered, insulted, scourged, spat upon, tortured physically and morally. The disciple follows the footsteps of the Master, and if you want to be faithful, then sooner or later the time will come for you to be a sign of contradiction.

Finally I would like to say a word about charity under such circumstances, for the "old man," to use St. Paul's words, would rather react according to the law of *talion:* an eye for an eye, a tooth for a tooth. But the new man, the man who lives in Christ, understands that this is not possible and that you must overcome evil with good. The best way to react is with kindness, respectful silence, patience, and forgiveness. It all has a reason in God's plans. He knows why, and he is the Master who knows how to bring good things out of what appears evil to us.

35. In 1950 you are only thirty years old, and you build a formation center for the Legionaries of Christ in Rome. Can you explain why and how you took this step?

During the year of 1948 the congregation kept growing stronger in terms of the number of vocations and the formation of the religious, but the criticisms were also on the rise to the extent that we had to give up the cowshed and house where we were living in the town of Comillas and move to the Cistercian abbey in Cóbreces, eight kilometers from Comillas. There, next to the monastery, the monks had a building — the Quiroz Institute — which they kindly leased to us for three and a half years, until 1952, when we were able to buy the present vocational center in Ontaneda, Santander. The Legionaries will always gratefully and appreciatively remember the kindness with which the priests and brothers of the abbey received us. The abbot, Father Luis Yagüe, knew us well and really loved us; he was the ordinary confessor of our students, and he and his entire Cistercian community welcomed us with the utmost kindness and charity. In 1950 the novices, juniors, philosophers, and theologians moved to Rome and only the brothers from the vocational center were left in Cóbreces.

How did we get to Rome, then? In 1948 after the congregation was canonically approved and established, the insistent accusations achieved their effect and a document was sent from Rome, from the Sacred Congregation for Religious, to Bishop Alfonso Espino y Silva of Cuernavaca ordering the congregation to be dissolved.

I was willing, of course, to obey the decision of the Holy See, because I have always believed that obedience to the legitimate authority in the Church is the path on which you find God's will and your own growth in holiness. All I asked my bishop for was time to duly carry out all the instructions, and above all to find the financial resources to make all the necessary travel arrangements since my seminarians would have to return to Mexico to continue in the Cuernavaca seminary or in some other diocese. While I was busy with this, it occurred to me I could go to Rome and ask permission from the Prefect of the Congregation for Religious, Cardinal Luigi Lavitrano, to bring a small group of seminarians to Rome to continue their studies there, and once they were ordained priests one of them could found the congregation and I would join the undertaking. What mattered to me, because I felt it in my conscience, was that God's plan in the congregation be fulfilled, not so much that I be the one to do it.

When I spoke to Cardinal Lavitrano for the first time, he was quite surprised because he knew nothing about the congregation being dissolved. He told me that he would do some research and then meet with me again. He did his research and sure enough found out that the dissolution was invalid since he, the Prefect, had been in the dark about it and had not signed the decree. So four days later he put me at ease, reassuring me that the congregation did exist juridically within the Church. However, he advised me to establish a residence in Rome as soon as possible so as to be close to the Pope and the Curia, since that would give them first-hand information about the state and development of the project. That was December 1948. I remember this interview with Cardinal Lavitrano took place on a liturgical festivity of Mary, but I cannot tell for sure now if it was December 8, solemnity of Mary's Immaculate Conception, or December 12, dedicated to Our Lady of Guadalupe. The interview with the Cardinal Prefect deeply consoled me and brought me tremendous peace, because once again it showed me by humanly tortuous paths God's will to forge ahead with the plan.

Cardinal Lavitrano himself introduced me to a construction company that worked for the Vatican, so that with them I could plan a college in Rome for our community. The project seemed a sheer fantasy since we had no funds for it. Supporting our students in Spain and Mexico had us stretched to our limit.

The following days I called on people the cardinal recommended to me, and that is how they offered me a beautiful property, twenty thousand square meters (roughly 4.5 acres) on Via Aurelia. Although I had no money at the time, I accepted and immediately phoned a friend in Mexico who had the means to donate the sum of money we needed. Thanks be to God, this person was generous and sent us the donation by check. That way, at least, we were able to buy the land. Right away we started working on drawings, and a few days later we signed the construction contract. To cover these expenses I returned to Mexico. I raised part of what we needed, but we still needed a lot more, so I took a trip to Venezuela to call on some people that a Venezuelan priest-friend of mine in Rome, Father Rotondaro, had recommended to me. Although it was difficult, I finally found substantial help: a woman of French extraction, Ana Cecilia Branger, who lived in the Venezuelan city of Valencia, generously donated a house on the French Riviera, in Cannes, for us to sell and with the proceeds pay for most of the college on Via Aurelia.

All of this meant that I was constantly on the move, but naturally I didn't fail to keep in touch with the religious, novices, and minor seminarians by letter, through the superiors and, as often as I could, through personal attention to each of them, to help them grow in their vocation to the priesthood and religious life.

The college in Rome was finished by fall 1950, but we still hadn't furniture or effects, which we put together over time. We brought a lot of the equipment with us from Spain, because they were much cheaper there. We had no beds or chairs for several months until we had enough money. We built a cowshed. With a few cows we got enough milk for the community. We also had chickens and a garden. The cowshed is still at our house at 677 Via Aurelia. Father Isaiah's orphanage in Primavalle gave us the kitchen utensils and dishware we needed. We lived very poorly, but God made sure nothing essential was ever missing, and all the religious were happy to imitate Christ in these external details too, and to be able to study in Rome, very close to the Holy Father.

36. The year 1950 was important in Pius XII's pontificate, being a jubilee year and the year he proclaimed the dogma of the

Assumption of Mary. How did you experience these events in Rome while founding your college in the Eternal City?

As I mentioned earlier, we built our college in Rome because that is what the Cardinal Prefect of the Congregation for Religious advised us to do. Even so, that had been my idea from the very beginning. I always wanted our men to be formed here, close to Christ's Vicar, because for me it was truly essential that our congregation stand out for its fidelity and loyalty to the Holy Father. My faith told me that only with the support of Christ's Vicar and his blessing and patronage could our congregation survive. In addition, it was my dream to offer Christ's Vicar priests who were entirely at his service and the service of the Church.

I had tried to transmit this spirit to our religious, and for reasons of faith we all loved the Holy Father deeply. So for all of us it was an extraordinary grace to know we could be nearer to him and participate a little more closely in his care and concern for all the particular churches.

As you rightly point out, our move to Rome providentially coincided with the jubilee year and the promulgation of the dogma of Our Lady's Assumption, which drew great crowds of pilgrims to the Eternal City to renew their faith at the places where the apostles Peter and Paul were martyred. All throughout that year, you could feel the catholicity of Rome like never before. Personally I wasn't able to be at the great events of that year, but I was present at the opening and closing, and I became aware of the graces a Holy Year implies for the Church. I thank God I was also in Rome in the Holy Years of 1975, 1983, and 2000, all of which were a special blessing from God for the whole Church and for myself in particular.

But the Holy Year of 1950 is full of unique memories, because that year I fulfilled my dream of coming with my religious to Rome so as to study at the best ecclesiastical universities and thus offer the Church an enthusiastic and well-trained band of apostles, holy priests, well prepared in every field, who could work for the good of the Church wherever we were needed.

37. You have lived in the preconciliar Church and the post-conciliar Church. What difference do you find between them?

The Council was a renewal of the Church, a return to her sources: to the gospel, to her living tradition. The Council wanted to bring the Church closer to the lives of contemporary men and women, and it brought in a breath of fresh air. As well, it enabled the Church to grow in self-awareness, in knowledge of the treasure of God's Word, in dialogue with the world, whose joys and sorrows the Church shares. I am thinking of the great dogmatic constitutions on the Church and on revelation, and the pastoral constitution on the Church in today's world. The Council invited the world to contemplate the mystery of the Church, the Spouse of Christ and the universal sacrament of salvation. There were no changes in doctrine; there was a desire to better understand today's world and be understood by it. The documents that came out of it were very beautiful and full of extraordinary doctrinal and pastoral richness.

However, we all know that some people took things to an extreme, supporting interpretations of the Council that agreed with their partial, subjective visions of the Church, which were not so much an authentic Church renewal as an excuse to question anything and everything. The famous postconciliar "crisis" was produced not by the Council itself, but by these interpretative trends that disfigured the face of the Church and took advantage of the Council to slip in their personal ideas about the Church.

Some currents that countered these radical interpretations likewise tried to draw an excessive contrast between the pre- and postconciliar eras, as if there had been a break or an unbridgeable hiatus between them, implying that after the Council everything or almost everything had changed or was to change, ignoring into the bargain the long and fruitful pontificates of Pius XI and Pius XII. However, before and after the Council there is a line of moral and doctrinal continuity in the Church that has not been broken. The Church's face has been rejuvenated under the guidance of the Holy Spirit. Thankfully, after a difficult phase we are now seeing the fruits of the Council in many areas of Church life. Along with the difficulties, which are never lacking, we can also contemplate with great joy the action of the Holy Spirit in so many lay associations, new religious movements, and fruits of true holiness — a case in point are the numerous martyrs, beatified or canonized, that John Paul II has raised to the altars — the numerical growth of the Church in Asia, Africa, and Latin America, the evangelizing fervor, the Christian solidarity in so many areas of social life.

Our attitude as Legionaries has always been to walk in step with the Church. That is why we had no problem embracing the Council, always avoiding extremes and the radical interpretations given to it. That is why we are and have always been careful to follow faithfully the instructions given by Paul VI and John Paul II, who with their authoritative Magisterium have guided the Church on the right path of Church renewal taught by Vatican II.

38. Early in the 1950s the Legionaries start their first apostolate, a school in Mexico City. How did the project come about and, particularly, why did you begin with a school?

The project came up providentially, just like all the other steps we took during the Legion's early years, and the steps we have been taking since. A woman from Mexico, Mrs. Flora Barragán de Garza, came to our college in Rome in 1951 and introduced herself. Her husband had died a short time before, and she had come to Rome to offer the Holy See a sum of money for the formation of priests. She had been received by Monsignor Giovanni Battista Montini, substitute for the Secretariat of State. Monsignor Montini already knew us, as I had had interviews with him several times asking his help to draft our constitutions properly. He suggested to Mrs. Barragán to come and visit us and offer the money for an apostolic project, and he gave her my name and our address on a personal visiting card. We agreed with Mrs. Barragán to use her donation to start the Legion of Christ's first apostolate.

The original project was to build a parish church, but while I was praying and begging God's light regarding the work we were to begin according to our charism, I saw clearly that what best suited our charism was an educational institution where we could educate children and young people in Christian values: the future parents of Catholic families, generations of professionals, industrialists, politicians, economists and so forth, who would help Mexico begin to find the way of Christian justice and charity.

The Legionaries' first apostolate was not exempt from hardship at its inception. Before it was born, Mrs. Barragán heard rumors from individuals of great moral prestige that completely discredited the congregation and me personally, insisting that we had not been approved by the Holy See. The Bishop of Saltillo, His Excellency Luis Guízar Barragán, backed Mrs. Barragán and unmasked the rumors, explaining that our congregation existed canonically within the Church, had diocesan approval, and would become a congregation of pontifical right once the Holy See had given it the Decree of Praise. Thus we were able to go ahead and purchase the land and start building the Cumbres school.

Directing and supervising this project took up a lot of my time and energy, but it was worthwhile since it would be the Legionaries' first apostolate and would set the standard for all those to follow. As I mentioned, we chose education because through children we would be able to do pastoral work of great value with their families and teachers. We could see on the horizon many possibilities for evangelizing society, though it would be by means of a small seed such as a school.

With the hard work and self-sacrifice of some religious (one of our first priests in particular, Father Faustino Pardo — *requiescat in pace* — who was one of the seminarians from Comillas who joined the congregation) we were able to build the Cumbres school and open it in 1954. The school marked the beginning of the Legionaries' educational work, which with God's help has steadily grown over the years.

39. Didn't the work that went into this and later achievements take you away from the work of forming your Legionaries?

The first apostolic projects and the fundraising for our formation centers meant making several trips, but my priority was always the formation of our young men. I always knew that the Legion would be its men, not its buildings. So I constantly exchanged letters with each of the men whom God had sent to the Legion to encourage them in their struggles and support them in their efforts to be holy and form themselves integrally. Whenever I was at our centers, especially Rome, I took on all the responsibilities that go with being a formator, even though in the early 1950s I already had very holy and zealous priests helping me: Father Antonio Lagoa as rector of the center for studies in Rome, Father Rafael Arumí as novice director, and Father Faustino Pardo as head of construction and later director of the Cumbres school itself.

In fact, one of the accusations made against me at the time was that I neglected the formation of our men. I believe in conscience that this was not the case. Within my limitations I always had a clear vision that the priority was to form the Legionaries thoroughly in every area, beginning with the spiritual and then proceeding to the human, intellectual, social, apostolic, et cetera. . . . Proof of this are my many letters, which the Legionaries later collected and printed in various volumes, whose constantly recurring theme is our men's formation in its every nuance.

The appearance of the congregation's first apostolates and the opening of new formation centers also occasioned envy and defamation. But this is something you simply have to take for granted in human life. All this helped me to do everything before God, not heeding the opinion of men but God's will. This principle has always brought great peace to my soul in spite of being continually misunderstood, defamed, and slandered. All of this is so very human besides, and God allows it so that we will seek him before all and above all.

40. Those were the very years, the fifties, when a difficult time in the life of the congregation began to take shape, which you have chosen to call the "Great Blessing." How did this situation come about, and what did it consist in?

Well, I believe all the trials God allows are ultimately blessings. I have always been struck by St. Paul's phrase: "All things work together for good for those who love God" (Rom 8:28). I believe that God's "blows" are blows of love. That is why I see that humanly dark period in our history as a time full of light, if you contemplate it in faith.

In fact, I can remember asking our Lord quite often during the hardest moments, in Madrid, why he was allowing all those trials. And one day, while I was at prayer before the tabernacle in the church of the Mercedarians on Silva Street in Madrid, I understood that I ought to raise my eyes and contemplate what was happening to me from a supernatural angle, from God's vantage point, from a faith-perspective, and not in an overly human, overly earthly way, because God's ways are not our ways, as the prophet Isaiah says. His ways cannot be explained by the light of reason alone, but by the other, higher light: the light of faith.

As I have been mentioning, even though we were a nonentity, by a mysterious design of God the congregation throughout its founding years aroused suspicion and criticism in certain churchmen, and they created a lot of complications for us. With God's help we got through these obstacles as best we could, and as a result we developed a deep spirit of unity and charity, which is the essence of Christianity and also of the congregation's spirit.

Those who did not look kindly on the embryonic congregation quickly understood that if this unity was broken, they would be able to destroy it more easily. This is what they tried to do. The wave of slander against me that reached the Roman dicasteries repeated the earlier slander of 1948 and included a new, very grave calumny, drug addiction, and brought about a series of canonical visitations.

No official written document ever reached me informing me of what was happening or giving me instructions. I received instructions directly by word of mouth and through third parties, and I was denied any possibility of defense. I was simply informed that I still held the office of general superior but was deprived of the faculty to govern, though I should keep working to sustain the congregation financially. While the canonical visitations were being carried out I was forbidden to have any contact with the Legionaries and was exiled from Rome to Spain from the last few months of 1956 onwards.

Two and a half years passed before I could return to the Eternal City. In the meantime I worked out of Spain, fundraising to support the congregation's various houses and paying for the construction of the new novitiate in Salamanca, Spain, and the Basilica of Guadalupe in Rome. When I telephoned Cardinal Federico Tedeschini, one of the cardinal-friends who encouraged and supported me so much throughout that time, he asked me, "Why do you keep on building that novitiate if you might end up expelled from the congregation, or if the congregation might be dissolved?" But I figured that if our situation failed to right itself, at least the building would be there for the Church to use. That's why I kept going with the project.

Those were tough years for the congregation and for me. But amid all the difficulties God's hand held us up, comforted us, and encouraged us to keep forging ahead. And since, once again, we plainly saw God's help and provident love amid these trials, we chose to call that period "the Great Blessing."

41. How and when did this period end?

In 1959, after almost three years, the visitators of the Holy See came to the conclusion that the accusations had been amply proven false. At last on February 6, 1959, I was fully restored to my functions as superior general. I am especially grateful to Cardinals Giuseppe Pizzardo, Gaetano Cicognani, Clemente Micara, Giovanni Piazza, and Federico Tedeschini, and to Bishop Giovanni Battista Montini; also to the two visitators, Monsignor Alfredo Bontempi and Monsignor Polidoro van Vlierberghe, a Franciscan from Belgium who is still alive — at present he is the bishop emeritus of Illapel, Chile. As the apostolic visitator appointed by the Holy See he sought the truth about the Legion and its charism without prejudice and with utter sincerity. Since then he has always been a loyal friend and wonderful defender of the congregation. I am also very grateful to Father Diego Bugallo Pita who worked as an adjunct in the Nunciature in Madrid and was a true friend, an honest and upstanding man, always faithful and unconditional.

I thank God for this period, which purified us and enabled me to practice Christian obedience. I have always believed in the spiritual fruitfulness of this virtue, which Christ lived to a heroic degree unto death, and death on a cross. No charism is authentic in the Church unless it bows to the gentle yoke of obedience. When lived in faith and love, this beautiful but difficult virtue opens up areas of true freedom and is a seal of authenticity on a Church charism. To teach myself to obey, I have carefully contemplated Christ's obedience to his Father in heaven, and this has sustained and encouraged me, especially when I have to accept trials and situations that are hard for human nature, though necessary in God's provident plan.

42. So this was when the Basilica of Guadalupe was built in Rome?

Ever since 1954 Cardinal Clemente Micara, His Holiness's vicar for the diocese of Rome, had asked me to build a church in Rome dedicated to Our Lady of Guadalupe. This project had a history. It had been proposed to other individuals and congregations, but for various reasons it never happened. Although we were also building the Cumbres Institute and the novitiate in Salamanca and in negotiations to buy buildings for our minor seminaries in Mexico and Spain, I decided to carry out the project, since it was a formal request from the Cardinal Vicar of Rome. Besides, I had always longed to build a shrine in honor of the Blessed Virgin. I began to ask for financial help from Mexican Catholics and, through Father Jorge Ruiz of the Querétaro diocese, I preached in various dioceses to that end. I continued to do so, always wanting to serve the Church, throughout the hard years of the Great Blessing. Thanks to God and the generosity of the Catholics of Mexico, the church was finished in 1958 while I was exiled from Rome. So, to my great sorrow, I couldn't be present at the inauguration on December 12, 1958. Several cardinals from the Roman Curia, however, attended the ceremony, as well as Archbishop José Garibi y Rivera of Guadalajara and many Latin American bishops. Pope John XXIII and John Paul II have visited the church to pray before the image of Our Lady of Guadalupe for the needs of the Church and of Latin America. It was Pope John Paul II who raised the church to the status of Minor Basilica.

At such times you are more aware than ever that you have been and continue to be an instrument that God uses to do his work, and the *Magnificat* springs spontaneously from your heart.

43. When did the Holy See definitively approve the Congregation of the Legionaries of Christ?

All religious congregations must go through a long process with various intermediate steps before being awarded the Decree of Praise (*Decretum Laudis*) by the Holy See. With this document, a congregation is no longer of diocesan right but becomes an institution of pontifical right. In our case the Decree of Praise was granted on February 6, 1965, twenty-four years after the founding. This decree is an act of recognition by the Holy See that the congregation has achieved spiritual and apostolic maturity.

By that time we had founded novitiates in Spain, Ireland, and the United States, and we were already running our first apostolates: schools and universities. The Prefect of the Congregation for Religious himself — Cardinal Ildebrando Antoniutti, whom I had met in Spain when he was the Nuncio there — came to our formation center in Rome on that February day in 1965 to bestow the Decree of Praise personally and to sing the *Magnificat* with us for all the great things the Lord had seen fit to do in our lowliness.

There still remained the approval of our Constitutions, which came on June 29, 1983. It was Pope John Paul II who granted the approval since the Congregation for Religious had referred the matter to him due to the fact that our Constitutions contained elements that required the Pope's personal intervention. The day after the feast of St. Peter and St. Paul, the Prefect for Religious, Cardinal Eduardo Pironio, a good friend of ours, signed the decree of approval in front of the community of Legionaries present in Rome, in the Basilica of Our Lady of Guadalupe. It is hard to express what that moment meant for me as founder. After forty-two years of labor to follow the interior call of God in my soul, the Church was authoritatively confirming, once again, that the path I had taken was God's will for me and for all those who were called and would be called to live this charism that God had raised up to serve the Church.

IV

The Legion of Christ:
Its Charism, Its Mission, Its Men

44. When people hear about the Congregation of the Legion-aries of Christ, one of their first questions, especially in Europe, has to do with the name, which in some countries sounds like a military organization. Why the name "Legionaries of Christ"?

Our first name was "Missionaries of the Sacred Heart of Jesus and Our Lady of Sorrows"; however, there were already a number of religious congregations with similar names; in addition, this name did not have the potential to convey to everyone an exact idea of our spirituality, and we did want our name to express our apostolic dynamism. That is why we looked for other possibilities. Around that time was when I met Pope Pius XII, in 1946. After I explained my plans for the congregation, the Holy Father quoted a verse from the Song of Songs (6:4, 10) where the husband evokes the beauty of his bride, "terrible as an army in battle array" (*"sicut castrorum acies ordinata"*). Naturally the Pope was referring to the combat of faith that St. Paul speaks of (2 Tim 4:7). The apostle himself begs Timothy to be a good soldier of Jesus Christ (2 Tim 2:3), and Ephesians 6 promotes the whole idea of a Christian's battle for the good: "Put God's armor on so as to be able to resist the devil's tactics" (verse 11), and he describes a Christian's armor: "So stand your ground, with truth buckled round your waist, and integrity for a breastplate, wearing for shoes on your feet the eager-ness to spread the gospel of peace and always carrying the shield of faith so that you can use it to put out the burning arrows of the evil one. And then you must accept salvation from God to be your hel-met and receive the word of God from the Spirit to use as a sword" (verses 14-17).

No one reads militarism into St. Paul just because he used these comparisons. Clearly the Apostle to the Gentiles is here trying to get across to his Christians that their life will be a strug-gle against evil, requiring them to clothe themselves with the Christian virtues that he mentions. Moved by the Bible verse that the Pope quoted, the passages from Paul, and the witness of the Cristeros who gave their lives for their faith, we finally chose the name Legionaries of Christ, which is intended to convey the idea of a well-organized, united, and compact group of men who are well prepared to serve Christ and his gospel, which as we know is the Good News of love, mercy, forgiveness, acceptance, and re-spect. Our name also certainly expresses the vigor, dynamism, and strength we should bring to proclaiming this message of salvation.

At the time I was unaware that countries such as France and Spain had military units with the name "Legion." It was princi-pally the discipline, strength, and effectiveness of the Roman le-gions that caught my attention — their cohesion and effective organization. We know from Church history that many of the men who spread Christianity throughout the empire during the first centuries of the Christian era were actually soldiers of the Roman legions. Since I wanted to embody the courage, devotion, and boldness of the men whom God would call to make his project a reality, I thought that Legionaries would be a good name, so that they would dedicate themselves with the same passion and con-viction to their mission of spreading Christ's Kingdom in society. Our name has nothing to do with any present-day military group or organization, of which I was quite simply unaware; it has to do with those Bible passages, the Roman legions, and the witness of the Cristeros who gave their lives for their faith. All this, and the words of Pius XII, came together in the name Legionaries of Christ. I said earlier and I want to repeat, our battle for Christ's Kingdom is a battle fought in love, peace, and service to our brothers and sisters. Our only desire is that each of them find the way to heaven and the fullness of his or her vocation in Christ. The Legion of Christ is a legion of love and peace.

45. How would you define the charism of the Legion of Christ?

Before addressing your question specifically I would like to recall the way in which the Holy Spirit throughout history raises up specific charisms to respond to the needs of the times. All such charisms are gifts from God to his Church; he gives them to specific men so that they in turn will transmit them to others, and in that way form what we call religious or spiritual families.

The secular press often tries to pit the various charisms against one another. This logic doesn't work on the spiritual level because these charisms do not conflict but rather complement each other. Each has its own mission to fulfill. Ultimately, all charisms work for the common good and serve the same faith of the Church.

Once that is clear, I think I can answer that the Holy Spirit has raised up the Legion of Christ to seek authenticity in fulfilling the commandment of charity among all people, which summarizes the message of the incarnation of the divine Word. Legionaries strive to spread this Kingdom of love in the world, in the various areas of society, by forming priests and laypeople who, imbued with the gospel spirit of charity, dedicate themselves to building a new civilization of justice and love by means of various apostolates. This means that the array of apostolates is quite broad, though the spirit that inspires them is one and the same. As a matter of fact we do not in principle rule out any type of apostolate that would help spread Christ's Kingdom in society.

To spread Christ's Kingdom in the world, you have to have a deep knowledge of God's love, the ultimate reason behind Christ's redeeming us. You have to live the authentic charity that Christ preached and demanded. You have to tell others about God's merciful love for all people by preaching the gospel tirelessly, so as to bring about the conversion of every heart, the spread of charity, and the building of a civilization of Christian justice and love. To practice true charity and ardent, generous love for Christ and the Church he founded, you have to give yourself generously to all, without barriers.

Therefore, the Legion of Christ and the Regnum Christi Movement strive to undertake those endeavors that in their depth and breadth will be most effective in establishing Christ's Kingdom among all people and in society, while maintaining utmost fidelity to the Church's Magisterium and full communion with the Successor of Peter, the Pope, and all the Church's shepherds who are in communion with him. Regnum Christi is conscious that our action will be effective if we achieve the Christian formation and apostolic deployment of those men and women who exercise the greatest leadership in the religious, cultural, intellectual, social, economic, human, and artistic spheres.

46. What does your spirituality contribute to the Christian spirituality?

Contribute? In Christ you already have everything. There are nuances — ways and forms of living — that explore a given aspect of the manifold richness of the mystery of Christ. Christ is the model for every Christian, priest or layperson. He is the supreme model that inspires all Christian spirituality. The Legion of Christ, as a Christian spirituality, revolves around the person of Christ. Right from the founding I kept very much in mind that Christ should be the supreme model, the standard, the one who would inspire our entire spirituality. In this sense there is nothing new. The gospel has already said everything. What the Legion of Christ proposes to the men and women who seek its spirituality is Christ himself. To be a Christian means to know, love, follow, and imitate Christ, and to preach his command to extend his Kingdom among all people. This is the marrow of our spirituality.

However, to imitate Christ in all his entirety is beyond the reach of man. For this reason the various currents of Christian spirituality explore different nuances of the manifold wealth of the mystery of Christ.

What the Legion of Christ wants to remind Christians of once again and more insistently is Christ's "new" commandment: "Love one another, just as I have loved you" (John 13:34). If as priests, religious, or plain Christians we do not live this commandment, we are outside the gospel, we are "playacting" Christianity. I don't understand Christianity any other way except as the sincere, authentic love for our brothers and sisters in imitation of Christ. Everything else — piety, devotions, ceremonies, rites, processions, and so forth — are forms of prayer, and if you do them with a sincere heart, they please God; but without charity they are meaningless because the spirit of charity is the backbone of the gospel message. If you sincerely want to find God, you have to enter through this door.

The true watershed of human history is the living of this commandment. Individuals or institutions that do not honestly practice charity are outside the truth of the gospel because you can't be living in the truth if sincere charity is missing. At the end of our lives we will be asked about love: if we have loved or not. All our other achievements and everything else we have done will be seen in relation to the great fulfillment of the new commandment of brotherly love. At least, that's how I understand the gospel. This is the only way there will be a deep change in the world because here, in my view, is the essence of Christianity, the great novelty of the gospel.

It is all well and good to pray, offer sacrifices, frequent the sacraments, but if you don't love your brothers and sisters, they are all empty because the essence, the marrow, is missing. If anyone thinks he's an angel because he is pious, yet speaks evil of his neighbor, is jealous of him, tries to trip him up whenever he can, doesn't help him when he's in need, then he is destroying what Christ came to build; he is simply acting out a farce, something that is not Christianity. Christ came to save us by love, to teach us the way of mutual love, forgiveness, reconciliation, and mutual respect and appreciation, how to give our lives for others, for our brothers and sisters.

To live in love we have to master our passions, our pride, our conceit, our laziness. Our passions lead us to charity's opposite: egotism. Charity, on the other hand, frees us from it. Just look at the lives of the great saints: They understood this, and they imitated Christ's love for us to the point of heroism, giving themselves unconditionally to their brothers and sisters.

In this vein the Legion offers for our imitation the charity practiced by the first Christians when they were still savoring, as it were, the newness of the gospel and were striving to know Christ and imitate him in their mutual love: "See how they love one another!" the pagans said. Love, the mark of a Christian, made them recognizable as such.

As you see, Christ-centeredness and charity are at the core of our spirituality and lead to another very important characteristic: our apostolic dynamism. Christ came to the world to save his brothers and sisters, and he sent the apostles and his disciples to preach this gospel of salvation. We emphasize the need to be active in our love for Christ, the Church and our neighbor out of our desire to imitate Christ, and out of true gospel love for others since they will find salvation in the gospel. We insist on translating our desire to love Christ and our neighbor into concrete acts of service and apostolate that go beyond merely good intentions. And in so doing, we choose the most effective ways, in order to do the greatest good for the most people.

Finally, there is an aspect I would like to underline, which, though not entirely new in the Church, still contains a degree of novelty. This is the importance we give to each person's integral formation, without overlooking any of its facets; we call it integral formation. I refer especially though not exclusively to human formation, since we believe that imitating Christ can't be limited exclusively to the virtues traditionally called Christian, the more spiritual virtues, neglecting the human ones, which are the basis on which the Holy Spirit configures Christ's image in a person. But once again I want to insist that both our apostolic dynamism and our integral formation spring from a sincere desire to live the commandment of charity to its utmost consequences. We want to tell our brothers and sisters about Christ because we love them. Since we love them, we want to be fitting instruments to transmit the gospel message through our integral formation. I repeat, without charity everything else is worthless.

47. What makes your congregation different from other congregations or religious groups in the Catholic Church?

This is an interesting question, but you understand it would take much longer than we have to answer it adequately, since we would have to take each congregation and movement one by one to point out the differences.

I would like, however, to mention that above and beyond the normal differences that you might point out among the various religious groups in the Church — those of a cultural, spiritual, apostolic nature — I think it important to understand what unites us all. In this sense I would like to recall the oft-quoted but always inspiring chapter 12 of St. Paul's First Letter to the Corinthians: "There is a variety of gifts but always the same Spirit; there are all sorts of service to be done, but always to the same Lord;

working in all sorts of different ways in different people, it is the same God who is working in all of them" (1 Cor 12:4-6). All the congregations and movements have the same purpose: to serve the Church. The same Spirit has raised them up, although each one serves according to the particular gift received. The person who tends the sores of a poor, dying person out of love for Christ serves the Church as much as the one who writes a book on theology for the same motive and with the same intention. What matters is that we are all here to build the Church, and that we respect our own and each other's charism as each one serves the same cause wherever God has placed us.

The annals of history speak of rivalries between religious orders and groups. I believe all of this is human. We all have to keep in mind that Christ's supreme prayer for the unity of believers should apply within the Church first of all. Thankfully there is a renewed awareness of this need. In recent years the heads or founders of the new Church movements have held regular meetings in Rome that are proving very fruitful towards achieving the kind of unity where differences are complementary and never antagonistic. In these encounters we have been insisting particularly on the need to encourage true gospel charity within each movement, among the movements, and in each person's relationships with others.

48. Earlier on you mentioned Christ-centeredness. I would like to know how the Legion of Christ understands it and why you chose to give your congregation this spiritual focus.

I already mentioned that the inspiration to found the congregation came to me on the feast of the Sacred Heart. From my childhood, especially under the influence of my mother, I lived in my home this devotion which, as you know, is focused on Christ's love for humanity. I remember our living the devotion quite spontaneously: we expressed it by receiving the sacraments of confession and Communion every First Friday and by imitating Christ's virtues, especially his charity. There were other traditions, too, such as praying the litany or enthroning an image of Christ in the home, but that was somewhat secondary. The most important was really to know, love, and imitate Christ. Later, during the Cristero war, as I also mentioned, I saw men — elderly, adult, and adolescents — die invoking Christ. For me, a relationship with Christ was something very natural and spontaneous.

Later, as time went by, I began to reflect in God's presence on what focus I should give to the congregation's spirituality. No matter how much I turned over and considered the lives of the saints and spiritual authors, I realized that in every case their holiness or wisdom ultimately came from imitating Christ and being deeply united with him. Therefore I didn't want our men to have any other model but Christ. With the passing of the years, as I became more and more experienced in forming priests and interacting with laypeople, I realized how attractive it is to present people with Christ. We often forget to talk to Christians about what is most obvious, which is to talk to them about Christ. When you preach to people, especially the youth, about Christ — the Christ of the gospel, true God and true man — they are captivated by the beauty of his message and the appeal of his person. If we truly believe that he is the Son of God made flesh, if we really believe what Vatican II says and John Paul II repeats so vigorously, that man finds the fullness of his vocation and his happiness only in Christ, then we would be less hesitant to proclaim him in all his beauty and with all the demands of his teaching.

Sometimes people start by talking about morality, about more or less abstruse doctrines. But I think what people (today and always) really want is to meet Christ personally, experience him vividly like the people in the gospel — like Peter, John, Matthew, Martha and Mary, Zaccheus, Lazarus, and so many others. The gospel shows us that their living encounter with Christ deeply touched these people, that their lives changed radically after they met him. True, not everyone was generous enough to follow him. Symbolic of these is the unnamed rich young man who preferred his wealth to following Christ. But those who did follow him were not let down.

I don't understand this Christ-centeredness in a romantic or theoretical way. It's an encounter. It's an experience. Ultimately it is a grace from the Holy Spirit. Our Christianity needs this living experience. People are tired of ideas and abstract notions. They need to give a meaning to their lives, and Christ can do this. And he does. When you aren't afraid of him, when you throw open the doors of your heart to him, then you know the happiness that comes from following him, even though you also know you have to carry the cross every day.

The Christ-centeredness I am describing is demanding, because it comes from the gospel. Let's not forget that while he lived on this earth he made the conditions to follow him extremely clear. He really "raises the bar," as they say in sports. He demanded that his own give themselves as radically and unconditionally as he. That is why I am not afraid to speak clearly and frankly to people, especially young people. And I think they appreciate it when I do. They are attracted by Christ's challenge. He wants to bring to light the very best that each person has inside. True, not everyone follows him. Today, too, we have our "rich young men." If Christ himself had this experience, of course it happens to us too. But what we can't do is water down the gospel, sugarcoat it, to each one's fancy. Christ is eternal. His person and his message are the same yesterday, today, and always. This is the Christ the Church and the Pope preach. This is the Christ we, too, want to preach.

49. Now that you mention being radical, some people think the Legionaries are too demanding, too rigid in their discipline, too serious in their formation. What do you think about this?

To form a person, and especially a priest, you have to be very precise, like making a fine watch. Nothing can be missing; all the pieces have to fit together and they must be put together properly for the mechanism to work. The formation of Legionaries is somewhat like that. If we want to form priests to be models of Christian life for the faithful, we need to ensure all the elements that go into the integral formation that a man consecrating his life in the Catholic priesthood should have: his human, intellectual, spiritual, and apostolic formation.

So it all depends on how you understand the terms "demanding," "rigid," and "discipline." Earlier I spoke of being demanding, but not of being rigid. I believe Christ was demanding with his own, but never rigid. When we say someone is rigid, it conjures up the impression that he is inflexible, unable to adjust to reality. Christ was realistic. He knew perfectly what was inside people, inside each person. That is why, even though he presented the gospel ideal with all its demands, he always understood people's failings, falls, and weaknesses. The most obvious case is St. Peter. Christ never lowered the ideal for Peter, not even after he denied him. Remember the wonderful passage where the two of them are on the shore of Lake Tiberias and Christ asks about his love: "Simon, son of John, do you love me more than these others do?" (John 21:15). But when Christ demands, he is full of motivation, affection, tenderness, sincere interest in the other person's good. It's in this positive vein that you can say the Legion is demanding with its members, because it presents them the gospel ideal in all its beauty. But the Legion, like Christ, understands the weakness of man, wounded by sin and full of shadows amid the brilliant light of grace. But I would neither apply nor accept the adjective "rigid," which smacks of intolerance, attempting to apply preconceived patterns without taking into account a person's actual situation.

As regards discipline, we would also need to clarify what kind of discipline we mean and how we understand the word. Some social groupings impose discipline externally, but that is not the discipline we are looking for. We foster a discipline motivated by love, with deep supernatural meaning, that will also be a means for apostolic effectiveness and formative ascesis. If you want to pray; or follow Christ who is poor, chaste, and obedient; or acquire a solid human and intellectual formation, you need to subject yourself to discipline. But this discipline is never a straitjacket. No one forces it on you. You yourself, given the specific purposes you seek, see the need to choose the appropriate way to reach the same. That is why we speak of motivated discipline and personal conviction. If discipline is merely external, it will only work as long as the structures that impose it remain in place, but once they disappear discipline will also. You build a man from within, from his will, freedom, and reason. This is where he needs to discipline himself voluntarily. If this is your understanding of discipline, then I would say the Legion esteems it highly, as long as it is guided by faith, love, freedom, and reason, as I just said.

Discipline also has pedagogical and spiritual value. As I mentioned, it has value relative to the goal you seek. You need discipline, for example, to study. If you want to learn a given branch of science systematically, you necessarily have to follow a measure of mental discipline and method. If you want to be effective in military undertakings, you need personal discipline. In this sense, discipline is a means to a goal. It is not the goal in itself. A student and a soldier both need discipline, not to practice it for its own sake but to achieve their goals more easily.

A Christian, too, needs discipline to pray and be virtuous. It is a necessary means. Besides, you see people today put themselves through the toughest discipline to stay healthy, for example, or simply to stay in good shape. No one criticizes their enormous sacrifices for these purposes that are good in themselves, so why should people criticize the discipline it takes to live the gospel? Christ was very realistic in this regard when he told his disciples to strive to enter by the narrow gate, since the gate that leads to perdition is wide (Matt 7:13-14). St. Paul himself employs the image of an athlete training to win his race and win a perishable crown. He concludes that he himself, seeking an everlasting crown, must strive that much harder than those who compete for a perishable prize (1 Cor 9:24-27).

A man who is preparing for priesthood, or is already a priest or religious, likewise has to maintain a personal discipline in line with his vocation. For example, if you want to live in priestly celibacy or take the vow of chastity you need the discipline in your lifestyle that will enable you to be faithful to that commitment. Not to know this would mean operating outside of a healthy concept of man — not just on the Christian but even on the merely human level.

I do not believe in discipline for discipline's sake, but I do believe that man, wounded by original sin, has tendencies that can lead him to evil. The Council of Trent, borrowing an expression from St. Paul, calls this concupiscence. In Romans 7, St. Paul vividly describes the inner battle waged in the theater of the human heart: "I cannot understand my own behavior. I fail to carry out the things I want to do, and I find myself doing the very things I hate . . . with the result that instead of doing the good things I want to do, I carry out the sinful things I do not want. In my inmost self I dearly love God's Law, but I can see that my body follows a different law that battles against the law which my reason dictates. This is what makes me a prisoner of that law of sin which lives inside my body. What a wretched man I am! Who will rescue me from this body doomed to death? Thanks be to God through Jesus Christ our Lord!" (Rom 7:15, 19, 22-24).

We all have to wage this battle against our passions. This is undeniable. Discipline, motivated by love for God, helps us to come out on top in this battle. All the elements of discipline that we use are there for a higher goal and motivated by love. This produces free and mature men, not men with complexes, stunted in their faculties or unfulfilled. Just take some time to observe the seminarians and priests who live the classical elements of Church discipline (the only kind that we demand), and see if they give you the impression of not living life fully. Quite the opposite: This discipline, lived in the balance given by faith and the harmony of the nobler faculties, helps them live what St. Augustine called *libertas maior*. They radiate freedom, composure, and self-mastery. They radiate freedom — be they Legionaries of Christ, regular Christians, or members of any other religious congregation or new community. When you practice discipline out of love and in an atmosphere of personal and community balance, it does not enslave, but liberates.

50. It's common knowledge that you chose to give the Legionaries a long and complete formation. Why did you feel this need?

To answer your question, let me briefly return to two topics we have already gone over: the charism of our congregation, and Christ-centeredness.

The formation that any association, including religious congregations, gives its members should be based on its goals. If our charism were to work with elderly people in retirement homes, we would have to give our members an adequate formation to enable them to understand the right way to treat the elderly to help them in the final years of their lives. Now, if what we want is to prepare men and women to imbue society with the Christian spirit, we must give our members the formation necessary to reach this objective.

For this reason, right from the beginning my idea for Legionaries was to give them a select, complete formation. And that takes time. You cannot improvise formation. I must say that I was tempted to ordain them more quickly so as to have more priests, especially during the early years. But I always knew that those easy shortcuts wouldn't solve the problem, but only put it off. I waited quite a few years to see the first Legionary priest ordained. The first to go through all the stages of formation is His Excellency Jorge Bernal Vargas, currently bishop of Cancún-Chetumal, Mexico. He had sixteen years of formation between the time he entered the vocational center until he was ordained a priest.

If it were only a matter of giving men a good intellectual preparation and a vague idea of what it is to be a Catholic priest, if it were only a matter of "churning out" priests, then priestly formation wouldn't have to take the time it does, and a Legionary's would seem very long. But if it's a matter of forming the man that God has chosen to be a priest in every aspect, and watching over him as he matures so that he becomes a priest after God's own heart, then we can't try to skip or rush through the stages of this evolution. And so we need to take the years required by the evolution of an adolescent, or a youth, or a person who joins as an adult, to complete his integral formation and come to bear the fruit expected of a Legionary priest.

Just as the nature of a tree requires certain phases for it to germinate, develop, grow, blossom, and produce its fruit, the nature of priesthood also requires time in order to form a priest well. You can't expect a tree to produce mature fruit in a year, or two, or three. We have to wait as long as the tree's nature requires to harvest ripe, healthy fruit. There is a similar process when educating a person or forming a Legionary. We have to wait, watch his evolution, watch the maturing process, see how he forms his intelligence, psyche, emotions, affections, personality, interpersonal skills, and so on. Then we reach the time we can say, "Now he can do it. Now he's mature. Let's present him to the Church to receive the sacrament of priestly orders."

Otherwise we could ordain our members in four, five, or six years and present them for priestly ordination, but the consequences would be very sad. It's better to wait as long as it takes for a Legionary to mature naturally and prudently, and attain his integral formation.

You see, I have always held that a priest's formation has to be integral. You can't limit it to one aspect or another. Sometimes the priests I met would have a superb intellectual formation, great scholars who knew theology, philosophy, and other civil or ecclesiastic sciences perfectly, but with no interpersonal skills or without a prayer life. Sometimes it would be the other way around: men who were very pious but lacking the intellectual leadership to guide their brothers and sisters to a deeper understanding of the faith. Seeing this, I always wanted the priests who would be formed in our congregation to imitate Christ in every facet of his personality. If we really wanted to help the Church, we were going to have to offer it priests who are formed in every facet, without neglecting any. To borrow a phrase from a well-known Italian song, a priest should be *impero dell'armonia*, where harmony reigns. Despite its apparent novelty in the Church this really is a return to our origins, because it means turning the priest's gaze once again to the figure of Christ, the perfect man, as the supreme model for his personal life and his ministry.

51. Isn't there a certain hierarchy to the various facets of a priest's formation? What do you think is the most important area of formation?

Yes, we could establish a scale of importance, and obviously spiritual formation has to be on top. Without a deep interior life, a prayer life, constant conversation with the Holy Spirit, deep communion with the mystery of Christ and the Church, a priest's life might well be packed with noise and activity, but it won't be worth a whit as far as salvation is concerned. A priest should live continuously immersed in the mystery of Christ. This comes from God's grace — God's grace and our cooperation, that is. It takes long years dedicated to forming your prayer-life, your personal ascesis, your understanding in faith of the mysteries of Christ's life, and slow, gradual maturing in your vocation.

To spiritual formation you then add the other aspects of formation. I wouldn't venture to put them in too rigid an order. God wants man to put his whole self into full cooperation with the action of grace, and no area of his person to be left out of this partnership with God and cooperation with his plan. If you neglect anything, however small, your formation will be incomplete, crippled. For example, if a priest neglects his human formation because he thinks it doesn't affect his holiness and ministry, the results could be disastrous — without the human foundation to provide the Holy Spirit with raw material to act upon and bring about holiness, that holiness will be very limited. Hence the importance of his formative years for a priest — and for any Christian. Hence also, because of the difficulty of such an undertaking, the importance of having an attentive, kind, demanding, patient formator on hand to encourage you, help you focus your efforts and overcome the times of discouragement that are always a possibility on the arduous path to priesthood.

52. In your book *The Integral Formation of Catholic Priests,* you really stress human formation. Why so?

I believe the basic reason I stress human formation for priests is that I always keep in mind that a priest is *alter Christus*. If we take seriously what Catholic dogma tells us — that Christ is perfect God and perfect man — it follows that whoever wants to fully identify with Christ in his vocation and mission cannot but work to be a "perfect man" like his Master. It is absolutely necessary to have an intense prayer life, as we have said, but that is no reason to neglect other aspects that may seem secondary, but which nevertheless shape the "complete priest." The various components of the human person form a deep unity. If you properly develop your mind, will, feelings, emotions, and interpersonal relationships, you are placing the foundation to reflect Christ as perfectly as possible in your life. Nevertheless, there are countless people without this human formation to whom the Holy Spirit gives himself, granting them an experiential knowledge of God as theirs to possess and savor.

Yet it is also obvious that a priest's human maturity — his psychological and emotional balance, keen intelligence, firm will, emotional composure — will contribute enormously to a much more effective apostolate. When we meet someone who is self-possessed, kind, noble, honest, welcoming, and consistent, this array of human values which make him a complete man attracts us to him. Christ certainly drew the crowds because of the strength that radiated from his divine person, but just as certainly his human personality was utterly overwhelming, even for his enemies.

From the beginning of the foundation I insisted strongly on these aspects, something novel at the time since it was generally held that a priest only had to have a high spiritual and dogmatic formation. But I saw that if these aspects were missing, there would be something in the priest that would not reflect Christ's image in him, and could even be an occasion for people to withdraw from him. I was overjoyed, therefore, to see this idea confirmed in the post-synodal exhortation *Pastores Dabo Vobis*, in which John Paul II calls human formation the foundation of all intellectual formation, acknowledging that without an adequate human formation all of a priest's formation would be deprived of its necessary foundation (n. 43).

Physical fitness is also part of human formation for us — as the Romans used to say, *"mens sana in corpore sano"* — and for this reason we always set aside some time for sports and exercise in our centers for formation and apostolate. We want our Legionaries to be in good shape. We believe that sports and exercise are a way to release energy and relax, and they are also formative. Team sports are especially helpful in developing social virtues: sportsmanship, respect for others, self-control, wholesome competitiveness, discipline, team spirit above personal interests, and so forth. Outings to the countryside, the sea, or the mountains are another type of exercise that can soothe your spirit, help you to find yourself, and contemplate God's marvelous creative action in nature. This is why we set aside a full two weeks every summer for community vacation, spent exclusively on hiking and challenging outings, plus a variety of sports for the purpose of replenishing physical and spiritual energy for the coming year. Our communities also take regular day excursions to the countryside; everyone or almost everyone — from the youngest to the oldest — participates, so as to get the exercise they need and share their spiritual or apostolic experiences with one another in an atmosphere of joy, charity, and brotherhood.

53. Related to the subject of human maturity is affective maturity, a hotly debated issue during and after the Council. Today it is again being addressed, especially after the priest scandals in certain countries. How do you understand affective maturity?

This brings us back once more to the principle we already stated: the confluence of grace and nature in the formation of every Christian, especially the priest. Affective maturity is the fruit of human effort cooperating with grace. We also start from the principle that the force of love and its affective expression are built into human nature. God chose to make man a rational being capable of giving and receiving love. No one is exempt from this natural necessity. Every person, according to his state in life, must fulfill his vocation to love. A single person, a spouse, a priest, and a religious will all do so in different ways, but no one can fail to make the rendezvous of love to which God calls him and for which he was created.

God does not call to priesthood men who love poorly. Rather, he calls those to whom he himself has given a big heart, large enough to embrace all men and women, bringing them grace and the message of salvation without favoritism or distinctions. But a priest is a man like any other, with affective and sexual tendencies like everyone else. If he gives up married love and the chance to form a family, he does so because he has received the charism of celibacy to give himself exclusively to the love of Christ and the Church. This unique vocation is a gift and not a limitation, as it might seem from a merely human point of view. In a world that displays hedonism, dominated at times by the erotic, celibacy for the sake of the Kingdom of heaven is a sign of God's presence in the world, of his grace triumphing over nature, and it is a summons from the world to come.

But this gift leaves intact our human nature wounded by sin, with all its tendencies and passions. And so, whoever receives it has to learn to integrate harmoniously his capacity to love and be loved with his condition in life. This implies channeling all his affections towards the priestly ideal that he has freely chosen in re-sponse to a call. This integration is neither simple nor painless. Our human heart spontaneously seeks a person of flesh and blood to love. The man who lives in celibacy has to accept this real, cru-cifying renunciation for the sake of an indescribably beautiful love: love for Christ, which unifies your personality and gives you the strength to overcome every kind of obstacle that could cross your path.

All of this implies a severe, motivated, but also joyful self-discipline: of your interior and exterior senses, affections, emo-tions, relationships with others — especially women. You can't be naïve and let seminarians indulge in uncontrolled affective expe-riences as if these didn't leave their mark on a man's psychology and emotions, especially when he's young. During the postconciliar years some seminaries were ruined because they let the seminari-ans have a social life exactly like laypeople, with the excuse that it helped them mature affectively. The seminarians were allowed to have girlfriends, take them out to the movies and the beach just like any other young man. What happened was, the normal ones fell in love and married them, and left their vocation to the priesthood. I think that if God calls a young man to follow him in the priesthood or religious life, it is an absolute injustice to deny him the means he needs to persevere in his vocation. Thankfully, many of these aberrations have been corrected, though not all of them, and we are still paying the price.

Affective maturity is possible for priests. It is possible with the help of God's grace. "Cut off from me you can do nothing" (John 15:5). It is possible with human cooperation that has to apply the necessary means to achieve it. With the example of so many, many faithful priests, Church history shows us that it is possible to live the gift of celibacy for the sake of the Kingdom of heaven, fully and with immense fruitfulness. Only when you see it like this, as a gift, and only when you know how fragile the earthen vessel is, in which you carry the treasure, will you be able to give the world the radiant word of the gospel beatitude: "Happy the pure in heart: they shall see God" (Matt 5:8).

54. You mentioned conversation with the Holy Spirit. How important is this in your life as a priest and founder in particular, and for Christian life in general?

The archbishop of Mexico City, Luis María Martínez, whom I was blessed to know personally, called the Holy Spirit the "great Unknown." We could apply to the Holy Spirit the Baptizer's words about Jesus: "There is one among you whom you do not know" (John 1:26). He is with us — the Paraclete, the Consoler — and we do not always acknowledge his presence and his action in our souls.

Ever since I was little, I got in the habit of talking spontaneously with the Holy Spirit, entrusting my problems to him and sharing with him my dreams and ideals. This has helped me very much to count on him whenever I have to make an important decision. The Church's tradition calls him "the soul's gentle guest" because he dwells in our soul and is always with us as our advocate and great consoler. He is there to give us his gifts, to enlighten our minds, to enkindle our hearts — so often mediocre and indifferent — with his fire. If you want to fulfill your vocation, no matter what it is, you need to get in the habit of listening for his quiet but clear voice and living your daily pains and joys in his company.

In my life as priest and founder I have found it very helpful to listen attentively to the Holy Spirit's inspirations and motions. Forgive the expression if it sounds too commercial, but for me he is a real partner in my efforts for the Kingdom and to be holy. I cannot do without him if I want to triumph in my life's investment. I need his "capital" to join it to the talents the Lord has given me to work for his Kingdom. The results of this friendship are beyond compare. If you want to go this road alone, you'll only get a few steps. But if you get beside the Holy Spirit, you will get where you are going in no time.

So I always recommend to priests and laypeople to pay him a lot of attention in their lives. This means that you have to bring silence into your heart so as to distinguish his voice from the noise of so many other worldly voices trying to drown out his word, but not only this; it also means you have to be docile and obedient once you have heard it. If you maintain this spiritual approach to life and are attentive to the Holy Spirit, you can be sure of success in fulfilling your vocation, whether you are a priest or a layperson.

55. Getting back to the Legion, some people criticize you for being too conservative, traditionalist, or elitist. What can you tell us in this regard?

First a word about criticism, and then I'll get to your question. We know there is such a thing as constructive criticism, when you are interested in somebody's or some institution's good and you point out certain things that ought to be improved. This is a positive kind of criticism, and we should all be open to it because it helps us to better ourselves constantly. Since every congregation or religious association is a human institution, it will always have aspects to improve. There is, however, another kind of criticism bred by envy, prejudice, or other twisted purposes.

You also have to remember that when people criticize the shepherds of the Church or the Church's institutions, it is often pretty shallow because the information they have is fragmentary or willfully distorted and manipulated. So when the Church comes up in a private or even public conversation, the first reaction is to trot out all the old topics — the Inquisition, Galileo, the supposed wealth of the Vatican, the pomp of the cardinals, and so on and so forth — the same ideas over and over since the end of the eighteenth century, handy catchphrases for the uninformed.

These criticisms often come from people or institutions with no supernatural outlook, without which you cannot have a deep understanding of the reality of the Church. From a horizontalist perspective, blind to the charism that celibacy is for the Church and for the world, priestly celibacy is mere repression, a disciplinary measure imposed by authority that the broad base of clergy need to rebel against. These see religious obedience as contrary to human rights because they fail to see the act of supreme freedom implied in placing your freedom in God's hands, following Christ's example. Church Magisterium is seen as contrary to the freedom of expression guaranteed by the democratic system. This all creates major confusion in the minds of ordinary people.

In addition, people are somewhat flippant and superficial in the free use of labels such as "the left" or "the right," "conservative" or "progressive," even though these terms properly belong to politics and can't be applied uncritically to an institution like the Church, whose mission is eminently spiritual.

These criticisms and prejudices, many of which are based on ideologies, are often picked up by the media, which amplify them and create trends of opinion that are negative towards the Church and Church institutions. With this I do not want to imply a low opinion of the work of journalists and media personnel who sincerely try to present to the world the truth of events. Many of them risk their lives as we have recently seen with the war in Afghanistan or the former Yugoslavia. Their mission is extremely important for society and for world peace. The Church itself is striving to train generations of professionally competent journalists who at the same time are aware of their mission and their ethical duties in the profession. In our apostolates we also contribute, however modestly, to this tremendous effort of the Church by creating in our universities schools of communication that follow the criteria just mentioned.

On this basis I will now answer your question. I think the criticism about our being too conservative comes from our desire to be faithful to God and to those who have authority in the Church — the Pope and bishops in their magisterial function. If that's the case, we won't be too bothered by being labeled as conservatives because our concern, more than the opinion people may have of us, is to walk in step with the Church without failing.

As regards elitism, it should be said that we seek the integral good of the human person, every person, be they rich or poor, wise or ignorant, regardless of race, language, nationality, or talent. This is the example that Christ left us in the gospel. Like him we approach people to bring them Christ's grace and redemption. We do not approach them for unworthy motives, economic gain, prestige, or any other reason. We want to reach everyone, and for that very reason, just as Christ chose a group of apostles to take his gospel to the whole world, we, too, begin by forming and training a given few, due to human limitations, so that their work will reach as many individuals as possible.

56. We know that the Legion's apostolic institutions seek to have a clear social outreach, especially in Latin America. Furthermore,

social education is mandatory in your schools and includes hands-on activities in service to the neediest. What is the Legion's position on the so-called social question?

This is a fundamental but very broad question that I am not going to be able to answer with the breadth it deserves. For an adequate response you have to work from the Christian principle of respect for the dignity of the human person that Pope John Paul II repeats so often. Christ came to redeem every human person; he came to offer salvation to all. As St. Paul says, for Christ there are no longer divisions between man and woman, slave and free, Greek and Jew (Gal 3:28; Col 3:11). In his eyes we all have the same dignity, the same value. He shed his blood and rose from the dead for each and every person. Furthermore, we know that he mystically identifies with those who have the greatest need, both materially and spiritually, as he points out clearly when speaking about the Last Judgment (Matt 25:31-46).

We have to approach the so-called social question from the principle of the dignity of every human being. With the globalization of information, the suffering and woes of individuals and nations that once could be kept more or less hidden are now paraded before our eyes every day. It tears your soul apart to contemplate all the world's misery, all its wars, injustice, hunger, unsanitary conditions, loneliness, the lack of social and medical assistance that so many millions of human beings suffer. In the face of this situation, only a truly hardened heart could remain unmoved.

Nevertheless indifference is a reality, and we can get used to living in cities where rich and poor virtually rub shoulders, one unaware of the other's miseries and misfortunes. Those who have the means have to do something to help our brothers and sisters. Injustice cries out to heaven and must be overcome. Something needs to be done, but something intelligent, possible, and good. We cannot overcome one evil with another, but as St. Paul said, "resist evil and conquer it with good" (Rom 12:21).

Historical Marxism attempted to provide an answer to this problem, which in Marx's time also surfaced dramatically together with the emergence of the proletariat in Europe. However, thanks to the undeniable facts history has provided, we now know that Marxism, however noble its ideal of man's equality and liberation from his material miseries, was based on a series of erroneous philosophical and anthropological premises that used hatred as the fulcrum for social transformation. Thus, its gospel was violence and class struggle. But, as Christians, we know that violence is not the appropriate way to solve inequalities because violence begets violence.

In addition, historical Marxism forgot the basic principle of social life: respect for the dignity and freedom of every human person. It attempted to establish equality by denying freedom, and that was the anthropological flaw that doomed it to failure. We are all aware now, and even the political analysts admit as much, that Pope John Paul II played a primary role in the fall of communism in the Soviet Union and its satellites by insisting on human rights and the value of religious freedom.

Marxism failed in its attempt, but the piercing social problems remain right there before us as a challenge for the Christian West. We can't play the ostrich, thinking we will solve the problem by simply ignoring it. But neither can we resort to solutions that are not gospel-based, such as those put forward by the proponents of certain brands of liberation theology that attempt a false marriage between the gospel and class struggle. Not to deny their possible good intentions: only God can judge what is in every man. But we can clearly affirm (as the Church's Magisterium does in two documents on the subject published by the Congregation for the Doctrine of the Faith, headed by Cardinal Josef Ratzinger) that any liberation theology that admits the Marxist analysis (and often, as well, certain elements of its underlying materialist philosophy) are incompatible with the Church's social doctrine.

Our focus in social issues is to apply the broad principles of the Church's social doctrine, trying to jog the consciences of the lay-people — especially those with greater possibilities due to their political, economic, or social status — so that they will apply them each one in his own field of action. This is slow work and not very flashy, but effective in the long run. By forming laypeople and projecting them into the apostolate, you can bring about very promising projects for social and economic development.

Since social sensitivity is something that a person develops slowly, especially during childhood, adolescence, and youth, we saw fit to make social formation mandatory in our schools, seeking to benefit the countries where we work and to form a Christian and social conscience in our students. The courses are structured to include practical, concrete activities that allow the students, from the last years of primary school on, to educate their human and Christian sensitivity, enabling them to provide effective remedies for the various social problems. We want to provoke in our students a culture of solidarity; not a merely sporadic reaction to injustice.

In the country where the Legion of Christ was founded alone, some twenty-one thousand teenagers and young people participate personally in social and community development programs on the outskirts of big cities and in the remote rural areas where you find the people most in need of financial, moral, and cultural support. We are talking about completely marginalized communities that live in extreme poverty. The young people go there to help them with medical care, hygiene, food, and housing, adding to the material help a heavy dose of brotherly love. They also teach manual skills and new farming techniques to help them increase their income for the daily needs of their families. It is edifying to see their efforts to gather building materials — bricks, cement, re-bar, metal sheeting, pipes — and then go out to the slums of the big cities on the weekends to be with their needy brothers and sisters and work with them to improve their life-conditions. The younger children help in orphanages, retirement homes, and hospitals, bringing love to orphans, the elderly, and the sick.

We have seen many things happen, which show us that if we form our young people in authentic human and Christian values, deeply sensitive to justice, with a will set on building a culture of solidarity, each cell of society will be a fruitful promoter of peace and harmony. There are many initiatives and institutions that Regnum Christi members or alumni of our schools and universities have created, that now provide effective solutions towards creating the conditions for peace in the fabric of society.

Out of fidelity to the gospel and the Church's teaching, the Legion of Christ will always be very alert to the social problems that afflict our world, and to the extent of our possibilities we will ensure that all our institutions and the people that are in contact with us will also be imbued with the same social concern. The Legion and Regnum Christi will always carry in the heart of our spirituality the same feelings of Christ for the poor and the dispossessed, the humble, and those who suffer injustice. Our efforts on man's behalf are a struggle for an authentic humanism geared towards opening man to the Good News, faith in Christ, and from there open him to the ways of justice and charity. But without settling for the quick fixes of violence and class struggle, for the simple reason that they are anti-gospel and anti-human. The class-struggle ideology has proven itself historically invalid with the thunderous collapse of the Marxist regimes. The fruit of Marxism was the spawning of new forms of violence and dictatorial, totalitarian systems that not only destroyed people's freedom but also ruined the economy itself. We seek rather the radical change of the human heart that comes from man's interior conversion when, under the influence of grace, he opens himself to faith in Christ and the needs of his brother. Our mission is to work to establish Christ's Kingdom in society by preaching the Good News of the Kingdom through entirely supernatural, transcendent action that changes hearts, building the foundation for a civilization of justice and love.

57. We have been discussing the Legion's charism. In the Church today there are many other charisms from the Holy Spirit that have taken shape in new movements or communities of various kinds. What is your relationship with these new movements and communities like?

Our guiding principle in our relations with other charisms that the Holy Spirit has inspired in the Church is one of deep respect, admiration, charity, and unity. First of all, respect and admiration: as the Holy Father said at the first great gathering of Catholic movements in Rome for Pentecost 1998, we are doubtlessly living in a new springtime of the Spirit. Alongside the disturbing fact of secularization, religious indifference, open hostility to the Church, and many other negative phenomena, we are experiencing a surprising reality in the appearance of a number of new movements and communities that are deeply renewing the spiritual life of a great number of the faithful.

The proliferation of these movements is yet another proof that the Holy Spirit is constantly at work, renewing the face of the Church. I have always admired God's marvelous action that is able to kindle a flame where to all appearances there were only spent embers. We saw the Holy Spirit at work in the eastern European countries when they were still under the domination of the Marxist-communist ideology. They were bent on tearing God from the hearts of men and society, but they weren't able to, because you cannot wipe out our desire for God through oppression, violence, or fear. To take a famous line from Don Quixote, you could say that "the spear never dulled the faith."

The same thing is happening in many Western European countries where materialism, hedonism, and spiritual indifference have wreaked havoc. Many decreed the death of God and the

Church. Nonetheless, amid the desolation these new groups arise, moved by a spiritual and apostolic dynamism, and challenge the bourgeois paralysis in which many Christians lived their lives. You may agree or disagree with their outward forms or methods of apostolate, or feel greater or lesser affinity for a particular spiritual trend, but it is undeniable that in these movements — I refer to those the Church has already authenticated with its authority — there is a new and powerful presence of the Holy Spirit's action, coming with his dowry of gifts to beautify the Church.

Our relations with all these movements are, thank God, very good and all of us together desire to achieve an ever-deepening ecclesial communion — that is, union with the Holy Father, the Church's Magisterium, the bishops, pastors, the various structures in the Church, and among ourselves. On the other hand, we cannot be naïve. Our communion doesn't mean we should all do the same thing, or follow the same methodology, or have the same nuances in our spiritual formation. The Holy Spirit is the one who causes diversity in unity. This means we have to respect each other, respect each other's charism, admitting their goodness and perhaps also their limitations, in order to help each other to build together the one Church of Christ.

The fact that there is somewhat of a tension between unity and diversity is by no means a negative sign. What's important is that each of us put the charism we have received at the service of the common cause, and not use it as an excuse to build independent fiefdoms; our charisms should help each one of us build the one Church. The movements, for example, cannot exercise their charisms outside the diocesan church or parallel to it. This means that the movements and communities have to integrate with the diocese, and correspondingly it also calls for the goodwill and a sincere desire to understand the charisms on the part of diocesan priests and the various church structures. An essential condition is charity and dialogue. This is not always easy since these charisms will at times contain pastoral novelties whose validity it is not easy to judge with certainty, for diocesan structures or organizations are apprehensive of groups that don't seem to integrate well with them. I believe, however, that John Paul II has done a lot to help the mutual understanding grow, to help on the one hand the charisms integrate with parish and diocesan structures, and on the other to help the latter to open up to the novelty of the charisms.

If we look at Church history, it won't surprise us that these tensions exist. When the mendicant orders appeared — the Franciscans and Dominicans, now universally recognized for their great contributions to the Church's holiness and evangelization — there were severe tensions as well. The clashes at the University of Paris are well known, where the teachers from the secular clergy refused to accept those belonging to these orders until the Pope himself had to appoint the first theology teachers of the new orders who were none other than St. Thomas Aquinas, a Dominican, and St. Bonaventure of Bagnoregio, a Franciscan.

We join John Paul II in his efforts to get the movements and new communities to know each other better and engage in mutual dialogue, so that in this greater knowledge we will grow in our respect for each other and collaborate effectively at the service of the Church. In the regular meetings that the founders and heads of ecclesial movements hold in Rome, there is a very beautiful atmosphere of communion in the Church; we have a great oneness of mind, and we have resolved to foster this spirit of unity and charity among the members of our respective movements.

58. The Legion and Regnum Christi, along with some of the new ecclesial communities, have been accused of being sects or cults that deprive their members of their freedom. Many would like to know how to answer this charge. What would you say?

I think you first have to define what you mean by a sect or cult. Following the criteria of some scholars of contemporary religious phenomena, not only the new religious communities but the Catholic Church itself would qualify as a sect or cult. We should remember that Christianity, in the Jewish world of its origins and even in the Greco-Roman world, was considered a sect of Judaism.

What danger do people perceive in cults precisely nowadays? Among others, the most basic is that the individual loses his personal freedom, his freedom to determine his own course in full knowledge and full consent. The danger of destructive cults is made manifest when they induce their members to mass suicide or all sorts of abuse, including financial and sexual. In a cult there takes place a certain loss of personality, in homage to a charismatic leader who holds the reins of power and decision-making.

In the Catholic Church and the organizations that form part of it — as is the case of the Legion of Christ, Regnum Christi, and the religious communities and associations the Church has approved — a person never loses his freedom, nor is their any exaltation of charismatic leaders. If there was anything Christ took into consideration in the people he met in his public life, it was their freedom. He didn't want to buy disciples or have them follow him grudgingly; he sought men who would give themselves to God and the Kingdom freely, spontaneously, out of love and out of faith — and, yes, give themselves totally.

However, for those who don't understand or have no desire to understand the nature of Christianity, it might seem like splitting hairs to make a distinction between cults and religious associations that truly respect one's freedom. Individuals and associations that have no love for the Church capitalize on this to attack some of the new Catholic movements, calling them cultish.

I think the best answer to this kind of accusation is to show that you always respect a person's dignity and freedom above all else, and that membership in a given association comes from a personal act of freedom and not from external interference. Since the Catholic Church, the Legion of Christ, Regnum Christi, and the ecclesial communities you mention all meet these conditions, the accusation falls under its own weight.

However, there is something I want to add here, since some use the idea of respect for people's freedom, a basic principle for Catholicism, to paralyze Catholics' evangelizing momentum and missionary spirit. Ultimately, they would like to keep Catholicism in the sacristy and church buildings, because everything that is really a wholesome effort to spread the faith in the public square in their view is sectarian action. You can't impose the faith; you mustn't. But you can and must *propose* the faith. If we don't, we will deprive many people of the beauty of an encounter with Christ. And besides, how else could we fulfill Christ's commission to go out to the whole world and preach the gospel?

Christ never forced anything on anyone. When the rich young man came to him seeking the way to eternal life and was not willing to give up all his belongings and follow him because he was a man of great wealth, Christ didn't recriminate, accuse, or force him. He had indeed invited him: "If you wish to be perfect, go and sell what you own and give the money to the poor; . . . then come, follow me" (Matt 19:21). "If you wish to . . ." and not "I oblige you to . . ." were his words. It was a question of loving more or loving less. Christ did not force him to love more. He doesn't oblige us to love more. He makes his proposal, and he then discreetly withdraws so that we can make up our own minds in complete freedom.

We must not let our evangelizing work be paralyzed for fear of being accused of sectarianism. The gospel is the Good News we have to spread. For some, however, it is an annoying message that reproaches their conscience and they would rather not have to listen to it — but the bearer of the good news, the prophet, cannot keep silent. It may irritate, but he will challenge their freedom while being very careful to respect it, because God is the first to show the utmost regard for our freedom.

59. Some people say that your formation is uniform, like a cookie-cutter, and all Legionaries look as if they're "cloned." What are your thoughts?

I think there is a family spirit among Legionaries, as is the case among the members of other religious congregations and apostolic movements. If we emphasize certain elements of human, intellectual, apostolic, and social formation, it would be truly abnormal if everyone turned out utterly unalike. But that doesn't mean they are the same, or "cloned," but as I just said, there is a family resemblance characteristic of the type of formation received. There is a deep communion in their spiritual faculties because they are guided by the standards of faith that come from the Church's Magisterium; there is a communion of ideals, interests, and formation.

It's logical that there be a resemblance. I believe Legionaries can be identified, thanks be to God, by their responsibility, seriousness, kindness, and joy. But each one has his own personality, his own character, his own individual manner. Do we resemble each other? Yes, like siblings in a family. But no two Legionaries are the same, as is also the case in families.

Actually, one of the characteristics of our formation is that it's personalized: God hasn't made any two people the same, but wants them to be entirely unique. So you can't have a cookie-cutter formation; you have to adapt it to each person. We apply this pedagogical principle to the formation of the students in our schools, but we apply it first to the formation of Legionaries. Within one style of priestly life there are as many variations as there are people being formed.

60. The Legion is also criticized at times because they say you produce robots, you all think the same, you do only what your superiors tell you with no other alternative, and so you stifle personal initiative and true freedom.

My reply to the previous question has already answered this one in part. I would simply add that if anyone says this, they definitely don't know the Legion, because everyone who does know it, and above all those of us who are in it, know this is false. Here, everyone can express his point of view. Everyone develops the capacities that God gave him. Everyone is pointed towards the apostolates that best suit his personality. And it is a lie that no one can speak up or propose anything in the Legion. All we ask is that they identify themselves and, as in any other congregation, that they act in line with our spirit as contained in the Constitutions. Not only do we allow personal initiative; we encourage it as a characteristic of personal maturity. I often tell the Legionaries and the lay members of Regnum Christi that initiative is the perfection of obedience. I pity the superior who has to take the first step in everything and give orders to makes things work! It means his community is dead. And if the initiatives — and there are very many, thank God — fall within our charism and seem feasible and appropriate, we accept and support them to the maximum. Proof of this are the hundreds of apostolic projects that Legionaries and Regnum Christi members have thought up and developed.

We don't impose anything above and beyond each member's commitment before God to live his religious vows — poverty, chastity, and obedience — and the vows that are specific to our congregation. But this is a commitment that each one takes on freely, without being forced, as a loving response to God, within the framework of the Legion, but moved fundamentally by love for God.

Within these parameters each one can and must try to develop, improve, and seek perfection. Some are more talented in one field, others in another. Everyone cannot do everything. So we try to assign to each of them the apostolic mission best suited to his talents, and we always encourage teamwork that each one enriches with his own contribution. Thus, a formation center has a team of formators with a rector, assistants, professors, administrators, and so forth, each complementing and enriching the others according to his God-given talents. Each one takes all the gifts that nature and grace have bestowed on him and puts them at the service of others and of the Church so as to fulfill as perfectly and effectively as possible the apostolic task entrusted to him, and each one responds in his spiritual life to God's immense gift.

61. You mentioned "our own vows," specific to the congregation. Are they secret?

No, not secret at all. Legionaries take them when they take the vows of poverty, chastity, and obedience that are more usual in congregations and orders. Besides these three vows we have a vow of charity and a vow of humility. The vow of charity is meant to safeguard and respect to the maximum our brothers in the congregation — especially our superiors — in our words and attitudes. With this vow a religious commits himself not to criticize a superior's actions in front of someone who is not in a position to resolve a given problem or conflict. But he is invited, if he thinks it appropriate, to express his views about a superior's governance to those who can fix the problem. Of course, the right person is not the receptionist, the telephone operator, the cook, or his fellow seminarian. Why not? Because they can't fix a thing, and the only result is to encourage intrigue, uncharity, and the destruction of the congregation's spirit of unity.

I want to clarify that this does not encroach on one's freedom of expression, but rather channels it. Anyone can freely express his problems or point of view about the actions or decisions of a given superior in the event he thinks these are mistaken, but he will not do so with those who are not in a position to remedy the situation, only with those who have authority over the superior to correct the problem. We only ask that the criticism not be made in the presence of those who are powerless to resolve possible conflicts.

In this way we foster the spirit of charity and unity among our religious, which is the very backbone of our spirituality, and hence we call it the vow of charity. It also helps us eradicate slander, and on the positive side it promotes the habit of always speaking well of others — focusing on their qualities, gifts, and virtues, disregarding if necessary their defects or errors, and creating for them an atmosphere of appreciation and welcome.

Our second vow is the vow of humility. In it we commit ourselves to humble service to our brothers, the Church, and the congregation; we avoid desiring and procuring for ourselves positions of responsibility; and we are joyful in whatever work obedience entrusts to us. We call it the vow of humility because this attitude of service takes constant mastery of our natural passion to be important, to stand out, and to attain positions through intrigue and playing dirty, as is unfortunately common in other institutions in civil, social, professional, or political life. It reminds us of our creaturehood, and that like Christ we have come to religious life not to be served, but to serve and to give our lives for the salvation of our brothers and sisters. Thus it is a major contributing factor towards the internal harmony of our communities and peace among all our members, with each one seeking to serve the others at all times, shunning the vain pursuit of honors, esteem, or recognition.

62. The Legionaries still believe in the value of vocational centers or minor seminaries, and have a number of them in several countries. Do you think it is possible to recognize a vocation to the priesthood at such an early age? How is the adolescents' freedom in their vocational choice to be respected?

We do still believe in the value of what we call vocational centers, or minor seminaries. For many years these institutions gave the Church select vocations, and enriched it with their holiness and apostolic zeal. The Church has never denied the value of such institutions; rather, it has supported them. However, many voices were raised during the postconciliar era claiming that minor seminaries didn't respect the teenagers' freedom, that it wasn't possible to discover a vocation at such a young age, and that teenagers should experience life or go to college before making a mature vocational decision.

I don't deny that the pedagogy followed in some of these seminaries needed to change in order to achieve a more open, more wholesome atmosphere, as well as a system that guaranteed civil recognition for the studies of those who didn't continue with their priestly studies.

However, and we are firmly convinced of this, it does not mean they should be shut down or that the Church should do without them. As I say, a renewal was perhaps necessary. But, unfortunately, many chose to close them, and thus to my mind we lost the possibility of presenting the priestly vocation to many teenagers whom the Lord really is calling. In this area, you see, you have to begin with a premise of faith: the Lord of the vineyard can call his workers at whatever hour he sees fit. In this parable, the owner of the vineyard called the workers at different times: early in the morning, at noon, early in the afternoon, and almost at dusk (Matt 20:1-16). He's the one who calls, when he wants, and how he wants. We cannot walk up and say, "Lord, call me any time after noon." Nor can we oblige him not to choose those who show up at the so-called eleventh hour. Why do we try to put limits on God's call? It's true that a child, an adolescent, a youth, and an adult perceive the call in different ways. God adapts himself perfectly to each person's psychology, age, and circumstances. It is completely false to say you can feel a calling to priesthood only when you are an adult, only after certain experiences (which are not always positive). The witness of so many vocations that have made it, men to whom God clearly showed he was calling them to his service when they were children or young teenagers, proves the contrary to be true.

On the other hand, it's true that you have to give teenagers all the room possible for them to make their choice the way God wants it to happen, that is, in an atmosphere of complete freedom. But freedom, for it to be such, also implies letting grace do its work in their souls. In other words, there has to be an atmosphere of prayer, openness to hearing God's call, reception of the sacraments, and the respectful, kind, and careful presence of the formators.

People often think that seminary rectors or formators "push" vocations. But they, like the one who has received the calling, are only listening to the Holy Spirit. They are quite aware that letting a youth go on in priestly life when he doesn't have the aptitude for a vocation damages not only him, but also the congregation and the Church. Some boys discover they do not have a vocation. Others discover that they are called to diocesan life, and they are pointed in that direction. Actually, we are justly proud there are now a good number of diocesan priests who went to our minor seminaries and discovered their priestly vocation there. What we are interested in is not the greatest number of vocations at any price, but genuine vocations, who will therefore be of service to the Church in the congregation, in a parish, or in other diocesan structures.

You also ask me how to respect a teenager's vocational freedom of choice. I think the answer is simple: the same way you respect an adult's vocational freedom. You never tell a teenager that he's got to follow his vocation under pain of eternal condemnation or anything like that. All you do is offer him the possibility to meet Christ personally to find out what he wants. Besides, if a teenager perceives God's call, he still has at least ten or twelve years to confirm or change the decision he has made, now as a fully mature young man. Also, since their studies are accredited, they will not experience problems transferring back into school if they don't continue.

In countries like the United States and France we were warned that vocational centers wouldn't work. And nevertheless there they are, with a good number of students. And you can see the boys are happy, fulfilled, healthy, overflowing with joy.

My experience of over sixty years working with priestly vocations brings home to me the marvel of God's grace acting in the soul of the chosen person, that surprises you and surpasses any human outlook. When I think about this, it reminds me of King David's calling, related in the First Book of Samuel. The prophet travels to Bethlehem because the Lord has revealed to him that he has chosen one of Jesse's sons to be Israel's king. Samuel sees Jesse's first-born and, going on outward appearance, thinks he is in the presence of God's chosen one. But God's answer to Samuel is very instructive: "Take no notice of his appearance or his height for I have rejected him; God does not see as man sees; man looks at appearances but Yahweh looks at the heart" (1 Sam 16:7). God does not judge as we do. His standards are simply beyond us.

I am, then, convinced that a teenager and even a child is capable of clearly sensing God's call in his soul. Obviously this calling must be studied and verified. The seed God sows in a young person's soul must grow and mature. This takes time, and his freedom needs space to make a proper choice. Does making space for true freedom mean offering a teenager environments that lead him to sin and thus distance him from God? Isn't sin the only real slavery? It is grace that creates space for freedom. This is the "space" we make in our vocational centers.

63. Moving on to another topic that also has to do with the Legionaries' charism: when people visit one of your formation centers they are struck by the green lawns, the cleanliness, sobriety, elegance, good taste, and harmony. Or if we consider some of your apostolic works such as your schools and universities, you have big, beautiful buildings, video-conference halls,

well-supplied laboratories and libraries, and so on. Some question how you reconcile all this with gospel poverty, which the Legionaries vow.

Yes, as you say our formation centers and our works of apostolate are, within the necessary limits, notably harmonious in appearance, with areas of architectural and natural beauty, without losing their functionality. I would like to mention that this places us in the Church's long tradition, which has played a truly humanizing role all throughout history, promoting true culture and the creation of beauty. Just think of the great Romanesque or Gothic cathedrals, the Baroque churches, the magnificent abbeys like Montecassino, the beautiful Carthusian monasteries, the monasteries and abbeys of all times. Since the Church is concerned with what is true and what is good, it cannot neglect beauty. The Church has always wanted to offer people natural spaces worthy of their dignity, and in sacred art especially, spaces where the natural and man-made are so harmonized that your soul feels spontaneously lifted to God. All this implies a particular view of man, the universe, and God. We believe the gospel is not at odds with things aesthetic and beautiful; indeed, it is their most authentic promoter.

If you observe more closely the buildings you mention, you will notice that they have what is necessary but never anything superfluous. There are other charisms in the Church that the Holy Spirit invites to give witness to a radical, and we could say "prophetic," poverty that strikes the senses. We very much appreciate these charisms God has inspired, because they help all of us understand that man does not live on material goods alone, but on every word that comes from the mouth of God.

But every religious congregation has a unique style of poverty. Our religious, for example, do not receive a monthly allowance, as is done in many other religious communities. If they need something for personal use, even a bar of soap or a pen, they have to receive it from their superior. They don't buy anything for themselves since by their vow of poverty they can't own anything. Their sole possession is the crucifix they receive the day they profess their vows. They put the gifts they receive at the disposal of the community, unless in some special cases the superior gives them permission to use them. Maybe no one knows this or sees it, but that's how it is. That's our way of living poverty.

But in addition we also place special emphasis on using well another basic good that God has given man: time. For us the good use of our time is part of our vow of poverty. Time is a precious, limited gift. Everyone, especially if he is a Christian and a religious, has the duty to use it responsibly and effectively, doing the most he can with it. I have always told the Legionaries that the good use of our time is part of our vow of poverty. As you can see, these are nuances with which each charism highlights one aspect or another of the imitation of Christ. But all religious because of their commitment to follow Christ, who was born poor and died poor, are committed to use material goods sparingly; to live unattached to what we have, be it little or much; to possess only what we need for our mission; to put our trust in the hands of the heavenly Father; to feel subject to the law of work just like everyone else; to be very careful to save; and to live in solidarity with those who suffer most from misery, hunger, war, and human injustice.

If you enter a Legionary's room, you will find a kneeler, a desk, a chair, a bed, the books he needs for his ministry, a simple wardrobe that fits into three drawers and a closet a few feet wide, and very little else.

But we don't believe that the spirit of poverty in our personal lives is at odds with using the most effective means that science and technology provide, which can help us achieve our objective of spreading Christ's Kingdom. For instance, if someone needs to go from Europe to America for reasons of apostolate and decides for the sake of poverty to go by boat and not by plane, he will certainly save a few dollars or euros, but he will waste a lot of time and perhaps many apostolic opportunities. In the gospels, Christ says something that should make us think: "The children of this world are more astute in dealing with their own kind than are the children of light" (Luke 16:8). Within the proper limits we should not be afraid to use the best means to do good, to spread the gospel, and to further Christ's cause. Our use of these means is dictated by the mission and not our personal ease or comfort. True, in using them we need to be prudent and moderate, aware that supernatural effectiveness in the order of grace does not depend on them but on our holiness and our personal union with God.

When we spoke about the Legion's history, we saw the material conditions it was born in: the basement of a rented house, minimal furniture, just a few chairs and desks. When we moved to Europe we had to live in a cowshed in the town of Comillas. When we moved to Rome to inaugurate the college in 1950, there were no chairs, desks, mattresses, or kitchen. As I mentioned, we borrowed the housewares from Father Isaiah at the Primavalle orphanage. As for food, we relied basically on what we got from the cows, chickens, and vegetable garden. Once in the first few years, as I already mentioned, I had to send the community to bed without eating because there was no money. In those first years we subsisted by going to the market in Mexico City to sell the milk we got from Mariposa, the cow we had been donated.

In the first three years of his formation, a Legionary spends an entire month of vacation working in the fields (harvesting coffee beans or lentils, weeding sugar beet, and so on) so that he can directly experience physical work and the effort it takes, especially in the fields, which is one of the hardest kinds of work. That gets us familiar with the working conditions of many of our brothers and sisters. We are used to austerity and poverty, and we know what poverty is like; but realism tells us that a complete formation and the development of effective apostolates at the service of the

Church require material goods, not for personal comfort but to spread the gospel with them.

64. Getting back to a topic you touched on earlier, the vocation: many laypeople wonder how to discern their vocation properly, regarding lay life itself as well as priestly, religious, or consecrated life. You have broad experience in this respect. What method have you followed, and what advice can you give someone going through a discernment process at a given moment in life?

From the time I was twenty, and made my first trip towards the end of 1940 to gather the first group of boys who would begin the Legion, I have constantly been in contact with young men making their vocational decision.

First of all I want to bring to mind something obvious: a vocation is a great mystery. I really like the title John Paul II gave his priestly memoirs on the golden jubilee of his ordination, *Gift and Mystery*. The vocation is a true mystery and a true gift. Mystery, since it is a light that is infinitely beyond us, and in the presence of this light our reason is too limited and inadequate to grasp it in all its depth. It's a mystery to be contemplated in faith from the perspective of love, with a sense of infinite gratitude and appreciation, generously embracing God's call. At the same time a vocation is an immense gift from God. Only in heaven will we be able to understand adequately how great and sublime it is.

I think of my own vocation, and also of the large number of teenagers and young adults with whom I have walked the path of their vocational discernment. I have to say that in every case, God's gift, the Holy Spirit's marvelous action in souls, has amazed me.

I take this as my point of departure simply to clarify that there is no one method to discern your vocation, though it is true that there are several elements you have to take into account in discerning. In my opinion it is a matter of discovering in prayer, in conversation with the Holy Spirit and with the person involved, the path God has in mind, what God wants for him or her. Yes, you have to take into account their talents; their human, psychological, spiritual and moral qualities; their upbringing, life-story, family; their leanings towards priesthood or consecrated life; and so forth. But once you have done this, there is a subtle interplay of delicate spiritual intuition on the part of both the person discerning and the one who guides and monitors him spiritually.

Once all the necessary human and spiritual qualities are present, it is absolutely necessary that the person discerning have a basic attitude of generosity, wanting to be generous with God, not wanting to haggle with him over the crumbs of his life. In my experience, discernment comes much more easily to those who are generous with God, and these have the necessary foundation to succeed in their vocations. Conversely, those who are miserly with God, drawing up long lists of all the things they have to give up in the world to follow Christ, more likely than not will end up like the rich young man in the gospel, going their own way without ever plucking up the courage to take on the adventure of following Christ. Generosity is not blindness. You can't go ahead if your reason, enlightened by faith, fails to perceive God's call. Generosity is a disposition of the soul that moves you to throw yourself totally into God's hands because you know they are powerful, loving, provident, and fatherly hands, and because you know that God is asking you to take that path.

Generosity is the basic attitude, but the whole choice has to be made in a climate of prayer. It is impossible to be able to discern your vocation correctly if you are not drawing close to God through prayer and the sacraments. You have to pray, insist, beg, knock, because God's ways are very many. Some perceive their vocation like an arrow of love: in a special instant of grace they perceive with clarity beyond doubt that God is calling them. For others, it is more difficult. They need to think it over more; they have to exert more their faith, intelligence, and will. Much depends on the makeup of your character, but also on the myriads of ways that grace acts.

The important thing is to be able to find God's will and follow it with all your heart. Never part ways with God's will. What I'm saying is true for marriage as well. How often people make the wrong choice in choosing a spouse because they simply didn't pray; it was a human choice that didn't at all take into account the Lord's will! If God's path for me is the priesthood, I'll head right for it, because I know that not only will I please God, but also I will find my own happiness and help many others find theirs.

A very important element in making the right vocational choice is to have the help of a spiritual director, to guide you and help you to see God's will clearly in total openness of conscience, heart-to-heart conversation, and complete trust. A good spiritual director helps you to steer clear of hazards and doesn't let you spin your wheels uselessly; he gives you courage, security, and confidence. For spiritual direction to be totally fruitful, the person discerning must be candid, docile to the guidance he receives, and open, so that the framework for the dialogue is a shared search for God's will.

65. You bring up spiritual direction. Many people today, somewhat disappointed with psychological consultation, are turning once more to spiritual direction. The image of the priest as spiritual director is being re-evaluated. Why do you think this is happening? Do you think spiritual direction is in fact necessary for a Christian following the call to priesthood or consecration?

As you say, in the years following the Council many people gave up spiritual direction and settled for psychologists, most of whom at the time were into psychoanalysis. Since priests were not, or at least not necessarily, specialists in psychology or psychoanalysis many people stopped asking them for their help in spiritual direction. I have nothing against a truly scientific psychology that is based on Christian anthropology, or at least respects the dignity and integrity of the person. You perhaps know that we collaborate with the Institute for Psychological Sciences near Washington, DC. We believe that psychology is a human science that can greatly help man discover who he is and identify the deep root of certain behavior. Furthermore, we have psychologists in our schools to help us know our students more precisely, the better to help them in their formation. There are several points in time during a Legionary's formation years when, as the Church stipulates, he is interviewed by a psychologist. He does detailed aptitude and personality tests so that we can get to know him in depth and thus be able to better guide him in his vocational decisions. We also have a chain of Alpha & Omega centers where doctors, psychologists, psychiatrists, and priests cooperate in addressing and solving family problems.

Psychology is very valuable as a human science, but it does not have the absolute value some gave it in the Sixties and Seventies, even in certain currents within the Church. Everyone knows of the Catholic seminaries that gave up spiritual direction for guidance sessions with psycho-spiritual consultants, that were an outright failure.

The loss of trust in the person of the spiritual director coincided with the boom in psychoanalysis and psychology, which, however, was not its only cause. It was also due to people's lack of faith in God's action through another human person. They said you didn't need to go through another person, who has his own defects and sins. Your relationship with God had to be direct, avoiding all those annoying mediations of the Church. "So many men between me and God!" exclaimed Rousseau. This, however, goes against a gospel principle that the Catholic Church has accepted and the reformed churches have de-emphasized: the need for human mediation in one's faith-life. Catholic theology has always emphasized the fact that God chose to save man through the mystery of the Incarnation. It takes faith and humility to accept this divine economy. True, God could have chosen another way, but this is the one he did. The Catholic Church's two-thousand-year history shows the wisdom of this economy, which helps us avoid the subjectivism we are so prone to when we venture into the paths of God.

The spiritual-direction crisis affected not only seminarians, priests, and religious, but Christian life itself. The Christian faithful, very many of whom had been in the habit of spiritual direction, some more formally, some less so, gave it up. Sacramental confession, too, was gradually abandoned. The net result was that spiritual direction fell into disuse in many places, and many Christians went astray on important issues of faith and morality.

Man, however, needs the help of another; it is not easy to walk alone. So now that the border between the psychological and the spiritual is becoming more defined, people are once again seeking the spiritual help they need, to live fervently in surroundings where it is not easy to live the faith. Spiritual direction has for centuries forged mature Christians, solid in their faith and firm in their consciences. After the time of crisis the waters are returning somewhat to their normal course. It should also be mentioned that now there are priests more willing to dedicate their time to spiritual direction, which is not easy; it takes selflessness and an ability to listen, empathize, and sincerely seek what is good for the other person.

You also asked whether spiritual direction is necessary for all Christians. I believe it is very helpful, but not strictly necessary for everyone, at least not systematically. Many of the faithful receive spiritual direction by regularly going to confession. But I would heartily recommend spiritual direction to everyone who feels that God is asking him to grow in his Christian life, to those who have committed themselves to live their baptismal vocation to the full in an ecclesial movement or association, and to those who have some sort of role guiding their brothers and sisters in the faith. In Regnum Christi we suggest spiritual direction to the laypeople, and they welcome it. Furthermore, since the proportion of laypeople to priests is very high, we train laypeople with special gifts to provide the service of spiritual direction, through which the Holy Spirit provides souls with countless graces of holiness.

66. Of all the virtues that a Legionary should have, which would you say is most essential?

This might seem like a difficult question, and it would be if Christ hadn't already answered it. I think I gave the answer earlier when I spoke about the Legion's charism, because for me it is very clear that for Christ the most important thing was love: what the Christians later called in Greek *agape*, which can be translated as charity. The Lord's supreme commandment, the one he gave us at the Last Supper: "I give you a new commandment: love one another; just as I have loved you, you also must love one another" (John 13:34). This is his "new" commandment, always valid and always new because love is never repeated, never exhausted; it is always creative. So it is clear that the essential virtue for a Legionary, as for every Christian, is charity.

The first Christians, along with St. Paul, grasped this very well: "If I have all the eloquence of men or of angels, but speak without love, I am simply a gong booming or a cymbal clashing. If I have the gift of prophecy, understanding all the mysteries there are, and knowing everything, and if I have faith in all its fullness, to move mountains, but without love, then I am nothing at all" (1 Cor 13:1-2). I have never trusted a Christianity that places great stock in pious practices but neglects charity towards our neighbor, or the self-styled "virtue" that consists in fulfilling religious or Church rules perfectly and then literally destroying people's reputations through criticism, detraction, or slander. Where charity and love are, God is there too. God cannot be where there is no charity, neither can authentic Christianity. Look at how simple it is, yet it seems so hard for us men to understand it.

The greatest revolution was neither the French nor the Soviet revolution. Both of these left a wake of death and destruction. The true revolution is the revolution of charity, the dividing moment of history: the Incarnation of the Divine Word. This is the revolution that changes the world, a community, a parish, a Church movement, whatever. The person who loves changes the world, at least a part of it. Love does not leave the world indifferent. So every Christian should seek above all else to love his brothers and sisters truly — love that is shown in actions, words, thoughts, giving your life for the other. You can't truly love God if you hate your brother, says St. John (1 John 4:20). The first Christians made this revolution, as have all those who understood Christ. The saints did; they lived charity heroically. Love gives life to Christianity because God gives life to it, and God is love.

I have also been able to see the value of this gospel truth throughout my now long life. I admit I sincerely do not understand the way some people live their Christian life when they devote themselves to riddling their neighbor in the back, gravely sinning against charity, because that is to destroy his honor. Truly I cannot understand. I know that we are all weak and exposed to sinning gravely. Sometimes we pay more attention to sins that shock our senses and our conscience more than others, like faults against the virtue of purity, but it seems that sins against charity, especially charity in our words (such as slander and detraction, or simply negative criticism) go totally unobserved by our conscience.

I have never stopped urging our religious to strive to live charity above all else; to make our communities oases of peace, pieces of heaven; to spend themselves and put everything into making others happy. But I believe that charity is the essential virtue not only for a Legionary but for every Christian. This is where we have to start our renewal of the Church, by committing ourselves to live, in a heroic way, charity among all who belong to the Church.

67. Obedience has come up several times. Some religious congregations have insisted a lot on it. From my knowledge of the Legionaries and what you mentioned about discipline, I can see obedience is important for you as well. Why? How do you understand this virtue, which today is somewhat discredited?

Obedience is important for us for the simple reason that it is a virtue that Christ lived from the first day of his life to the last: "obedient unto death," St. Paul describes him, "even the death of the cross" (Phil 2:8). Christ redeemed us by his redemptive obedience — a filial, never servile, obedience to his Father in heaven.

Our modern culture finds obedience hard to accept because it regards it as an assault on freedom, which many people today see as the supreme, defining value of the human person. Actually, obedience doesn't go against freedom because when you obey out of faith and love, you make an act of supreme freedom: you freely choose not to exercise your freedom independently of your lawful superior. Hence, we do not encourage blind obedience, but *motivated* obedience. Seen from the perspective of faith, obedience is truly liberating. Merely servile obedience, on the other hand, does go against human dignity.

To understand this, you have to move to the supernatural level. From a merely human point of view, religious obedience might perhaps seem senseless or harmful to human dignity. But this is not the case with Christian obedience, as is shown by so many cases throughout Church history and the life of every religious.

Yes, obedience is difficult precisely because it is the oblation of what is most noble in us, our freedom. It is like a burnt offering: you offer God your most intimate and personal possession, your ability to choose for yourself. But it is never a blind or servile offering. Christian obedience, like Christ's, is always filial.

Christ Is My Life

Throughout my life the Lord has frequently allowed me to exercise ecclesial obedience. Doubtless it is hard for human nature, but it always bears fruit in God's ways. In this regard I always remember my mother's uncle, Blessed Rafael Guízar Valencia, bishop of Veracruz — the one I told you accepted me into his seminary. When he was still a young priest in the city of Zamora, his bishop suspended him *a divinis* without any explanation. He was full of life and immersed in apostolic activity, doing missions that brought about mass conversions; hundreds and hundreds of people went to him for confession. His apostolic zeal was boundless. However, he aroused envy and resentment in others, who spread grave calumnies concerning him and the bishop gave them credence. Overnight his priestly ministry was brutally brought to a halt. For more than two years he went to Mass at the parish where he had once presided, with the small-town gossips pointing him out as a corrupt priest. He spent those years in total silence, obeying and bearing with the injustice, waiting for God's time to come. When someone invited him to leave the diocese and work apostolically in another, he answered: "God put me here. This is where I must bear fruit." Those were years of tremendous interior suffering for him, totally unjust but very fruitful. Those years would bear fruit in his later ministry as a priest and as a bishop.

Another well-known case in church is Father Henri de Lubac. In the early Fifties his superiors asked him to give up teaching theology since it was suspected that some of his writings sided with the *"nouvelle théologie,"* a theological current condemned by Pius XII in his encyclical *Humani Generis*. Around that time he wrote a very beautiful book on the Church, *Meditation on the Church*,[4] penning wonderful pages on obedience in the Church and the Church as Mother. His obedience and his merits as a theologian

[4] Published in English by Ignatius Press under the title *The Splendor of the Church*.

were later recognized by Pope John Paul II, who made him a cardinal.

Obedience is a Christian virtue. Christ practiced it to the point of heroism. The fact that today's mentality holds it in less regard does not mean that obedience is bereft of value. It has no value if it is servile or practiced out of fear, but it has immense value if it is guided and directed by love, as is the case with Christ's obedience to his Father in heaven.

68. You mention opposition between the Christian spirit and the spirit of the world, and yet Vatican II speaks of the need to move towards the world and understand it, if the Church is to save it. Many people are not sure what attitude a Christian should have towards the world, opposition and rejection or closeness and understanding. Which does the Legion of Christ opt for?

This is a very interesting question because it is true that many people are confused in this regard. I think the confusion might stem from the fact that "world" as used in the bible and daily life can have either a neutral-positive connotation, or a negative one. In the Bible you sometimes find "world" used to mean whatever is against God and the spreading of Christ's Kingdom. St. John often uses it in this way in his gospel and his letters (see John 15-16; 1 John 3:13, 5:19). But there is also the other meaning, where the Bible speaks of the world as all people or even all the beings God has created. In this sense the word is neutral, with no moral connotation.

If you give the word the first meaning, both Sacred Scripture and the great authors in Christian tradition speak of a battle between the world and the gospel, between the world's standards and God's, giving rise to a war to the death that will end in the definitive triumph of God's Kingdom. The Book of Revelation, for instance, uses symbolic language to describe this battle that grows fiercer as the end of time approaches and concludes with the victory of Christ and the redeemed. No doubt, if you want to be consistent with your Catholic faith, you will find yourself at odds with other "worldly" ways of thinking, and you have to be ready to be a "sign of contradiction." The gospel proposes a prophetic message that does not follow the norms of this "world." Hence St. John could say in his first letter: "You must not love this passing world or anything that is in the world. The love of the Father cannot be in any man who loves the world, because nothing the world has to offer — the sensual body, the lustful eye, pride in possessions — could ever come from the Father but only from the world; and the world, with all it craves for, is coming to an end; but anyone who does the will of God remains forever" (1 John 2:15-17).

Those whose mission it is to preach the gospel at times feel tempted to adapt it to the standards of this "world," to make it softer, more accessible — some would say more "human." The ethical norms that derive from the gospel commitment are intolerable to the mentality of this world. People cannot understand a life lived according to the gospel, radically and with complete consistency. It would be very easy to offer a gospel trimmed down to suit each person, an *à la carte* gospel that people would accept without a problem. But the gospel is always a stumbling block for the world. St. Paul understood this very well, especially after his failed attempt at preaching in the Areopagus at Athens, when almost to a man they walked out on him at the mention of rising from the dead, which was unthinkable for the Greek mentality. So, some time later, he wrote to the Corinthians: "If it was God's wisdom that human wisdom should not know God, it was because God wanted to save those who have faith through the foolishness of the message that we preach. And so, while the Jews demand miracles and the Greeks look for wisdom, here are we preaching a crucified Christ; to the Jews an obstacle that they cannot get over, to the pagans madness, but to those who have been called, whether they are Jews or Greeks, a Christ who is the power and the wisdom of God" (1 Cor 1:21-24).

Ever since the early centuries of Christianity, Christ's disciples realized that they would inevitably be poles apart from the world around them. The gospel tries to change the world's mentality and bring it into line with Christ's teaching. The world rejects the gospel, which it sees as an enemy of its outlook and values. In this sense you can — as the Holy Father does — speak of a struggle for the world's soul, which lasts down to our own day and age. Christ was well aware of this, and clearly stated that he had not come to bring peace but the sword. He knew very well that his message was revolutionary, that it demanded one's very best, but that the darkness would not be willing to admit defeat so easily: "The light shines in the dark, but the darkness could not grasp it" (John 1:5).

As Legionaries we want to contribute to the Church's mission to save the world — understood in the neutral sense — which we should love as Christ did. But we also know that our action, like that of everyone who sides with the gospel, will clash with the standards of the world understood in the negative sense, which will make us in its eyes a sign of contradiction.

69. You speak of struggle, battle. Some people think that such an attitude is exaggerated and goes against the spirit of our times — open to tolerance and accepting of diversity.

We have already touched on some aspects of this topic. Let me now add that I understand warfare in the biblical sense. In the gospels and the letters of St. Paul and St. John we find texts calling us to live geared for battle. It's a special kind of battle. It's not about waging holy wars, not at all. I said earlier that our Legion is a Legion of love and peace.

In his Farewell Discourse Jesus speaks to his disciples of all the hardships they will have in the world, and invites them to trust in the final triumph: "Be brave: I have conquered the world" (John

16:33). St. Paul, for his part, describes what he calls the "armor" of a Christian's faith: "Put God's armor on so as to be able to resist the devil's tactics" (Eph 6:11). Man's life, especially a Christian's, is presented as a struggle against the spirit of the world, his passions and the evil one. It is a law of life. It's about fighting for the good, for values, truth, kindness, the Church, God's Kingdom. "To fight" means that we have to work for the gospel. True as it may be that God's grace always has primacy in Christian life, we have to correspond to it, and in the absence of this reply God "has his hands tied" as it were, because he wants us to be his free and responsible coworkers.

The battle for God's Kingdom may at times be intense, but it is never fanatical or intolerant. As I said earlier, what God most respects is man's freedom, and whoever works for the gospel should respect God's way of doing things. But that doesn't mean that man doesn't have the right to have the gospel preached to him, to be invited to live it — and that an apostle doesn't have the duty to preach it. The invitation to believe leaves freedom intact, and offering the gospel never breaches the intimacy of conscience.

Tolerance has to be properly understood. To be tolerant means to respect the opinion of others on political questions, their view of the economy, of reality, their religious creed. But a society must not falsely tolerate what damages or wounds human dignity and man's fundamental rights. So tolerance, important as it may be, can never be the only or the ultimate defining norm in a democratic society, which should be founded on a set of shared values that all are bound to respect — in other words, values that derive from nature and human dignity. The militancy we are discussing is no threat to proper tolerance; rather it symbolizes the passionate love with which Jesus' disciples work to spread the gospel of salvation.

Father Marcial Maciel was born in Cotija de la Paz, Michoacán, on March 10, 1920. As a child he witnessed the persecution unleashed against the Church in Mexico.

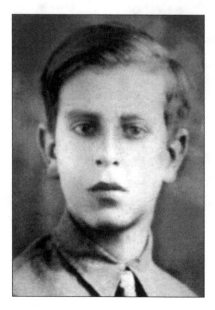

Marcial Maciel at the age when he felt called to become a priest.

Maura Degollado Guízar (1895-1977), Father Maciel's mother, who is presently in the process of beatification for her exemplary life as a Christian wife and mother.

As a seminarian, Marcial joined the group of Catholics who actively took part in opening the churches of the city of Orizaba that had been closed due to religious persecution.

The Congregation of the Legionaries of Christ was born on January 3, 1941, in the basement of this house, 39 Turín Street, Mexico City.

The first Legionaries in their makeshift dining room in the garden of the young congregation's second house, located at 21 Victoria Street, Mexico City, in 1941.

Father Marcial Maciel was ordained a priest on November 26, 1944, by the bishop of Cuernavaca, Monsignor Francisco González Arias, at the feet of the Blessed Virgin Mary in the Basilica of Our Lady of Guadalupe.

In 1946, five years after founding the congregation, Father Maciel takes the first group of Legionaries to Spain to study humanities and philosophy at the Pontifical University of Comillas.

The first Legionaries to go to Spain ready their new dormitory:
a cowshed in the town of Comillas, Santander province.

Love for and loyalty to the Holy Father are hallmarks
of the Legionaries. In this photograph Pius XII receives
a group of Legionaries accompanied by Father Maciel.

John XXIII, the "Good Pope," visits the Basilica dedicated to Our Lady of Guadalupe in Rome, built by the Legionaries at his request.

The Holy Father Paul VI showed his special affection, goodwill, and fatherly closeness to the congregation, giving it unconditional support in carrying out its charism. He granted the Decree of Praise in 1965.

*The Holy Father John Paul II in his most recent
visit to the Legionaries' center for higher studies
in Rome: another manifestation of his fatherly
love and his appreciation for the Legion.*

*The international network of
Helping Hand schools provides free
education to the underprivileged.*

In 1970 Paul VI entrusted the Legionaries with the pastoral care of the new prelature of Chetumal (now Cancún-Chetumal) in the state of Quintana Roo. It is situated in the southeastern part of Mexico's Yucatán peninsula, covers more than 19,890 square miles, and has a population of 1,132,433.

When the Legionaries first arrived, the Chetumal prelature had only eight churches. In thirty-three years, the Legionary missionaries have built 343 churches and oratories, and have founded eighteen schools and two universities. This photo shows First Communions in Cozumel's Corpus Christi Church.

The Anáhuac University, the Legionaries' first, was founded in Mexico City in 1964. It currently offers twenty-five Bachelor's programs, twenty-two specialization programs, twenty-seven Master's programs, and six doctoral programs. It has seven thousand registered students.

The Regina Apostolorum Pontifical University in Rome was inaugurated on September 5, 1993. There are currently 2,820 students in its Theology and Philosophy faculties and the world's first School of Bioethics. Cardinal Angelo Sodano, His Holiness's Secretary of State, blessed the new installations on December 31, 2000.

Training center of the Legionaries of Christ in New York, USA.

The International Pontifical College, Maria Mater Ecclesiae, in Rome is for diocesan seminarians, especially those who will be seminary formators in the future.

*Closing Mass of the "Megamissions." Each Holy Week the
Regnum Christi Movement organizes humanitarian and
evangelizing missions for the poorest of the poor. In the year 2003,
in Mexico alone, some sixty-five thousand missionaries took part.*

*The Holy Father John Paul II ordained sixty Legionary
priests in Saint Peter's Basilica on January 3, 1991,
the fiftieth anniversary of the Legion's foundation.*

The Legion of Christ is a constantly growing congregation. Here is a glimpse of the community in Rome when the Holy Father visited the Legionaries' formation center on March 18, 1998.

The Holy Father held an audience for Regnum Christi members in Saint Peter's Square on January 4, 2001, for the sixtieth anniversary of the Legion of Christ's founding.

V

Regnum Christi

70. Alongside the Legionaries of Christ there is the Regnum Christi apostolic movement. Why did you decide to associate this movement to the Congregation of the Legionaries of Christ, and what is its purpose?

When I felt the Holy Spirit move me to found the Legion of Christ on that First Friday, the feast of the Sacred Heart in 1936, I clearly saw that the Lord wanted me to gather a group of people who would go throughout the whole world preaching the gospel of his love. Since my milieu at the time was a seminary, I logically began to share the idea with my fellow seminarians, but at the core of the inspiration the charism was not restricted to the men who would later be the Legionaries of Christ. It was for all the men and women, including diocesan priests, who wanted to share my long-ing to bring every last corner of society and every last heart the message of God's love, made known in Jesus Christ.

That is how Regnum Christi gradually emerged, as a Catholic movement of apostolate to establish Christ's Kingdom in the world; and fundamental to Christ's Kingdom, what stamps us as Christians, is charity. Hence the name. I drafted the first statutes in 1959, but not until the first groups of Legionaries were formed and we began to start our apostolates was it possible to gather the laypeople to give them the spiritual and apostolic formation that would enable them to live their Christian and apostolic vocation deeply. Regnum Christi emphasizes the spirituality of baptism, because at baptism a Christian receives not only all his dignity but also his commitment to grow in holiness and evangelize. Later, when the Second Vatican Council reminded all Christians of their call to holiness and apostolate, we already had our first lay members working along the same lines as the spirit of the Council, which came as a confirmation of our spirituality.

Regnum Christi's charism is the same as the Legion of Christ's; it is the means for the Legionaries to do their apostolate. In Regnum Christi we insist on the apostolic nature of the Christian vocation. Christ sent his apostles out into the whole world, not so that each one would keep the treasure of the gospel for himself or put it under the table, but to place it out in the open, where it could shed its light on everyone in the house. In his encyclical *Redemptoris Missio*, Pope John Paul II reminds us that "faith grows when you share it." When you are convinced about your faith, you can't help sharing it, and when you share it, your faith itself grows stronger. This isn't the only trait of Regnum Christi's spirituality, but it is one of the most important, and it has moved the laypeople themselves, aware of their Christian vocation to be light of the world and salt of the earth, to start countless apostolic projects that spring from their desire to share the treasure of their Christian faith with others.

The Holy Father has confirmed Regnum Christi's spiritual and apostolic charism on several occasions, recently in a letter he saw fit to send me on March 2, 2002. In this letter, the Pope recalled that in Regnum Christi diocesan priests and laypeople want to live their spiritual commitments more intensely, following a Christ-centered spirituality, based on a fervent sacramental life and firm loyalty to the Successor of Peter and all the shepherds of the particular churches; this spirituality helps them to travel firmly the road that leads to the holiness to which all Christians are called.

In the same letter, the Pope mentions his esteem for Regnum Christi's apostolic zeal, reflected in our many schools and universities, our work with families, the associations that aid the neediest of society, the projects that spread the Christian spirit in the media — all of which Regnum Christi promotes in order to build a civilization of justice and love.

A concrete proof of the Holy Father's appreciation and goodwill towards the lay Regnum Christi members is the plenary indulgence they can obtain several times a year if they comply with the established conditions. Regnum Christi members can obtain a plenary indulgence on their incorporation day, on the liturgical memorial of Our Lady of Sorrows and on the Solemnity of Christ the King, when they yearly renew their intention to continue fulfilling the resolutions they made on joining the Movement. We see this grace that the Holy Father has granted to us as yet another invitation for each one of us to strengthen our friendship with God, our sacramental life, and our desire to establish Christ's Kingdom.

71. You just mentioned the role given to laypeople in Vatican II. Do you think this is a sign of the times? On the other hand, how can the laity and priests keep their roles without creating friction or confusing their respective duties?

There's no doubt that the role laypeople have assumed — especially after Vatican II, but also before it in an incipient way — is a sign of the times by which God is clearly pointing his Church in the direction to go. In the whole undertaking of Catholic Action, promoted by a number of Supreme Pontiffs throughout the twentieth century, the Holy Spirit was visibly at work, asking laypeople to take on more co-responsibility in the Church. Little by little, lay movements — many of them springing up after the Council — began emphasizing laypeople's protagonism in Church life. The Council decree *Apostolicam Actuositatem* was quite clear and explicit in describing the tasks that fall to laypeople in the Church's apostolate. *Lumen Gentium,* moreover, vigorously reminded the Church of the universal call to holiness, which includes laypeople as much as priests since the Christian vocation itself is essentially a vocation to holiness, no matter what state of life you live it in.

It is important, though, to avoid making the laity like clergy and making priests like laity, hazards that have not always been avoided. Today there is a certain tendency to water down the distinction between laypeople and priests or deacons, to the degree that some can't understand why laypersons do not exercise ministerial functions. These tendencies become abuses when they fail to make the right and necessary distinction between clergy and lay. While on the one hand many would like laymen to take on specific functions of the priest, on the other some priests having lost their identity try to find it by behaving like laypeople. I think we must avoid these extremes. We can strike a balance: a fruitful cooperation between priests and laity, where each keeps to his proper functions and works for the good of the Church. There is a wonderful complementarity in which each respects the other and follows the specific vocation to which God calls him.

I see this clearly in the various Regnum Christi apostolates we have started. Priests have their own duties: They celebrate the Eucharist and the other sacraments, and leave to the laypeople a wide range of activities in which they are often much more effective since they are in the world as leaven in the dough. Regnum Christi trains the laity, gives them a thorough formation, and then gets them, in proportion to each one's abilities, to undertake apostolates that meet the Church's needs. We do not set any limits as to the types of apostolates we can do. Not that we do every kind, but in principle we are open to doing whatever would help establish Christ's Kingdom and be of service to the Church. And since the laypeople are very enterprising and the needs are many, they

come up with all sorts of initiatives, and not just in the necessary and traditional areas such as families, the media, education, or missions. Our laypeople have begun initiatives in areas such as assistance to homeless children, defense of the environment (with a Christian view of the earth), training in trades and crafts for underprivileged youth and adults, medical clinics, food banks, support for single mothers, cultural foundations, musical groups, full-time evangelizers, promotion of peace and harmony between nations, et cetera. It is amazing to see the laypeople's initiative when they burn with the desire to spread the truth of the gospel to their neighbor.

I believe that cooperation and mutual trust between laity and priests is essential for the good of the Church, because laypeople need the presence of priests to offer them the bread of God's word and the Eucharist, God's forgiveness through the sacrament of reconciliation, and all the divine life that flows through the sacraments. Besides, closeness to and trust in a priest not only helps Christian families fully live the spirituality of the sacrament of matrimony, but has the added importance of helping the children grow in esteem and respect for priests. In some countries the fact that a priest doesn't have a presence among families has aggravated both the family crisis and the crisis of religious and priestly vocations. Through their presence as shepherds in the heart of the family, priests strengthen the faith of the family members, and with their prayers and advice they often prevent painful separations and divorces. The absence of priests from family life makes a distant stranger of him who was consecrated to dispense the Eucharist and the sacrament of forgiveness, and is completely devoted to serving God and the Church. It enriches the priest to have contact with laypeople, with their experience in the professional life. Laypeople expect from priests a warm welcome, understanding, closeness, and the witness of fidelity. To separate priests and laity or to fail to distinguish their functions can be devastating for the Church. A balanced relationship, where each respects the other's vocation, can give the Church great vigor and enrich it with the complementarity of these two kinds of vocations.

72. What do you have to do to join Regnum Christi? How do you go about it, and what commitments do you take on?

People normally get to know Regnum Christi by way of its works or because they know a member. Some of these people, after coming into contact with this ecclesial entity, wonder about their own Christian life — whether they are living it fully, if they could do more, pray better, or know Christ and the gospel better. In a word, they begin to feel a certain desire to leave behind what might be a mediocre living of their faith, or they simply feel a longing for greater fullness.

That is how God calls some to live more in depth and more responsibly their Christian life, their baptismal commitment. The next step is simply to write a letter asking to join Regnum Christi. After an appropriate time of preparation and a spiritual retreat they renew their baptismal commitment, fully aware of what it is, during a special Celebration of the Eucharist. In joining Regnum Christi, you commit yourself to a renewed effort to live your Christian life better, to deepen your prayer life, to partake of the sacraments frequently, to live in charity towards your neighbor in word and deed. Regnum Christi also offers you specific ways and means to reach the fullness of your Christian vocation, such as spiritual direction, team meetings for formation and motivation, short courses in spirituality, and spiritual exercises.

Membership also implies doing some apostolate to serve the Church, each according to his or her possibilities. Some people are kept housebound by sickness; their apostolate will be to offer their prayers and sacrifices to the Lord. No one can truthfully say, "I have nothing to give to Christ's Kingdom." We all have something to give to others, be it little or much, because God gave it to us first.

In my experience these people, at varying rates depending on the pace of grace and each one's responsiveness, steadily renew and strengthen their faith. And their faith in Christ and love for him grow to be very important in their lives, gradually transforming them without their realizing it, spurring them to break out of the pen of their selfishness and go out to meet the needs of their brothers and sisters and of the Church. As you see, what Regnum Christi is looking for is very simple: It wants each member to be a Christian convinced of Christ, to live his baptismal vocation fully, and to be eager to share his faith with others. That's all, nothing more and nothing less.

73. You keep stressing that the Christian vocation is a call to apostolate. Is this the root of Regnum Christi's apostolic dynamism?

I think Regnum Christi members have taken seriously Christ's words that we read at the end of the gospels according to Matthew and Mark where, before ascending to heaven, Christ left his disciples a command, to go out into the whole world and preach the gospel (Matt 28:19; Mark 16:15). It is an explicit command, not an option or one of many possibilities for his disciples to choose, depending on their inclinations. The way it is expressed and the solemnity of the occasion give it all the force of a command that the Lord gives his own before ascending into heaven. The apostles understood this very well, and the proof is that all of them began carrying this mission out under the Holy Spirit's guidance. That is how Christianity spread. It is true that a person is persuaded to accept the faith by a gift from the Holy Spirit. But that doesn't relieve us of our mandatory duty to give witness with our lives, to preach, to announce, to set the light on a stand so that it will enlighten all those who come to it.

In times past Christians were forbidden to witness to their faith. In recent times the communist regimes tried to stifle the spread of the gospel with violence and repression, but they failed in the attempt no matter how harsh their persecutions and punishments. In modern democratic societies, the attempt is sometimes made to silence and discredit the Christian proposal by resorting to the clichéd topic of the errors Christians have made, or pronouncing that preaching the gospel goes against freedom of expression. It is curious to behold how a society that tolerates every bizarre idea objects to the gospel's being preached and sometimes denies it citizenship within the democratic system. Obviously those who can't bear to hear the message of the Church will not put it that way, but ultimately the implicit reasoning is that only those voices in favor of a permissive society where license reigns are admissible, while the Church, which goes against this mentality, is accused of being authoritarian and anti-democratic.

However, the Church cannot remain silent. It cannot cease to announce the Good News of the gospel. I believe the desire to announce Christ is the reason Regnum Christi members — and the members of many ecclesial movements that share the same concern — want to live their Christian vocation dynamically. The same motive is what ultimately drives John Paul II to make his apostolic journeys to the local churches, and what moved St. Paul to preach the gospel to the ends of the known world of his time. The Apostle cries out, "Woe to me if I do not preach the gospel" (1 Cor 9:16) because he feels prisoner of the mission to announce the gospel to one and all, in season and out of season (2 Tim 4:2).

Apostolic dynamism comes from within, when you are convinced that the message you have to share with others is the saving word, a message of salvation in which another's eternal destiny is at stake. That is why St. Paul could say that charity urges us on (2 Cor 5:14), because we feel the urgent need that Christ's saving love reach all people. When your faith is real you can't hold back Christ's message. You have to announce it. Then there is dynamism. I think that people in Regnum Christi understand this aspect of Christianity, and consequently its members aren't content with just living the faith more or less, but want to share it joyfully and enthusiastically. I believe we are all aware that we must give Christianity, especially in traditionally Christian countries, an air of freshness, vigor, and joy. It's true that Christianity requires serious ascetics and discipline, which we have already discussed, but it is no less true that Christianity, which is above all a personal experience of Christ in the very depths of your soul, produces immense joy beyond words. Christ himself, in the gospel, tried to bring this out in the parables of the treasure and the pearl of great price. When a man discovers the treasure of the gospel, which is Christ himself, he goes and sells all he has because he wants to buy the property where the treasure is, and this he does not grudgingly but with his heart full of joy. Believers are deeply joyful people; their joy is not at all shallow, nor is it exempt from great trials, sufferings, and sacrifices. But the soul is content, serene, and joyful because it knows that it possesses the precious pearl, the gospel (see Matt 13:44-46).

Christ himself told us that the Kingdom of heaven is continuously dynamic: It's like a mustard seed, growing day and night, even though at the beginning it is the smallest of seeds. This is the vitality we see in the early Church, in the lives of the apostles, martyrs, and confessors — in a word, in the lives of all who embrace the gospel message and make it the life of their lives. Therefore, as the Council decree *Apostolicam Actuositatem* reminds us, the Christian vocation is in its very essence a vocation to the apostolate (n. 2). This is the thrust of Regnum Christi's spirituality: to help the baptized who are its members to live to the full their vocation to be Christ's apostles in the world today.

74. If I understood you correctly, earlier you mentioned diocesan priests belonging to Regnum Christi. Is that possible?

In our mind Regnum Christi is a large family where laity and priests can live their spiritual and apostolic commitments, each according to their particular vocation and mission. Thus, there is also room for diocesan priests who want to live their priesthood with the help of the Regnum Christi spirituality, as long as they have the proper permission from their bishop. These diocesan priests remain incardinated in their dioceses and continue to fulfill the ministry their bishops entrust to them for the good of the local church, dedicating some time to the spiritual and formative activities that Regnum Christi offers, such as spiritual direction, retreats, courses on theology or pastoral renewal, priest-conventions, et cetera.

These simple activities for formation and perseverance do much to help the 725 priests who take part in them, since now more than ever priests are menaced by an increasingly hostile world and need a fraternal atmosphere to live their vocation and keep their priestly ideals intact. In addition, a good number of bishops and four cardinals have opted to benefit from Regnum Christi spirituality. Getting together to renew their spiritual life, sharing apostolic experiences, nourishing themselves by reading and reflecting on God's Word together, adoring the Eucharist together, also having times for wholesome recreation are all of great support and encouragement to carry on with their daily battle to be faithful, to serve Christ and the Church with undivided hearts, and to renew the first love that moved them to follow their vocation to the priesthood. For their part, the zeal of these priests, their holy lives, their desire to serve the Church, and their pastoral methods greatly enrich Regnum Christi, in the mutual sharing that takes place among family members.

75. I understand that Regnum Christi runs a fascinating program called Full-time Evangelizers. Can you tell us something about it?

From an early age I realized that many regions had not been evangelized and were deprived of the spiritual care they needed because there were too few priests. Sometimes lay catechists ran activities that were very praiseworthy but also very limited, because they lacked both the training and the time. So we decided to provoke an interest in some laypeople that had the possibility of dedicating themselves full-time to evangelization

At the present time there are more than a thousand lay evangelizers working full-time in three countries: Mexico, El Salvador, and Venezuela. In turn they minister to approximately forty thousand catechists in some six thousand rural communities of seventeen different native ethnic groups. Their main work is teaching catechism, ministering pastorally to families, preparing the faithful to receive the sacraments, and visiting families home-by-home to help them live their faith better. They work for the new evangelization in a professional way. Their profession is to evangelize. We give them appropriate training in catechetics, pastoral work, and even theology to enable them to fulfill their mission. In this way they are a support and a multiplying factor for the priests' work. Their evangelizing work brings not only spiritual but also cultural improvement, and has paved the way for social and humanitarian projects inspired by a new Christian awareness.

76. How does mission work, such as you do in the State of Quintana Roo, Mexico, fit into your apostolic charism?

In principle, any way to preach the gospel is part of our charism, and so when Paul VI asked us to take over the Cancún-Chetumal Apostolic Prelature in 1970, we very willingly agreed, seeing his request as God's will, made known to us through Christ's Vicar.

Paul VI named as the first bishop of the prelature Father Jorge Bernal Vargas, who was the first Legionary priest to go through all the stages of formation, including the vocational center. Twenty percent of the Legionary priests who exercise their ministry in Mexico do so very zealously in this mission diocese. It covers a vast area, over twenty thousand square miles, and has a population of 1,132,433 — mostly Mayas. Since the establishment of the mission territory, Legionary missionaries have built 343 churches and chapels of ease, a number of schools, clinics, refugee centers for the fifteen thousand Guatemalan refugees fleeing the forty-year-long civil war in their country, housing complexes for those who lose their homes due to the frequent hurricanes that strike the Caribbean, and so forth. The distances they cover are great, and living conditions for the missionaries are not easy. Some live in villages buried in the jungle, difficult to reach. They learn the Mayan language to be able to carry out their ministry effectively since many of the people do not speak Spanish. They also have to be very prudent and discerning to judge whether or not certain of the Mayan ancestral rites can be accepted and if they are compatible with the requirements of the Catholic faith. Thanks be to God, their work has been very fruitful, helping the Maya adapt to the requirements of today's civilization while respecting their traditions. In the past thirty years, their humanizing presence has enabled the native populations to live in peace and harmony and avoid clashes and conflicts, which unfortunately have occurred in other states in Mexico.

77. How can a person live the gospel and the great apostolic ideals that you mention in their daily life? How does he overcome the force of routine that always threatens to ruin great spiritual and apostolic ideals?

You bring up an extremely important aspect where faith is put to the test: everyday life, with its monotony, its annoying and boring repetition, all the petty conflicts that hurt us deeply, the letdowns, all the grayness that seem to unsaddle our highest ideals. Nevertheless, it is in daily life that a Christian grows in holiness and shows whether his love for Christ is merely platonic or able to affect his whole life.

My experience as a priest has brought me into contact with many people, a lot but not all of them young, who were fascinated by Christ. His great ideals moved them, and they wanted to follow him. Then daily life set in, and unfortunately I knew not a few who were unable to overcome the small trials of every day. For this reason I have always insisted that faith in Christ and love for Christ are not a matter of mere emotion, feelings, a one-day bloom of enthusiasm. Faith has to take flesh, become reality, become "flesh of my flesh" in real life. If not, it's just make-believe, castles in the air.

That's why it is absolutely necessary for faith to permeate every aspect of your life: your work, your family, your relationships, your rest and relaxation, and so forth. We shouldn't make false dichotomies in life and lay down artificial boundaries between the various aspects of our life and our faith. Either you believe or you don't. Either you live according to your faith or you don't. Christ doesn't allow for halfways in the gospel. He asked his disciples clearly for wholehearted dedication that left no room for mediocrity. He wants it all because he gives it all. So, to answer your question, you overcome the force of routine by totally, constantly, authentically giving yourself, and that takes the constant exercise of true love.

78. Why does Regnum Christi give so much importance to the family apostolate?

If, as we were saying, our faith ought to shape our whole life, and a very important part of life is the family, we must conclude that if we want to evangelize deeply, we must evangelize the family — which is the natural space where a person comes into the world, is brought up, lives, and develops his affectivity, emotions, and openness to others. Christ himself chose to live in a family, the Holy Family of Nazareth. There, in the surroundings in which he chose to share our human nature, he learned the Jewish prayers of his time; he learned, from the point of view of his human nature, about the great mysteries of life and the human being.

That is why we give priority to families in our apostolates. We have established, and with God's help will continue to do so, family centers that provide family members with the nourishment their spirits seek, where families find support in these times of grave moral crises in which strong winds threaten to break up marital fidelity and family unity.

For the human person it is fundamental to be born, live, and die in a harmonious family. I don't mean to say that there must be no problems or difficulties. Of course there will be, as is logical and natural. But faith in Christ helps families to stay united, to support the members who are weaker or suffering more, to feel one another's joys and pains as their own, and find in one another the acceptance and affection that we all need for our normal emotional development. When faith and charity permeate natural family relationships, this allows the family members to live the theological virtues in a completely spontaneous way, a profound joy reigns in the home, the bonds of affection grow stronger and rise to a new supernatural level where the person finds a deep harmony and balance.

79. What activities and centers does Regnum Christi have for families?

Their activities are many, and they depend to a great degree on each place and the members' initiative in each country. Along with schools, which we have discussed, one of our first apostolates in Mexico was dedicated to the family: *Familia Mexicana*, or FAME. Similar initiatives have arisen in other countries, such as *Familia Unida* [United Family] in Chile, *Desarrollo Integral de la Familia* [Integral Family Development] in Spain, and so on. These programs offer formation to all the members of a family from grandparents to youth and adolescents, and they help each family to become truly a domestic Church, where the gospel is lived out and a simple, spontaneous encounter with God takes place.

There is a beautiful family apostolate in the United States as well, FAMILIA, which stands for Family Life in America. It was started with married couples who realized that they needed to be really solid in their faith if they were to strengthen their family unity. Working with their directors, they put together a program of Christian education based on the principal encyclicals of John Paul II, not only on the subject of families but also on other topics basic to the faith. Thousands of families participate in this formation program, and they also commit to some form of apostolate, to the extent their situation allows. The program, which was originally prepared in English, has already been translated into other languages and is quickly growing in other countries of North and South America, Oceania, and Europe. The participants tell us that when faith becomes more vigorous, family life is deeply renewed — a fact confirmed by reliable studies done in several countries.

Another very interesting initiative that we have begun is *Edificar la Familia* ["Build Your Family"]. Tens of thousands of couples have taken these courses. It's a formation program that helps parents approach motherhood and fatherhood maturely and responsibly. People put years of study into preparing for their career, yet they get hardly any specific preparation as fathers and mothers. They assume that nature takes care of this. But our society is so complex and the problems that parents have to face in raising their children are so new that if they aren't adequately prepared, parents are overwhelmed and don't know how to take up these responsibilities. Today's parents, for instance, weren't brought up on the Internet, and now their children have easy access to this medium, which as we know is not devoid of risk for their moral and religious life. What should their attitude be towards this and many other new challenges in an ever-more-globalized world? Or, how will

they educate their children in their emotional and sexual maturing process? In our times it is not at all easy to live out conscientiously the call to parenthood. The resources these programs offer are spiritual as well as technical, helping people to face new problems from the point of view of the Christian faith.

We also live our commitment to families through the John Paul II Institutes for the Family, which we run in three cities in Mexico. These institutes, which depend on their headquarters at the Lateran University in Rome, train specialists in family-related topics, who in turn become competent teachers and professors in this field. We have also started Master degrees in family studies in several of our universities.

Finally, I want to underline that we think it is very important for people to live their faith in the family: to pray as a family, and even to do apostolate as a family. An experience that has been very fruitful is what we call *Missionary Family*: the whole family, parents and children together, participate in evangelization programs in rural areas or missionary territories that are without sufficient pastoral care. It is very beautiful to see whole families go out to evangelize and share their faith, and how the children sense intuitively their vocation to be apostles to other children, and often even to their own parents.

80. Some of the activities you've mentioned, and even the spirit you do them with, seem very similar to activities that other Catholic organizations do. To someone who doesn't know the Church, all these organizations seem almost identical, and yet each one has its own spirit, its own history, and its particular aims. Why so many organizations? Isn't it a little confusing for the faithful? Wouldn't it be simpler if each Catholic were just committed in his own parish?

The Holy Spirit, not men, guides the Church. The Holy Spirit enriches the Church with a great variety of gifts and charisms that offer the faithful the one Christian spirituality, the one gospel, from different perspectives — each one of them a different, possible way to grow in holiness. Neither I nor any of the founders of ecclesial organizations or movements tried to invent something. We have tried, within our own personal limitations, to be faithful to an inspiration that came from on high and has been confirmed by the competent Church authority. If any of us had set out to found his own thing, So-and-so's Movement or Father Maciel's Movement, we would have failed. If the Holy Spirit has chosen to inspire this treasure of gifts, it's because they will be of help to the Church, and he wants to make the greatest number of possibilities available so that by one means or another people will learn to know and love Christ. We can say it is of no great importance whether they come to know and love him through Regnum Christi or another ecclesial organization or the parish. What does matter is that Christ penetrate each person's heart and transform it.

I believe that the diversity of gifts beautifies the Church, just as the various shades of color blend and beautify a landscape. They would be in error if each of these organizations tried to monopolize salvation or give themselves an absolute value they don't have. Each is there to serve the Church, and has meaning only in the Church, for the Church, and as part of the Church's supernatural and human mission. Outside the Church they would be pointless.

The Holy Spirit, who has inspired each one of these charisms, also suggests to each person a path to holiness that fits his or her circumstances and characteristics. If you have received a specific calling to strive for holiness in one of these movements or organizations, you are duty-bound to be faithful to your movement's spirit, because that is the direction in which the Holy Spirit is calling you.

As regards the relationship between movements and parishes, we encourage Regnum Christi members to participate actively in their parishes, to be of help to their parish priest in whatever way they can, and to support parish activities. The Regnum Christi commitment should never be a reason to distance yourself from your parish; on the contrary, it should stimulate you to be a better parishioner. The Catholic Church is structured in dioceses and parishes, and while we should not create other parallel structures, we can offer our help to form, organize, and commit apostolically the Christian faithful who make up the parishes. That's what the movements with a true Church spirit do. On their part, parishes should also be willing to welcome all the Catholic movements and organizations that the proper Church authority has approved. Above all else we have to seek the good of each of the faithful and of the Church in a spirit of communion, letting the Holy Spirit do his work and taking steps to be complementary to one another, to serve the Church better.

81. A major area of apostolate for the Legionaries of Christ and Regnum Christi is the education of children and the youth. When talking about your history you discussed how this first field of apostolate got started. Can you comment now on its development, its challenges, and the results you see?

As I mentioned at the beginning, our first apostolate was an educational undertaking, the Cumbres Institute, opened in Mexico City in 1954 thanks to then Monsignor Giovanni Battista Montini, later Paul VI, who recommended us to Mrs. Flora Barragán de Garza, a generous woman who saw God's hand acting in our humble congregation. Before starting this apostolate I prayed a lot and begged God's light as to what I should do, since I was aware that the first apostolate would set the course for the generations to come, and the other apostolates that we would open over the course of time. I thank God and the men who faithfully and selflessly worked with me to start the school, that this first apostolate achieved its goal of educating its students with very good results and offering them and their families the light of the gospel.

Soon other people asked us to open new schools in Mexico City and other cities in Mexico, and later in many other countries.

In 1964 the first of our universities opened it doors, the Anáhuac University in Mexico City, in which we sought to blend a humane approach to the sciences with academic excellence. In its nearly forty years of operation it has garnered a well-earned recognition both nationally and internationally. Entire generations of professionals have gone through its halls and now provide competent service to the country in the various areas of social and economic life.

We presently run twenty-two universities and centers for higher studies and 154 schools. The results have been very positive, for which we thank God. We seek to form the students integrally, in all the facets of their personality, always holding up as their model Christ, who is perfect God and perfect man. Our schools have a high level of academics, but in addition — and this is most important — we give the boys and girls a balanced, harmonious formation that strives to blend faith and reason, nature and grace. Over time our pedagogical system has become more and more professional, and we now have teams of people who help assure the very highest-quality education and excellence in our schools.

We have a pedagogical consultation center with an international staff of experts in the various subjects. At this center that has branches in Europe, North America, Central America, and South America, we develop our formation curriculum, textbooks, teacher's guides, and teaching tools, and we offer courses of ongoing training for teachers and provide the technological infrastructure for schools. Thus we can more easily maintain our commitment to reach the highest educational standards.

In our eyes, the students' faith-formation is of paramount importance, while respecting the beliefs of those students who profess non-Catholic religions. The education we offer includes education in the faith as an element in integral formation. Legionary priests exercise their ministry in our schools as spiritual counselors so that our students have easy access to the sacraments of the Eucharist and reconciliation, and have a priest available to talk to. Our schools also offer a wide variety of activities such as religion classes, retreats, conferences, pilgrimages, and summer courses, et cetera, so that the children, teenagers, and youth can open up spontaneously to the faith as the natural surrounding in their lives.

As I remarked earlier, we try to give everything that has to do with religious education a personalistic approach, based on the figure of Christ. This means for each one to meet him face-to-face and establish a relationship of friendship and love with him. If this doesn't happen, laws and disciplinary norms will lack true pedagogical value since there will be no deep-down motivation to live their demands.

We set great stock in young people. John Paul II says over and over that they are the hope of the Church, and it's true. Sometimes they are falsely caricatured as being uninterested in religion or the search for transcendence, as if they only looked for private forms of religiosity, some more occult than others, and systematically rejected the institutional Church. This is false, as the massive participation in World Youth Days proves. Young people search for truth and love. It is true that today, as always, they are barraged with provocations to give up their search: the deceiving dreams of fleeting, transitory happiness, less costly but less authentic. It is also true that many of them retreat into the easy solution of drugs, sex, or consumerism; but many others are generous, they give all they have, and they place themselves at the service of their brothers and the Church. I believe that the key to success in working with young people is not to be afraid to offer them the gospel pure and simple, with all its demands. That's what Christ did with his disciples, and he provoked loyalty and devotion that often culminated in martyrdom. Some, perhaps many, will not accept the gospel ideal, but many others will. It would be an error not to present the gospel with its demands for fear that they won't accept it, to try to deceive the young people and deceive ourselves with gospel substitutes. That is not what young people want, nor will it make them happy.

82. What do you think is the key to Pope John Paul II's success with the youth? Their enthusiasm for him could be explained easily enough when he was young and strong, but how can you explain it now that he is eighty-two, tired, and ill?

I believe, as he himself just said in Toronto [at the July 2002 World Youth Day], that he has a young heart, and the young people catch on to this right away. We could wonder what a young heart is. Having a young heart means being open to what is true, good, beautiful, and noble — to high ideals. The young are open to life, to love. They want to build a new world; they want to change the world their elders have bequeathed with its wars, injustice, and false relationships. We've all gone through a stage where in one way or another we wanted to change the world. John Paul II is a man, a Christian, and a priest who believes that we can change the world for Christ, and his faith is contagious. You can perceive it almost physically. There is no other human explanation. No other leader in the world is so acclaimed by the young. He is a living witness to what he preaches. He believes in the beauty of a world with Christ, and that is what attracts young people.

When all is said and done, what is the Pope's message to youth? The gospel. What did he speak to them about in Toronto? The Beatitudes. It was as if the Sermon on the Mount were being proclaimed all over again, not by the shore of Lake Tiberias, but in the modern industrial and cosmopolitan city of Toronto. But the message is the same: there is a world where truth, beauty, and love are possible. That world is the Kingdom of heaven that is won by those who weep, are persecuted, seek peace, are pure of heart, are poor in spirit, and seek justice.

The Pope's physical exhaustion has merely emphasized what St. Paul calls the "power of God" that shines in man's weakness. And young people see him more as a witness than as a teacher. Paul VI was so right when he said that today's world believes and follows witnesses more than it does teachers, and if people listen to teachers, it is because they are witnesses. For young people, the Pope is a witness: he is a man who has been faithful to his faith, to his vocation, and to himself; a man who saw firsthand the horrors of Nazism and communism, the two great plagues of the twentieth century, and who could believe, hope, and love through all those painful situations.

For youth the world over, John Paul II is therefore a summons, a model, an inspiration, a guide; a true spiritual leader who proposes without imposing, who strides ahead without fear, blazing the trail. Beyond his physical illness and weariness, his person radiates the mystery of God, who is Love; the passion to communicate Christ's gospel; and the desire to bring each man and woman, each young person, a message of faith and hope.

83. Among Regnum Christi's apostolic initiatives, "Youth for the Third Millennium" especially attracts young people. Thousands and thousands of young men and women interested in sharing their faith participate in the program. Can you tell us what it is all about?

It's something very simple that happened spontaneously. As you know, Mexico is a country especially coveted by the sects, which receive handsome financial backing, mostly from abroad. Once I was in my hometown, Cotija de la Paz, Michoacán, and I heard that a sect was going to organize a mission there, going door-to-door. I was sure that the bulk of the town would not accept them, but some would — for economic reasons, or out of ignorance, or because they felt more accepted, or for whatever reason — and abandon their Catholic faith without realizing it to join a non-Catholic church. The Regnum Christi laypeople looked for a preventive solution, to get there first and strengthen people's faith, to remind them how important it is to stay faithful to their Catholic faith, and even to give them some basic education so they could answer the sect members. They reported to the parish priest, the young people did the mission, and the experience had excellent results, thank God, in terms of strengthening the people's faith and renewing their joy to be Catholic.

These mission experiences were repeated in other places on weekends, with students from our schools and Regnum Christi groups. Later on, the young people offered to give up their Holy Week vacation [spring break] to spend the time doing missions. We gave them adequate preparation, spoke with the pastors from towns that were particularly affected by the sects, got permission from the bishops, and the young people went to be missionaries for a week, with Legionary priests for the sacraments and doctrinal support. The young people's experience was so intense, and the people welcomed them so warmly, that year after year, larger and larger numbers of young people have chosen to have the same experience.

At present, they go not only to towns where sects are more active, but also to the more remote communities, where priests rarely make it; they also go to prisons and to some of the worst, most hostile slums in the big cities. In Mexico alone this year fifty thousand young people and families had this missionary experience in twenty-two States, reaching more than three thousand native communities. We have also done missions in Africa (Ivory Coast), Lebanon, Bosnia, Romania, Brazil, Canada, Belize, Chile, Argentina, Italy, Spain, France, Germany, Ireland, the United States, Colombia, Venezuela, and others — a total of twenty-five countries. We have seen the great truth of the Pope's words in

Redemptoris Missio: "Faith is strengthened when it is given to oth-ers" (n. 2). Besides preventive action against the sects, the mis-sions have substantially helped the evangelizing process of many regions that priests couldn't reach for lack of time. As well as the laypeople involved during these missions, twenty-five percent of Legionary priests worldwide participate, helping the parish priests administer the sacraments in these missions of evangelization.

Whole families also started going on the missions, and that's how *Missionary Family* started. The entire family participates. As I explained earlier, everyone, parents and children, support one an-other in the mission. Young people and families thus have a whole new experience: spreading the faith as a family, an experience that transforms them, too, as they realize how important the faith is for people, and how it can make them totally happy even when they're materially poor.

The participants receive appropriate preparation so that they can work effectively. Not only are they taught the doctrinal no-tions of their Catholic faith and given information about the most important sects, so that they can explain the differences from Catholicism, but they also receive an adequate spiritual for-mation, which is the motor that keeps their apostolic momentum going. Here again you see the importance of the person of Christ, as Catholic tradition presents him. When you make the experi-ence of Christ and see how life changes with him, you want to share with others the joy of having found what your heart was looking for.

84. Before continuing our discussion of Regnum Christi's initia-tives and apostolates, I want to go back to a more essential point: why the name? What does the name have to do with your spiri-tuality and apostolate?

The name *Regnum Christi* describes its purpose very well: to es-tablish Christ's Kingdom in our society. To preach to all people the coming of this Kingdom is the ideal that inspires each member's actions in formation and the apostolate.

The synoptic gospels show us how Christ himself announced the Kingdom's coming when he preached: "The time has come, and the Kingdom of God is close at hand. Repent, and believe the Good News" (Mark 1:15). Christ's coming is the coming of God's Kingdom in the world. When Pilate asks Christ if he is a king, Christ does not deny it. Instead he responds, "It is you who say it. Yes, I am a king. I was born for this, I came into the world for this: to bear witness to the truth; and all who are on the side of truth listen to my voice" (John 18:37-38). Regnum Christi members work so that this Kingdom of love, truth, life, grace, and peace will come to the world, to all the structures of society, economy, work, and of the family. Christ's Kingdom is a gift, but men and women can work together to help this gift become a reality, we can pray for it to come. That is why we take our motto from Jesus' prayer, the Our Father: "Your Kingdom come!" It is a petition because we know that the Kingdom is a gift from the Father, but we are also aware that God seeks coworkers, people who will offer their lives to make the Kingdom a reality, even now in this life. This is how Christ's words are to be taken: "The Kingdom of heaven has been subjected to violence, and the violent are taking it by storm" (Matt 11:12). The "violence" Jesus speaks of is not physical, because we know he never liked to use physical violence, not even in self-defense. He speaks of another "violence" that consists in "wresting" from God the necessary graces for the Kingdom of heaven to become a reality here on earth, the "violence" that an apostle must do himself to master his passions and overcome the ruses of the evil one and the world's seductions.

Regnum Christi members believe in the reality of Christ's Kingdom, which has already begun in this world and will come to its perfection in the next, a Kingdom that is present in the Church. They battle and strive so that Christ's Kingdom will be a reality and imbue the life of society, transforming people's hearts, but also changing social and legal structures — to the extent that this is possible here on earth — bringing them more into line with the gospel principles of justice and charity.

85. I hear that you have in Regnum Christi men and women who live in chastity and complete availability for apostolate. Is that true?

We think of Regnum Christi as a large family in which there are various complementary vocations. One of these is the vocation of the men and women who by a special call from God dedicate their lives entirely to spreading Christ's Kingdom, living the evangelical counsels in the form of promises, and devoting themselves completely to the apostolate. In spirit they are men and women who want to serve the Church in Regnum Christi with their whole soul and their whole body, putting their professional talents and qualities exclusively at the service of the Kingdom and its interests. Likewise, they receive an appropriate professional and apostolic training so that they can work in or direct Regnum Christi's apostolates.

The women dedicate themselves mostly, though not exclusively, to directing girls' schools and educating girls and women in Christian life. For this, they receive specific preparation in pedagogy, psychology, philosophy, theology, and pastoral work, as well as a deep spiritual formation. Their mission is very sensitive and important, since they are dealing with the formation of women in cultural circumstances abounding in confusion as regards the identity, vocation, and mission of women.

The men also do exemplary apostolic work in their own professional fields or in spheres where apostolic action properly belongs to the laity. These men, totally dedicated to apostolate in Regnum Christi, act like yeast that steadily transforms the dough. They combine human talent, professional expertise, and intelligent, imaginative apostolic zeal to get the gospel message to penetrate all the sectors of the social structure, even in places that seem indifferent or even hermetically closed to the gospel. Their contribution is decisive in Regnum Christi's various apostolates, especially as directors of institutes for higher studies and as corporate managers of our institutions.

Members dedicated full time to apostolate in Regnum Christi live in teams in formation centers or centers for apostolate. Their total availability to help build Christ's Kingdom makes it possible for us to carry out many apostolates that would otherwise be brought to a standstill. Their great apostolic zeal, deep charity, generous dedication to their work, joyful self-giving, fidelity in their relations with God, and love for the Church are a testimony of exemplary lives for Legionaries and the rest of Regnum Christi members, encouraging us all to live with the same attitude of faith, love, and dedication.

86. Some people have the idea that Regnum Christi and the Legionaries of Christ are exclusively dedicated to the Christian formation of leaders, and so they accuse you of elitism. What truth is there in this?

Although we already discussed this topic, I would like to repeat that Regnum Christi is here to serve man, every human being, without distinction or discrimination of any kind — the reason being that Christ came to save man, to save everyone. Race, nationality, or tongue mattered nothing to him. He is open to everyone, because we all need him. We, who try to be his disciples, cannot be less universal in our outlook than our Master.

Regnum Christi wants to reach everyone, but as a method for its outreach it chooses to form laypeople who will transform their surroundings. The idea is that these laypeople themselves will be apostles to their neighbor in their natural element, be it the home, university, their circle of friends, according to each one's profession:

a doctor in his hospital, a teacher in his school, a worker in his factory, an entrepreneur in his business, a merchant in his shop, and so on.

For this transforming action to be effective, you need to have in-depth formation and deep convictions. Only then can the yeast transform the dough. The gospel shows us that Christ's method was similar. Though he spoke to the crowds and took pity on them, he chose only twelve apostles and a group of disciples, who later became educators and guides for the others.

This does not imply that Christ discriminated in any way or was elitist. The apostles were not great leaders at the time Christ called them. But he gave them a quality formation, and thus they became guides for the rest after a slow process of education in the faith. Regnum Christi is open to everyone, but it invites each one to be a true guide in the faith for his brothers and sisters, to lead them in the way of the gospel, to present to everyone the face of Christ.

We do not think of this as discrimination or elitism. We want to reach everyone, but we begin by forming a few so that we have a multiplier effect, following a tactic of effectiveness that Christ himself used. We admire and support other movements with other apostolic methods. As I mentioned, this multiplicity is a gift of the Holy Spirit, who inspires complementary charisms within the one Church, all of them working for the common good. The important thing is for all to be focused on building the Church and spreading Christ's Kingdom, united in charity and truth.

87. Why does Regnum Christi put so much emphasis on educating entrepreneurs and businessmen in the Church's social doctrine?

As I said, we don't exclude any social class from our apostolic work, but it is obvious that businesspeople have a great potential as multipliers. They are in a position to apply the Church's wealth of social teaching to their businesses, their radius of action can become very wide indeed, and they can improve the living conditions of thousands of workers and their families.

Without a doubt, in today's society the economy plays an ever more important role in the lives of nations and peoples. If you want to create the right conditions to renew society, you clearly have to imbue those who are the driving force in the economy with Christian and gospel principles, so as to bring about a culture of solidarity, and humanize the market laws, which are governed by the interplay of supply and demand. The global and national economies grow more and more complex, and not even the experts themselves completely understand them due to the amount of variables at play. But it is clear to see that those who drive the economy, in the private or the public sphere, are in a position to make the concrete economic choices that affect the well-being of many individuals and families.

Our interest is to teach these people the wealth of Christian social doctrine so that it inspires them to take concrete decisions that will lead to a just society. The facile populist interpretations of what has been called the "preferential option for the poor" caused people to neglect the Christian formation of the leading classes in some countries — more specifically in Latin America — as the post-synodal apostolic exhortation *Ecclesia in America* acknowledges (n. 67), with the resulting loss of a Christian presence in the process of lawmaking and enforcement.

Some businesspeople may have the impression that the Church condemns their kind of economic activity, as if the Church thought that capital was bad in itself. It is true that capital should be subordinate to the value of man, who should be the center of economic life. But that does not mean demonizing capital. Capital can and should be used to generate new wealth and create new sources of employment. Christians who possess material wealth should feel God's call to put it to productive use in service to society, seeing themselves more as administrators than absolute owners of their wealth. I have met quite a number of businessmen estranged from the Church because some pastors caused them a conflict of conscience by telling them it was against Christian life to own capital. Yes, Christ does speak out against those who have disordered attachments to this world's riches, pulling their hearts away from the goods of heaven. But at the same time, in the parable of the talents, he invites us all to do business with the gifts he gave us and make them produce as much as possible for others.

I know many businessmen who act with an acute Christian social awareness in all they do. They reinvest their profits so as to create new jobs or improve their workers' living conditions. As the Pope says in the paragraph of *Ecclesia in America* quoted earlier, "With renewed fervor and updated methods," it is necessary to "announce Christ to leaders, men and women alike, insisting especially on the formation of consciences on the basis of the Church's social doctrine." This is no easy task, because business directors are pressed for time and are pressured by many urgent commitments, making it hard to find time to dialogue with them. But it is necessary if you want to evangelize the business world, where a country's economic and professional life transpires.

For this reason, some of Regnum Christi's many activities are geared precisely for businessmen, to offer them a new vision of economy, based on ethics and solidarity, to help them build businesses that are more human and therefore more Christian. As you can easily see, the kind of Christian formation we try to give the heads of businesses ultimately benefits the workers and employees.

This doesn't mean, however, that we don't do activities directly with the workers as well. For instance, a program that has had significant results is *Asociación Pro-Superación Personal* [Association for Personal Improvement], which promotes human values among the wives of workers and employees in third-world countries. The association was founded by wives of businessmen who were conscious of their social mission and wanted to do something personally to help with the formation and integral improvement of workers' wives. The Association works through individual businesses to offer them courses in human formation and professional training, an indispensable basis for any evangelizing action. The program already has eighty thousand women enrolled and works out of some three thousand centers in various countries. All this was made possible by motivating a group of people to learn about the Church's social teaching more thoroughly and start applying it. Because this group of people was ministered to spiritually, they have achieved what they never even dreamed of when they started. In reality all they did was simply try to apply the principles of Christian social teaching to their social milieu according to their concrete possibilities.

88. In some of your answers you mention being effective. That sounds more like a business tactic than a principle taken from the gospel.

That depends on how you look at it. It's true that effectiveness is all-important in socioeconomics. When you're contracted to do a job, you have to be effective — if not, you risk being fired. The business mentality applies this principle of effectiveness so things run well. To speak of effectiveness in establishing Christ's Kingdom might seem like commercializing the spiritual. Yes, we do use the term "effectiveness," but with reservations, since you don't measure gospel effectiveness with the same parameters as you do the economy.

I am perfectly aware that the parallel between the economy and spreading God's Kingdom in the world is not entirely adequate, and has its real limits. But I have often wondered to myself why is it that a person, a businessman, will squander so much talent, energy, reflection, and action on his business, all to earn a few euros or dollars, and we, when we want to do something for God, don't seem to have the same determination and energy or invest the same intelligence into our work. What's wrong? The children of darkness, Christ tells us, are more astute than the children of the light (Luke 16:8). I think this word from Christ invites us to take the creativity and good means that people apply in their human enterprises and put them at the service of the gospel. To use these good means for the great enterprise of God's Kingdom is profoundly gospel-based. You put all the capacity of your intelligence and will at the service of what is good. All your creative energy. If effective problem-solving is a principle in economic life, why not apply it to doing good, to Christ's Kingdom?

Of course, gospel effectiveness is different from human effectiveness, but in spite of the differences, a person working in an apostolate cannot overlook the elements of human effectiveness, half-do his job, or do it badly or unprofessionally. I believe we must use all human skill, the best, the most professional, for God's works, for the Kingdom. Some might view this as cheap pragmatism. In my book, I repeat, as long as effectiveness is not the absolute value or understood in the wrong perspective, it comes from the gospel. Grace needs nature. Before being holy we have to be human, and in the normal dynamics of grace, Christ's Kingdom cannot go without serious, responsible human cooperation. God wants us to throw out our nets for a catch, and apply the proper skills as we do so. It is up to him to give the results, but we cannot exempt ourselves from doing all we can to get the best fruits.

89. If Regnum Christi develops a social consciousness in its members, I assume it has created social initiatives that reach out to the underprivileged. Do you have these kinds of initiatives?

In his first letter, St. John says "If a man who was rich enough in this world's goods saw that one of his brothers was in need, but closed his heart to him, how could the love of God be living in him?" (1 John 3:17), and "A man who does not love the brother that he can see cannot love God, whom he has never seen" (1

John 4:20). Our Christian life would be sham if we didn't turn our faith into concrete works to provide our neighbors with effective help. This is what we try to teach the laity. This issue is so important for us that in most of our schools and universities we have a mandatory course in which we form the social consciousness of the students so that from their teenage years they commit part of their time to helping others.

Once the laypeople develop a social awareness, they themselves realize that they can't be indifferent to their brothers' and sisters' needs. I thank God that there is a growing number of initiatives that include a wide variety of areas: children, women, food distribution, building houses, health, education, human development, et cetera.

For example, in the area of education and helping children, we have a series of programs that offer formation to impoverished children and teenagers. These include the *Mano Amiga* [Helping Hand] schools, where we give children the same kind of education with the same methods and pedagogical system as the other schools run by the Legionaries of Christ. Other education programs, like *Lazos* [Links], find yearly sponsors for a child's education. Other associations offer scholarships to children and teenagers who can't afford the full cost of their education. In others cities we have *"villas asistenciales"* [Support Homes] to help children in underprivileged areas, taking in and educating orphans or street urchins, and offering teenagers vocational training and if necessary helping them to overcome drug addiction or alcoholism. In Brazil, where the problem of the *meninos de rua* [street urchins] is especially critical in mega-cities like Rio de Janeiro and São Paolo, the *Tertio Millenio* [Third Millennium] program offers medical assistance, education, and psychological and spiritual help to children who for various reasons don't have a family dwelling and are forced to live on the streets of destitute neighborhoods. These and other programs benefit around sixty thousand children and teenagers, as well as their families, since they also offer parents courses in human formation and workshops for learning arts and skills that will help them get jobs.

Not only Latin America benefits from this kind of social work. In Europe we also have the *Villaggio dei Ragazzi* [Boys' Town] in Italy, an educational complex near Naples with a total of 1,200 students, many of whom have serious family problems. In Paris, Cardinal Jean Marie Lustiger turned over to us *Le Chantier*, a center for social assistance which ministers to around three hundred children from immigrant or needy families.

As regards healthcare, in areas with large native populations we have opened a number of hospitals that offer practically free medical consultation and treatment. The medical missions of our universities and Helping Hand Medical Missions, organized by Regnum Christi members in the United States, send about a thousand doctors to Latin American countries to offer health services and evangelize in rural zones in the Third World where they don't have the necessary health infrastructure.

Sometimes our social aid is a response to natural disasters such as earthquakes, floods, and hurricanes. This is the case with the *Centro Integral de Desarrollo Comunitario* [Integral Community Development Center] housing project, which now benefits a thousand families. The first CIDECO village was built near Mexico City for the victims of the earthquake that devastated Mexico City in 1985. Later on others were built near disaster sites such as Acapulco, after hurricane Pauline, and San Salvador, after last year's earthquakes. Each of these housing complexes contains homes for the victim families, a school, a church, commercial and recreational facilities, a police station, a clinic, a trade school, a sports and culture center, and other necessary social services.

To the above you have to add the work we do to promote women, such as the *Yoliguani* projects (a Nahuatl word meaning "the gift of life" or "that which lives eternally") and *Origen* ["Origin"], which gives psychological and sexual guidance to young women, especially pregnant single mothers. Our food distribution programs, such as *Un Kilo de Ayuda* [A Kilogram of Help] and *El Amor Nos Une* [Love Unites Us], provide food for roughly twenty thousand families and over twenty-one thousand children in approximately four hundred rural communities. We also have projects that help the native communities in the Maya region and Oaxaca State.

Many of these initiatives would not be possible without the many voluntary organizations that have grown up around them to organize the young people who want to dedicate part of their lives to social work or Christian charity. By now almost 340,000 people have participated as volunteers in social action programs of all sorts.

In doing these projects, valuable help comes from our "coworkers," young men and women from Regnum Christi who volunteer to do one or two years of apostolic work, going wherever the Church needs them most. Thanks be to God, the groups of coworkers get bigger every year, and it is my desire that the great majority, if not all the young men and women in Regnum Christi, have the grace to participate in this very enriching kind of experience.

I could keep on listing many more initiatives in the area of social action. When the laypeople are spiritually motivated, they are capable of working wonders to fulfill their desire to serve their neighbor. As Legionaries of Christ, our task is to educate them in Christian social awareness so that each one will take responsibility for the talents God has given him and use them to serve his needy brothers and sisters.

90. I've heard that teamwork is highly emphasized in Regnum Christi. Why do you believe it is an important principle for the apostolate?

Well, teamwork has many values, also for the apostolic life. When you want to do something great, you need to combine the actions of different people, and it becomes vital to coordinate efforts, to accept sincerely what others have to offer, and to acknowledge their areas of experience. Teamwork gives a dimension to communion that is accessible to the individual. Teamwork provides an adequate channel for the social need that everyone feels to join with others in projects and ideals. In addition, Christ chose a team of men to form them as disciples. He could have chosen a number of men separately and taught each one individually, but he didn't. He wanted the apostles to form a body, a collegiality in which there could be discussion, dialogue, sharing of ideas, and mutual enrichment.

Teamwork is essential if you want to be effective in your apostolate. Pity the priest who is not capable of working on a team with laypeople in his parish, or organizing an activity with young people or families, who wants to do everything on his own without delegating responsibility to his coworkers. And besides, it's a great help to the individuals when they can share faith experiences together, as a team. Christians often feel somewhat isolated, alone, in our secularized society. It revitalizes your spirit to get together and share experiences, to encourage others or be encouraged by them. So team life for us isn't just a contributing element to apostolic effectiveness, but also to perseverance; it's a stimulus for our faith; it's a way to feel we are part of the Church, vitally linked to other members of Christ's Mystical Body who share the same ideals. In this way, teams provide the atmosphere you need to live the faith spontaneously: you pray together, you do apostolic projects, you receive formation, you strengthen the bonds of charity, you accept your brother for who he is, and you help him in his spiritual and even material needs.

91. When you spoke about the Legionaries' spirituality you emphasized Christ-centeredness and gospel charity. Do these same characteristics apply to Regnum Christi? Is there any

other element of Regnum Christi spirituality that you want to highlight?

Between the Legion of Christ and Regnum Christi, as I mentioned earlier, there is a deep oneness of purpose and spirituality, although how you live it depends on whether you are a priest or a layperson. So Christ-centeredness is at the core of Regnum Christi spirituality. Christ is not only a model for priests. Christ is the Way, the Truth, and the Life of every Christian. We hold up the attractive figure of Christ to the laypeople as well, to be their ideal in life. Many people think themselves Christians because they were baptized and maybe received the other sacraments, but no one ever taught them the way to a profound, personal experience of Christ.

This reminds me of a gospel scene that has always impressed me: the cure of the woman with a hemorrhage (Mark 5:25-34). The gospel writer tells us that the woman had been ill for twelve years already and had spent her money on many doctors to no effect; on the contrary, she only grew worse. When Jesus is on his way to Jairus's house to cure his daughter, the woman manages to work her way through the crowd around Jesus and touch the hem of his robe, firmly convinced that just touching Christ's tunic will cure her. Even though she felt weak and it was hard getting through the wall of people that almost prevented Jesus from moving, she manages — who knows how? — to touch Christ's garment. And she is instantly cured. In commenting on this passage, St. Augustine says, "The woman touched him, the crowd pressed against him; what does 'touched' mean if not 'believed'?"[5] This gospel scene helps me visualize how we can "be" with Jesus and yet fail to "touch" him by faith. A lot of people are called Christians simply because their name is the baptismal register. But you only "touch" Christ when you enter into intimacy with him, when you

[5] *In Iohannis Evangelium Tractatus*, treatise 26, par 3.

explore his heart, when you are able to understand who he is for you and grasp his infinite love for each and every person, his desire to save us, his longing to see us all in the Father's abode.

I am strongly convinced that if Christ is loved little, it is because he is unknown. Interior, experiential knowledge is a grace from God, something we can humbly ask for in prayer. Regnum Christi wants to present a Christianity centered on Christ. Once he enters your heart, once your faith has "touched" him, many other things become clear; you accept his laws, and you acquire a new outlook on the Church and its commandments and moral norms. We often start back-to-front, trying to get people to accept a cluster of external norms before there is an inner knowledge of Christ. The only way to this knowledge of Christ is to get in touch with him through prayer, the Eucharist, the sacrament of reconciliation. This shows us the importance of those means that help us to pray, such as spiritual exercises, retreats, or eucharistic adoration.

You could say the same about gospel charity. Christ's new commandment is not only for priests. It's for everyone. We must all love one another as Christ has loved us. That is why we also propose to the lay Regnum Christi members the beauty of charity, for them to live it in their thoughts, words, and deeds. As far as Christian life goes, any ascetic effort or apostolic initiative not motivated by love is useless. Christianity is authentic when there is charity. Where you find charity and love, there you find God. Where there is no love, God is absent. It's simple. There's no alternative. I have always detested the fake Christianity, full of sighs and pious resolutions, that is not well-founded on the rock of charity. As St. Paul says, charity does not pass away; it does not end. Even the other two theological virtues, faith and hope, will pass away, but charity is eternal. You could say that the person who lives charity in a certain sense is already living in eternity.

In general, we also propose to the laypeople all the Christian and gospel virtues we mentioned when discussing the formation of

Legionaries, situating them naturally in the specific context of the layperson, who has to live them in the midst of the activities of this world, though without living in this world. They are in the world like leaven, like yeast in the dough. Their mission is therefore essential if Christ's Kingdom is to be established in the fabric of society, the various professions, the economic and social structures, culture, art, and so forth. The layperson's mission is beautiful. Regnum Christi helps them to discover and carry it out; it gives them the tools to be true to their Christian faith amid the normal difficulties and obstacles that anyone immersed in worldly affairs must face.

92. In recent years the Legion of Christ and Regnum Christi have spread notably in the United States. To what do you think this is due?

From the Legion's early years, I sensed that in the not-too-distant future God's providence would help us found apostolates in the United States and enjoy the firm support of this pioneering, responsible, and religious nation. With this in mind and since there weren't any English-speakers in the Legion, I was keen on founding in Ireland so that we could then go to America with Irish priests. Our presence in the States goes back to 1965, the year we rented a small house that became our first novitiate in the country, located on the Atlantic in Woodmont, Connecticut. Our first steps there were modest, since we had limited personnel and were still adapting to a new cultural environment. Those were also the years of the student protests of '68 with their corresponding impact on the Church. But by the beginning of the Eighties we were in a position to invest more people and were able to start Regnum Christi groups more systematically and consolidate our formation centers. We moved the novitiate from Woodmont to Orange, and later, in 1982, to Cheshire, all in Connecticut. Vocations began to increase: generous young men ready to give their lives for Christ and also to help the Church in their country or wherever the Church was most in need. In those years as well, we opened a vocational center or minor seminary in New Hampshire, and later, in the Nineties, a center for higher studies in philosophy and theology, in Thornwood, to the north of New York City. Little by little, thanks to the zealous, systematic, and well-organized work of our priests and the American Regnum Christi members, we've been able to grow steadily both in terms of vocations and in terms of apostolic work, in many states.

I believe that an important factor in this growth is the strength of the often large, Catholic families who really want to live their faith. It has given me great satisfaction to see these American Catholic families with a healthy pride in their Catholic faith. They know what it means to be Catholic, and they want to identify deeply with what they are, with the greatest respect for others' differences. Vocations to priesthood and consecrated life develop spontaneously in these Catholic homes, and all the family members naturally want to be actively committed in some form of Catholic apostolate. These Catholics know how to practice the great principles of Christian life and translate their baptismal commitment into concrete institutions and initiatives. These are laypeople who accept their vocation as baptized Christians; in their very generous and practical way they come up with a broad range of initiatives that they themselves carry out under their pastors' guidance.

That is how in a relatively short time, we've been able to increase considerably our work in schools, the number of retreat centers, prayer groups, clubs for children and teens, and other apostolates in the media, with families, and in campus ministry, in many different states. It is very edifying to see the dedication to the apostolate and their prayer life of these laypeople who take their baptismal commitment very seriously and responsibly: parents who spend their spare time leading clubs for children or teenagers, moms who teach CCD, college students who spend their weekends on youth missions or running programs for teens, and so on.

Despite the stereotyping that associates Americans with materialism and consumerism, my personal experience is that a huge portion of this nation has an authentic religious feeling, a deep sense of the transcendent, and a great openness to spiritual values. I don't deny that in American society today there are obstacles, even grave ones, that can lead them away from the gospel ideal; nevertheless, the spontaneous openness to God that there is in the great majority of the population is a priceless foundation in the effort to open their hearts to the action of God's grace. All this is deeply rooted in the American people. Today there are many who are determined to build their lives and their nation on solid foundations, people who are committed to renewing the authentic American character in individuals, families, and society.

There is no doubt that the United States, above and beyond its material wealth, possesses great moral and religious potential, and so I also believe that the responsibility weighing on the shoulders of its leaders and on every citizen is also very great. We know Christ's words: when much is given, much will be required (see Luke 12:48). The Catholics of North America are called to contribute decisively to the new evangelization in the third millennium, not only in their own nation but the world over. It is largely up to them whether or not the globalized culture that has been taking shape in recent decades will respect the life, liberty, and dignity of each person and nation.

93. The Legionaries of Christ also do a lot of work with young teens. You yourself started the Legion of Christ with thirteen of them. What is the secret to touching the souls of adolescents, who are at a very sensitive stage in their development and often reject everything, even religious values?

Christ Is My Life

Providence decreed that the Legion begin with thirteen adolescents. I myself was a twenty-year-old when I began the Legion. Working with adolescents is exhausting but exhilarating. It's exhausting because adolescents are charged with surplus energy and an educator has to be with them always in everything they are up to. You can't follow them from a distance, because they are not yet fully mature and they need an adult to guide them. That's why it is very demanding work, even physically — ask any educator who teaches adolescents, or any parent of young teens. But it is exhilarating because their souls are still receptive and, with the utmost respect for their freedom, you can instill in them many human and Christian values.

I think the secret to working with adolescents is to believe that you can trust them, that they are open to the great ideals of life: they have huge reserves of generosity, and they will respond eagerly to what you ask of them — as long as you give them a motivating ideal. From the point of view of faith, this ideal is friendship with Christ. At this stage of their lives they are very sensitive to this value; they have high esteem for true friendship, and if they grasp that Christ is their real friend, they are willing to give him in return their own friendship with total selflessness.

As they traverse these sensitive years in their lives, we prepare them to open up to authentic values so that they will not stray so easily into behaviors that go against their Christian faith. In ECYD [Education, Culture, and Youth Development] and in our formation clubs, which are part of an international network, we provide adolescents with a wholesome atmosphere of fun, friendship, sports, apostolate, and formation under the watchful guidance of parents and expert educators, and with the presence of priests for their spiritual needs.

Our experience has been very positive, though it is not easy work, especially because adolescents are extremely malleable, for good and for evil, and there are many other alternatives available that can easily lead them astray. So we believe it is also very important to be in contact with their parents. Without unity and constant communication with them, what we do in the clubs can easily be lost. Many parents understand this, and then the results are very good. Others give into the pressures and easily leave their children adrift, directionless, at the mercy of circumstance, without a guide to motivate them, guide them, and point them towards the good. Worse still, in some cases there are parents who facilitate their drifting away from Christ.

To achieve the integral formation we want to give adolescents, and prepare them for a mature life as human persons and Christians, our clubs offer quite a wide variety of activities: summer camps, spiritual retreats, works of Christian charity, sports, excursions, camping, and so on. For us, sports are a very important educational tool. Every year we hold the Friendship Tournament in Mexico, which draws about six thousand athletes, not to mention other countries. It's wonderful to see these young athletes from our schools and clubs together with another twenty-five thousand people, between classmates and families, in an atmosphere of wholesome competitiveness and friendship that sports provide. They remember these formative elements for the rest of their lives, and the principles they learn become their sure guide and support in the complicated problems that adult life sometimes brings.

VI

The Church

94. I would like to switch now to topics that have to do with the Church today, beginning with Pope John Paul II. When did you first meet him? Did you know him before he took the Chair of Peter?

I had only heard of him. But to tell the truth, like many Western Europeans, we had heard very little about the bishop of Krakow, at that time a city behind the iron curtain and therefore quite a mystery to us.

I had always admired the Polish people's faith. Despite persecution and history's turns of fortune, they always found inspiration and strength in the Catholic faith during the hardest times in their nation's history. I got to know His Holiness much better during his first pastoral visit to Mexico. It is common knowledge that this visit was fundamental for the direction John Paul gave his pontificate, and it filled him with enthusiasm to reach out personally to the various churches, something the Holy Father repeatedly remarked to journalist Valentina Alazraki, and as she put it in her book *Juan Pablo II el viajero de Dios* [John Paul II, God's Traveler]: "The Pope's heart was taken with Mexico, not only because it was the first visit of his pontificate but also because our country was the discovery for John Paul II of the enormous importance for him to have contact with the faithful, and above all, the discovery

of the direction that his pastoral activity was to take in the future."
He marveled at the fervor and devotion that the Mexican people
showed throughout those days.

I was blessed, along with other Legionaries, to be able to help
organize certain aspects of his visit, and I was able to greet him
several times in what was at the time the Apostolic Delegation. It
was a very sensitive visit because the Holy Father was supposed to
inaugurate the work of the Third Conference of Latin American
Bishops in Puebla, and some proponents of liberation theology
wanted to use the situation to manipulate the Church's Magisterium. On the one hand the Holy Father had to affirm the ideals
of Christian justice, but on the other he could not accept the
Marxist analysis or its underlying doctrine it as the way to inter-
pret the Church's situation. In perfect Spanish the Holy Father
gave a very balanced discourse that laid down precise guidelines
for the bishops who were to begin the working session, and the resulting Puebla document is now one of the most important reference points for pastoral issues on the continent.

It was in those grace-filled days for Mexico, when the country
received a visit from the Successor of St. Peter for the first time in
its history, that I was in a position to appreciate close up the extraordinary human and spiritual stature of Karol Wojtyla, the man
whom God in his providence had called to govern the Bark of Peter in the last decades of the second Christian millennium. The
Pope was aware that his encounter with the Mexican people was a
moment of intense spiritual experience for the country's Catholics.
The country obeyed with blind faith when the Vicar of Christ,
Pope Pius XI, ordered them to end the armed hostilities between
Cristeros and government forces. My uncle, General Jesús Degollado Guízar, was the one who signed the peace agreement. In
1979, despite living under a regime that did not legally acknowledge the Church, Mexican Catholics did enjoy relative religious
freedom, or at least a degree of respect, and they were able to

celebrate their faith even though the rights of the Church and her ministers were not fully recognized.

The memory of this faith-encounter was indelible both for Mexican Catholics and John Paul II. On the one hand, John Paul II was heartened and encouraged by the warm and affectionate welcome that the Mexicans gave him. On the other, the Mexican people, "always faithful," just like the Pontiff's native Poland, was confirmed in its robust, constant faith. From that moment you could say there has been a kind of mutual attraction between the Pope and Mexico, so much so that he has visited the country five times, thus confirming the deep bonds that have developed between them both.

In the course of those days full of feverish activity at the Apostolic Delegation, and enjoying the kind welcome of Monsignor Girolamo Prigione, then Apostolic Delegate, I saw firsthand the great gift that God had given the Church in John Paul II.

95. This first contact — how did it continue over the years?

I spoke with John Paul II on a number of occasions, especially in Rome, in official audiences and in private encounters. Whenever I'm close to the Pope I feel closer to Christ, so I remember very fondly each and every meeting. One occasion that was very important for our congregation was the definitive approval of our Constitutions. Vatican II asked all religious congregations to review their Constitutions to adapt them to the Council's new norms. Though our Constitutions didn't require any special adjustments, we submitted them just as we were asked to, to the Congregation for Religious and Secular Institutes, at the time headed by Cardinal Eduardo Pironio. Our Constitutions contained some aspects of governance, administration, and discipline that needed special approval from the Pope.

He personally gave his approval to everything. For me, this approval, which I received straight from Christ's Vicar, meant the culmination of a lifetime of effort to fashion the project that I had carried in my heart since I was sixteen, which I began in response to an inspiration from God. I always knew for certain that if the work was God's, it wouldn't be without the Pope's total support. And the various pontiffs I have had the grace to know during my life, beginning with Pius XII, have given me, through their words and deeds, the close and constant support of the Successor of Peter.

At other times I have had the grace to dine with His Holiness at the Apostolic Palace. These are moments of intimate and spontaneous conversation about our shared interests. The Holy Father also invited me to participate as a special guest in a number of synods of bishops to discuss the formation of priests, religious life, the Church in America, as well as the Conference of Latin American Bishops held in Santo Domingo in 1992. In His Holiness's second trip to Mexico he invited me to travel with him on the plane as part of his entourage. He has received us in special audience when the congregation held each of its ordinary general chapters, always pausing to give some words of encouragement afterwards. He has come to visit us several times in Rome, either at the parish of Our Lady of Guadalupe or at our college on Via Aurelia Antica, staying to have lunch or dinner with the community. Every time, the Holy Father has expressed his unconditional support for the Legionaries of Christ and Regnum Christi, confirming us in our mission to establish Christ's Kingdom in the world, and always encouraging us to keep working for the good of the Church.

One very special touch was when he ordained sixty Legionaries to the priesthood in St. Peter's Basilica in Rome on the fiftieth anniversary of our founding. He also gave us a special audience on January 4, 2001, still during the Holy Year 2000, for the sixtieth anniversary of the foundation.

These are all signs of the special fondness he has for us and the hope with which he looks to the Legionaries and Regnum Christi.

From each of these encounters, besides a renewal of my faith and love for Christ, I take away a desire to confirm my fidelity to the Church, not to leave the Holy Father alone in his efforts to bring Christ's message to as many men and women, our brothers and sisters, as he can; to be with him, as much as possible, in his dedication, his suffering, and his love for the Church.

96. What most impresses you about Pope John Paul II?

God wished to give a gift to the Church and the world in John Paul II. His exceptional human gifts are there for all to see: the balanced character and keen intelligence, his gift for personal relations, the ability to analyze problems, his human leadership, and so on. You could also add other qualities: his memory, his gift for learning languages, his capacity for work, his physical vigor in spite of the wear and tear of age, his determination and will, his exquisite appreciation for beauty and art, his refined poetic intuition, the vigor of his thought, the serenity of his spirit, his patience in adversity.

This extraordinary combination of qualities in John Paul II makes me reflect on and contemplate his life, his actions, his Magisterium, his mission; it is grist for long and deep meditation, and it leads me to the mystery of God. My contemplation of how he has guided the Church during these crucial times in the history of Christianity and Western culture, and his role even in political history, has been a true light for my path and in my own exercise of governance.

But above and beyond all this, I see in John Paul II a man who deeply believes in Jesus Christ, hopes in him, and loves him with all the strength of his priestly heart. He is a man of deep prayer, a true man of God who is able to see everything with a supernatural spirit; he senses the heartbeat of God in the world and in the Church, and he is in love with his vocation as a priest and apostle. In sum, you could say he is a holy man, a giant in the faith, a great pontiff, a doctor of the Church, an untiring shepherd, an artist in the way he makes contact with individuals, groups, crowds, the ecclesiastical world, and civic powers. His importance is unmatched in the history of the twentieth century and the dawn of the third millennium. God in his providence reserved him for these times of confusion and disorientation in faith and values.

97. Besides John Paul II you also knew other popes. What experiences did you have with them?

The first pope I met personally was Pius XII, at a private audience in Rome. I was very young, twenty-six. His presence radiated a special power, a halo of deep mysticism. It was he who first confirmed and blessed the idea of the Legion and encouraged me to go ahead. I was also able to meet John XXIII a number of times. He was kindness and welcome personified, a big heart with room for everyone. I first met Paul VI when he was working as substitute for the Secretariat of State in the Vatican. Pius XII recommended that I call on him to examine the Legion's Constitutions together. With his fatherly advice he helped me greatly in this task and in others, also when he was archbishop of Milan. As Pope he made time for me whenever I asked him. He was a man of penetrating intelligence, highly prepared intellectually, with exceptional sensitivity, who never wanted to hurt anyone in the least. He suffered greatly in the wake of the Council with the problems that afflicted the Church. The group of self-styled progressives, especially after *Humanae Vitae*, accused him of betraying them. Those who called themselves conservatives accused him of abandoning the Church's tradition. He was a martyr-pope whose lot it was to live one of the most difficult times for the Church in the twentieth century. I never had a chance to meet John Paul I personally because of the brief duration of his pontificate. However, I was deeply struck by his humility of heart and his simplicity, expressed in his open smile that won over everyone.

98. You yourself lived through the difficult times following the Council. What can you say about that critical time in the Church's history?

As we all know, the Second Vatican Council was a time of grace in which the Catholic Church was deeply renewed, and drew from its wellspring — ever-living because the Holy Spirit nourishes it — new strength to face the challenges of the modern world, with its changes in science and technology, culture and society. The in-word at the time was *aggiornamento:* to update the Church so that Christ's message could penetrate the modern world more incisively. Great bishops and theologians toiled on magnificent documents like *Lumen Gentium, Gaudium et Spes,* and the Council's other constitutions and decrees.

From the time of the Council itself, great opposing trends were already forming within the Church, the so-called progressives and traditionalists. Some thought the Church hadn't gone far enough, others thought it had gone too far and betrayed the deposit of the faith. But in general, the Council was welcomed enthusiastically as a tool that God was giving the Church for its renewal.

The problem with the Council wasn't so much its teaching, which was crystal clear, but rather the deceitful interpretation and alteration of its teaching and spirit. Unlike other councils, held before the media acquired the power to influence events, Vatican II was presented to the world by the media. You mustn't forget that the media, with all the good they're called to do by forming and informing, often go after the trivial and sensational news-piece, which distorts the presentation of realities that can be difficult to understand, as is the case with everything to do with issues of Church teaching and discipline. And so the Council reached the mass of the faithful more through what the newspapers, magazines, radio, and TV said about it than through the Council documents themselves, which only a few experts read and reflected on.

Moreover, the progressive current tried to corner the market on the Council's interpretation. Not only that; they thought the Council Fathers had been too timid in addressing issues such as liturgy, priestly celibacy, women's ordination, and so forth, and it was their role to draw every last conclusion that the Council itself hadn't dared (so they thought) to state. In the name of the spirit of the Council they set out on a whole series of theological, liturgical, and pastoral adventures that the people's faith paid for dearly, and many were led astray. Both male and female religious life suffered especially, as interpretations of the vows arose that were a far cry from the spirit of the Council, clearly expressed in the decree *Perfectae Caritatis*. They started to speak of dialogued obedience. They encouraged or allowed a whole series of experiences that supposedly lead to affective maturity, arising from questionable psychological theories that sometimes doubted the very possibility of living a celibate life fully. In a word, there was terrible confusion and all because these groups betrayed both the letter and spirit of the Council.

The consequences were not long in coming: Thousands of priests left their ministry, many seminaries and religious congregations lost a good number of their members, the faith-life of God's people was weakened terribly, and a seemingly unstoppable process of secularization shook the Church to its very foundations.

Pope Paul VI suffered deeply over all this. On many occasions he went right to the problem, pointing out the deviations and false interpretations given to the Council, but few listened to him. At one point he caused a stir in the media by even speaking in a public address of the smoke of Satan that had filtered through the cracks into God's temple, the Church.

Throughout that time of grave confusion and error, which saw the collapse even of those thought to be solid pillars, we tried to take always as our guide the voice and word of the Pope. We were attentive to see how he interpreted the Council, what he said and did, to try to follow his instructions faithfully, even the smallest. As a consequence, this gave us much internal peace, great security amid what the Italians were calling the *buio* [darkness], and many blessings from God. We had a beacon of light and truth in Rome. All we had to do was pay attention to it. Sadly though, many others failed to follow these same guidelines and preferred to go their own way. Not everyone agreed with our attitude. There were misunderstandings and we were criticized by those who thought us too "Roman," too conservative, not open enough to the new times. We didn't pay much attention to this criticism because what we wanted was to keep in step with the Church, not with the latest best-selling theologian, to follow the pace that the Holy Spirit was setting in the Church through the Vicar of Christ, the authorized interpreter of the Council documents.

99. In those years, as you mentioned, many seminaries ended up almost empty. What experience did the Legion have?

The winds of these warped interpretations of the Council reached us too, but thanks be to God, we had a sure reference point in the word of the Holy Father, and we didn't go through a vocational crisis. Young men kept coming, eager to serve Christ authentically in religious life, which implies renouncing the world and your own passions. We have always been completely frank with everyone about what following Christ really implies. I don't think it right or just to deceive a young person, who makes the generous act of wanting to follow Christ in priesthood or religious life, by offering him a worldly lifestyle. The logical reaction is, "I could have had this at home. I needn't have bothered."

But as I said, throughout that period the Lord kept us united in charity, faith, and obedience; loyal to the Council, its texts, and its spirit; in communion with the Holy Father and the bishops; praying for those who chose other paths, suffering for them and the Church, but full of hope that one way or another the devastating time would come to an end. In those years many people would visit us and leave with their enthusiasm renewed; it restored their strength and hope to see a large group of young men wanting to follow Christ and go preach his gospel with all their hearts. And they didn't see any sad or disheartened faces. Quite the opposite.

I want to emphasize that we are not partial to tradition because it's tradition. We are only partial to the Church's authentic teaching, expressed in the councils and in the writings of the popes and the bishops in communion with them. The Church, master in humanity, as Paul VI's famous saying goes, is also very realistic. Realistic because she knows human nature through and through and understands that some naive proposals will not work, simply because man is wounded by original sin, which has affected his mind, his will, and his affective and emotional world. But by the same token we believe in the goodness of human nature, which has not been destroyed but only affected by sin, and in the amazing, surprising action of God's grace. This anthropological realism sheds new light on man, spurring him to conquer great goals, though all the while he is aware of his weakness and fragility.

That is why during those years you might call ill-omened we experienced peace, serenity, constant growth — despite the fact that vocations were harder to nourish, especially in Europe, due to the grave postconciliar crisis that affected the vast majority of the countries on the Old World.

100. Do you see any solution to the problem of secularization you were talking about?

The possible solution I see to the problem of secularization is living the Catholic faith authentically. To teach people again to believe with a simple faith, which is not to say childish or irrational, but one that accepts the greatness of God's mystery and the limitations of man. Recently I happened to be in Mexico when the Pope canonized Juan Diego, the Mexican Indian to whom the

Blessed Virgin appeared to ask him to speak with the bishop of Mexico City at the time, the Franciscan Juan de Zumárraga, and ask him to build a church on the hill where she appeared to him. I was deeply struck by the gospel passage chosen for the canonization, taken from Matthew, chapter 11. It tells how Jesus, on seeing how the simple people accepted the message of the Kingdom of heaven he preached, while the scribes and Pharisees, the wise men of his time, rejected or simply ignored it, exclaimed: "I bless you, Father, Lord of heaven and of earth, for hiding these things from the learned and the clever and revealing them to mere children. Yes, Father, for that is what it pleased you to do" (Matt 11:25-26). It applied perfectly to this simple Indian from the humblest class in those days, to whom Mary had chosen to appear.

This is the disconcerting way God acts, to teach us the great lesson of humility, because the soul of a humble man like Juan Diego is prepared and ready to accept the message of God, who turns away the proud and welcomes the humble.

Leaving aside its other cultural and historical causes, which also have their importance, from a religious point of view I think secularization is the result of dull and lifeless faith. People drift away from God because they believe less, because they think their problems are all going to find a solution in technology, science, their own knowledge, and not in God. If we are not humble and fail to acknowledge the region of supernatural mystery that puts us in contact with a reality that goes beyond us; if we refuse to recognize our creaturehood and make ourselves the center of the universe without any ties to God, defining ethical norms for ourselves, what is good and evil without any reference to God's revelation; we will be doomed to increasing secularization, which will only make man more miserable. I don't deny that the secular sphere has its own measure of autonomy, nor do I suggest a return to a Church that gets drawn into it. I am referring to the need that today's society, and each person in particular, has to rediscover the value of faith, which is not the enemy of reason. John Paul II was so on target in writing the encyclical *Fides et Ratio*, which begins by affirming that faith and reason are the two wings that lead us to the knowledge of truth! The modern world tried to keep only one wing, reason; you can't fly, nor can man rise to the knowledge of truth, on only one wing. We need both. Faith alone is not enough either, it would lead to a dangerous fideism. We need the use of reason, God's wonderful gift, and faith, which embraces God's revelation of his mystery in humility and awe.

So to return to the essence of your question, I think the process of secularization is reversible since man can always open up to the message God sends him, and embrace it in faith and gratitude. That doesn't mean it will be easy or that we know exactly how it might happen. What I do believe is that Christians should look at the present situation with immense hope, as a challenge. The problem of secularization calls for hearts on fire, apostles who are willing, like the great evangelizers of Europe and the first centuries of Christianity, to give their lives if necessary so as to share the great gift of the gospel with their brothers and sisters; to help them to open themselves to the gift of faith, which does not mutilate our intelligence but rather liberates it by helping its eyes to see the fullness of divine truth.

101. More than half of all Catholics live in the Americas. In the apostolic exhortation *Ecclesia in America,* John Paul II looks to the American continent — Latin America especially, but also North America — with great hope for the future of evangelization and Christianity. You were born there. Do you share his hope?

I look to the Church on the Latin American subcontinent, and, generally on the whole American continent, with great hope. No one can deny the serious problems afflicting Latin America, especially as regards social justice, the stability of the political regimes, and the economy of the various countries; the problem of the native peoples' integration in the various spheres of society; the solution to problems you could call endemic in some countries, such as corruption, drugs, guerrilla warfare, and so forth. These are very delicate situations that have no easy short-term solution, requiring time and changes in mentality and culture. But you can also see that the great majority of these countries have held on to their human and Christian values. For the most part, people are open to the faith. They connect with God spontaneously and sincerely, they are rich in popular devotions and missionary enthusiasm. I think their ability to perceive God's presence and their openness to the faith can be of great help to other churches, especially in Europe, where the spontaneous sensitivity to religious values has been partially lost.

The faith of the people in Latin America, however, has to be better formed. That, in turn, calls for well-formed, zealous priests and holy formators of priests. At the Holy Father's request we began a series of initiatives to help dioceses form their future seminary formators. Thankfully, there are vocations. I am thinking, for example, of seminaries like the one in Guadalajara, Mexico, which has one of the largest enrollments in the world.

To provide a solution to the scarcity of formators, the International Pontifical College *Maria Mater Ecclesiae* was founded in Rome over ten years ago for seminarians who in the future might be rectors, formators, or spiritual directors in seminaries. At present it has a student body of approximately three hundred, and has already formed more than two hundred priests from twenty-five countries. Two years ago we opened a similar formation center in São Paulo, Brazil, at the request of the president of the episcopal conference and many of the country's bishops. Training seminary formators will make possible the better preparation not only of priests but also laypeople in Latin America, and this may give added thrust to the missionary expansion of Latin American Catholicism.

I also see signs of hope in the Church in the United States and Canada. The Church in the States has suffered, but it will surely emerge purified and strengthened from this pain and suffering, and the great store of religious feeling in the American people, shown in the wake of the tragic events of September 11, 2001, will produce a deep desire for holiness and fervor, not only in the clergy but in all Catholics.

As for Canada, I am also hopeful that World Youth Day, held recently in Toronto, will leave a mark of deep renewal in the Church, as happened in France after World Youth Day 1997. The postconciliar crisis deeply affected the priestly, religious, and lay life of the Church, above all in the French-speaking provinces, with their Catholic majority and rich tradition of missionary activity, social assistance, and charity. We all see with great joy and hope that the Church in Canada has once again begun to find the path of a living and expansive faith.

102. You are Mexican and you know the Church in your country firsthand. John Paul's latest trip to Mexico to canonize Juan Diego occasioned harsh polemics among some churchmen. On the other hand, the people flocked to receive the Holy Father, perhaps more intensely than ever. Mexico seems to be a country of contradictions. As a Mexican deeply familiar with the Church in Mexico, what can you tell us about the Church's current situation there?

The question is complex, and a complete answer would require more time than we now have to encompass all its aspects and nuances. Yes, as you say, Mexico is a country of contradictions. President López Portillo defined it to the Holy Father on his first visit to Mexico: "Holy Father, Mexico is surreal." To judge fairly the situation of the Church there, you have to remember the past. The history of the Church in Mexico, especially since the country's independence, has been difficult. There were persecutions, a cruel war of religion, the Cristero War, which left much martyr's blood in its wake. The Church has suffered in silence, living in faith the tragic events that convulsed the Mexican people. But the blood of those martyrs has blossomed in a living faith, deep respect for priests, a fond, supernatural love for the Pope, and faithful devotion to the Virgin of Guadalupe. In his first pastoral visit to Mexico, the Holy Father had occasion to remark that the Mexican people, like his homeland Poland, had remained "always faithful."

The favorable religious situation stands in contrast to other problems, some old and some more recent. The political situation is still not stable enough, since Mexico has recently moved to a regime of greater democracy and not all the nation's institutions are adequately prepared for it. Great strides have been made, but it will be a long transition. The economy is still struggling to overcome the chronic crisis that has lasted some decades. We need better living conditions for the great masses of the population, especially the millions of natives. All of this provides an enormous challenge for the Christian social conscience.

After many years of anomalous relations with the Vatican, the Constitutional reforms and the agreements of 1992 re-established full diplomatic ties between Mexico and the Holy See. That caused a new public position for the Church in our society and a greater leading role in the country for the bishops and the Episcopal conference. The problem of the sects still causes concern. Most of them come from the United States, are well-financed, and have invaded many poor neighborhoods in the cities and large rural areas, winning many followers in recent years.

As far as the internal life of the Church goes, within the Church in Mexico there have never been in our history serious problems of dissent from the Magisterium, although in recent years you can perceive a more critical trend in some circles. The recent polemics you referred to regarding the historical existence of Juan Diego are a sign of that.

Very positive and typical of Mexico has been the episcopacy's unconditional, heartfelt loyalty to the Church's Magisterium. Thanks be to God, this loyalty still comes through today. The declarations of the episcopal conference are a sample of this, as is the wonderful pastoral letter written by the Archbishop of Mexico City, Cardinal Norberto Rivera Carrera, on the canonization of Juan Diego.

A very special grace given to the Mexican church is what has been called the Guadalupe event. The apparitions of Our Lady of Guadalupe have had enormous repercussions on the evangelization of the country and of the continent, as the most reliable Church historians acknowledge. Along with their Guadalupan devotion, the immense majority of Mexicans love and honor the Holy Father.

I consider these two facts to be a very special supernatural gift that God has granted the Church in Mexico to share with other churches throughout the world. In this respect John Paul II's words during his second-last visit to the country in January 1999, come to mind, when he asked the Mexican Catholics to make theirs a missionary faith; in other words, to share it with other peoples and churches. I think the Church in Mexico has a lot to share with other churches, and as the Holy Father requested, their faith must become more contagious and missionary, and I hope it does, more strongly so every day.

103. When you were still young, at twenty-six, you traveled to Europe and saw with your own eyes the situation of the Church in many countries on the Old World. Were you scandalized by a faith perhaps more tepid and rationalistic than that of your native Mexico? Do you still hope in the European church? Do you think it still has anything to contribute, or will it be re-evangelized by the younger churches, Asia, Africa, or Latin America?

Yes, I must admit that the contrast between my country, Mexico, and Europe was quite a shock at first. I arrived here with the simple, credulous faith of a small-town boy. But it was this very faith that helped me understand the cultural differences and view them as merely accidental. Beyond these differences, I am convinced that man, in the depths of his nature, is the same, and his thirst for God is rooted deep within his soul, beyond all social, economic, cultural, or racial differences.

I marveled at the wonderful cultural and evangelizing achievements that Europe had wrought all over the world, for we shouldn't forget that America and other continents were evangelized by the immense reserves of faith on the old continent.

It is true that in Europe, especially after World War II and after Vatican II, the faith suffered great damage because of the crisis we spoke about earlier. I confess I find it very sad to see beautiful churches full of artistic treasure mostly empty or visited only as if they were museums, out of merely historical or cultural interest. The magnificent legacy of cathedrals, the achievements in culture, art, architecture, music, and literature inspired by the Faith over the centuries is witness to what was in the hearts of Christians of past centuries.

But now it is our turn, in the present generation, to build new temples where God is adored in spirit and in truth, temples not necessarily made of stone but rather those inner sanctuaries built by Christian holiness, wherever you find a person who lets grace take possession of his soul. Europe has built this type of temple in the twentieth century as well, and continues to do so. They may be less visible, but there they are nonetheless, eloquent witnesses to deep faith and great love. I mean martyrs such as Edith Stein and Maximilian Kolbe, the martyrs of the religious persecution in Spain and of the communist oppression in Russia, Poland, Lithuania, Hungary, the Czech Republic, Slovakia, Romania, Bulgaria, and others, and the martyrs of the Nazi extermination camps. The Holy Father, a son of this continent, also comes to mind.

Christ Is My Life

Yes indeed, it seems as if Europe has been drifting away from Christ, but I find that the embers of the faith have not vanished. I know thousands of young people who seek him, who want to give themselves to him, who thirst for something lasting. You have the two million young people flooding the streets and plazas of Rome during the Jubilee Year 2000. This year I participated in youth and family encounters in France and Germany, and the number of participants and their enthusiasm deeply impressed me. The marvel of Christianity is that when it looks as if the faith has been extinguished, it springs back to life without anyone really knowing how, like the mustard seed that Christ speaks of in the gospel. It is enough for one man or woman to let the gospel take over their life, and the seed grows, multiplies, and bears fruit. Proof is the case of a woman like Mother Teresa of Calcutta, from a European country where the faith was persecuted for decades; she was physically small and frail, but the enormity of her faith moved her to found a religious order, now spread across the five continents, to serve the poorest of the poor. And you have the new realities, many begun precisely in Europe, such as Renewal in the Holy Spirit, the Focolare movement, the Neocatechumenal Way, Communion and Liberation, Schönstatt, the Sant'Egidio community, Opus Dei, the Emmanuel community, the community of the Brothers of St. John, Canção Nova, and so on. And don't forget the pastoral renewal in so many parishes and dioceses, and the radiant example of many of the Church's shepherds in Europe.

Yes, the crisis exists and causes concern, but I am not pessimistic because we can almost touch with our hands the powerful work of the Holy Spirit, who never ceases to help his Church. So I have great confidence in the church of Europe, which still has a vocation to evangelize and be missionary; she has given the Church great saints, she is the cradle of outstanding and saintly theologians and profound Christian philosophers, and she has a centuries-old tradition of creativity in the faith and apostolic activity.

On the other hand, I also think that we who received the faith from those missionaries, true giants in the faith who left their homeland to go to the distant lands of America, have a debt of gratitude: to do all we can to help the Christian faith flourish once again on the European continent in all its intensity.

104. Giving in to the temptation of a typically journalistic question: do you think the next pope will be European or maybe Latin American?

I'm not the proper person to answer this question. The Holy Spirit is. He always surprises us, journalists too! There is something to what they say in Italy, "He who enters the conclave a pope comes out a cardinal."

105. The Latin American subcontinent has been home to a theological current that met strong opposition: liberation theology. After years that generated vast amounts of theological literature it seems now to be less active, especially since the Vatican documents penned by Cardinal Joseph Ratzinger and the fall of the Berlin wall, although it hasn't died out completely. What opinion does this current merit? Do you think it will come back to life again?

The documents you mention make key distinctions regarding liberation theology. It wasn't condemned *en masse*, only in the aspects of its doctrine that reduce the salvation message of the gospel and the Church to a purely socioeconomic liberation of the people, as well as its interpretation of Scripture and dogma, based more on the Marxist analysis of reality than on the Bible or the Church's tradition and Magisterium.

Liberation theology's insight was to place at the center of theological reflection one of the fundamental concepts of the Christian faith: the concept of liberation. But both the sacred Scriptures and the documents of the Church have always understood that Christ came to liberate man from sin and death, and they never gave this liberation a political interpretation, despite having to resist certain authors and doctrines that would. Even in Christ's day, some of his more nationalist disciples may have interpreted Christ's work politically. It's enough to recall the reaction of the Emmaus disciples who had hoped Jesus would liberate Israel from Roman domination (Luke 24:21). The concept of liberation is very close to salvation, which is central to Christianity. The Word became man for our salvation, as we recite in the Creed. To save us means first and foremost to free us from sin and death, and not only or mainly to free us in a merely economic, political, or social sense. This doesn't mean we are not supposed to seek the living conditions that befit our dignity as human beings. That, too, is part of the gospel message, but you can't reduce liberation to those aspects alone.

You also have to keep in mind that the real social injustice many Latin American countries live in is a thorn in the Christian conscience. It is logical that faith should want to respond to this pressing problem of poverty, the economic gap between rich and poor and so many social injustices that cry out to heaven.

However, none of this justifies turning to an atheist philosophy like Marxism, which failed precisely where it boasted being strong: in praxis. The inhuman practices of the communist regimes caused the great statue with feet of clay to topple in a few years; it was like their symbol. The Holy Father, in opening the Puebla conference, also provided principles to tell apart the various currents of liberation theology. These helped the bishops enormously in discerning what was correct and valid in these trends from what was totally unacceptable, such as violence and class struggle.

What we all can and should learn from liberation theology is its concern for creating a more just society, guided by the principles of the Church's social doctrine. In this regard, through Regnum Christi we do all we can to spread this wealth of teaching, which has any number of applications in economic, social, and political life. We have to educate the Christian conscience of the leading classes of Latin America, as the apostolic exhortation *Ecclesia in America* recommends (n. 67), so that the grave social problems afflicting the continent will receive a swift response within the channels of Christian justice and charity.

106. The Legionaries of Christ recently opened a Pontifical University in Rome, *Regina Apostolorum*. Is opening this academic center the expression of a desire to start a new theological current in the Church?

Actually the center began for more practical reasons. We had a very large number of students studying at the pontifical universities in Rome, creating more than a few logistical problems. So we thought of asking the Holy See for authorization to open our own center, since we already had enough professors to cover the formative curriculum in philosophy and theology. That was in 1991. The Holy See granted the permission and a while later, in 1993, it become a Pontifical Athenaeum, which now has three schools (Philosophy, Theology, and Bioethics), an Institute for Religious Sciences, a center for forming seminary educators, a number of Master's programs in Psychology, Faith and Science, Environmental Sciences, and a wide variety of other cultural initiatives. The Holy Father and also other figures of the Roman Curia, such as the present Secretary of State, Cardinal Angelo Sodano, have given us invaluable support in making this project a reality.

In 2000, Cardinal Sodano himself personally inaugurated our university's new facilities in Rome. Although it has not been open for long, the enrollment is high. If you count the various schools, institutes, and master's programs, more than 2,600 are taking classes at our university this academic year. We plan over time to open new schools and institutes so as to provide the Church with priests, male and female religious, and laypeople solidly formed in the various disciplines and faithful to the Magisterium.

Getting back to the heart of your question, what I can say is, thanks be to God, we already have highly competent and qualified professors writing for the university's journal, *Alpha-Omega,* and publishing books in their areas of expertise. We are not trying to start a new theological current, creating useless rivalries between schools of thought. We seek to study and examine deeply the revealed truth, guided by the Church's Magisterium and living tradition, engaging the people of our times in dialogue and finding answers to the many questions that arise in the various fields of learning. St. Thomas Aquinas is a model for us, as the paragon who successfully combined attentive listening to God's word, *auditus fidei,* with logical, coherent rational reflection, *intellectus fidei.* We don't follow blindly all the Thomistic theses, some of which with the passing of time may have become outdated in particular and secondary points; St. Thomas inspires and guides with his love for the truth, his rigorously logical reflection following the principles of perennial philosophy, his openness to the new problems of his day, his unshakable loyalty to Church Magisterium, and his pastoral intention in his studies.

The way we do theology at our university is certainly not the one favored by the exponents of the so-called "parallel Magisterium" who either ignore the voice of the Magisterium or accept it as just another theological opinion. We favor the deeply ecclesial nature of theology by which theologians are not proprietors of the deposit of faith, but serve and conserve it with reverence and respect, open to the new problems that arise over the course of time.

At some meetings and congresses on Catholic theology, it seems as if everyone wants to avoid at all costs referring to the Church's Magisterium, as if it entailed giving up the scientific nature of theology. They prefer abstruse reflections that instead of connecting with today's culture actually seem to pull away from the common man, his problems, and his vital concerns. Our theological endeavor is based on faith and anchored in the Church's long tradition, open to the world and man, willing to engage science and philosophy in dialogue, and markedly pastoral in its approach, but without renouncing to reflect deeply on great theological themes such as the Trinity, Incarnation, creation, grace, eschatology, morality, et cetera.

107. What line of Philosophy do you take at your university? Also St. Thomas?

St. Thomas inspires us in philosophy also, insofar as his thought stands out for its vigorous reflection on being and its principles, its forceful logic, and its sincere quest for the truth. But we do not want to remain entrenched in a thirteenth-century philosophy as if thought had come to a standstill back then, ignoring the new philosophical problems that have challenged human reflection since Descartes, and later Kant. But you cannot question that St. Thomas laid the foundation for the great marriage of reason and faith that took place in the thirteenth century and produced such great benefits for human thought, theology, and the Church itself. John Paul II emphasizes the importance of Thomistic thought in the encyclical I mentioned earlier, *Fides et Ratio,* while he also points out other great thinkers who created a body of true Christian wisdom in their day, in both the East and the West.

In philosophy we try to give our students a coherent vision of what reason can tell us about God, the world, and man. To do this it is necessary to accept a serious, well-substantiated philosophy of knowledge and demonstrate that the intellect can indeed discover truth. That is the only way to ground a metaphysics that is open to being and its principles. As long as philosophy refuses to accept the possibility of metaphysics, the road to understanding reality will remain closed. We also emphasize philosophical anthropology, which is so important as a basis for moral issues, especially in bioethics. In other words, we study the classical branches of philosophy in a consistent and systematic way so that it can also be a support for theological reflection and sow more certainties than doubts. Therefore, in explaining philosophical systems we always provide the students with parameters so that they can judge philosophical problems on the basis of solid criteria, thus discovering the elements of truth there, and also the possible errors.

Reading *Fides et Ratio* (which many authors, including non-Christians, hail as a true defense of reason), it strikes me to see the force with which the Holy Father defends the realist philosophy of being, without which you are exposed to absolute philosophical, moral, and religious relativism. Interestingly, it is the Church that stands up and defends the value of human reason and philosophy, in an age when an overdose of rationalism has led modern thought to forms of irrationality at times truly errant.

108. When the Holy Father addressed the Legionaries of Christ on the occasion of the Jubilee Year 2000 and the sixtieth anniversary of your founding, he spoke of "a passionate love for the Church" as typical of the Legionaries' spirituality. How do you conceive this love, and where did this trait of your spirituality come from?

To answer you, allow me to return again to the topic of Christ-centeredness, which characterizes the spirituality of the Legionaries of Christ. For us — and I think for every Christian — love for Christ should define our religious personality. If we are Christians, we should know Christ, follow him, and love him. Love for the Church arises as a factor of our love for Christ, because the Church can never be thought of as an addendum to Christ. He himself chose to identify with the Church. The Church is Christ's Church, and to love Christ is to love the Church. St. Cyprian's words are well known: "You cannot have God as your Father unless you have the Church as your Mother."[6]

---

[6] *De cath. ecclesiae unitate*, 6: PL 4, 502.

The oft-repeated slogan from the Seventies and Eighties, "Christ yes, the Church no," is unacceptable. It is theologically false. I cannot accept Christ without accepting his Mystical Body, which is the Church. So, passionate love for the Church derives from passionate love for Christ. Personally, I received the grace never to look on Christ and the Church as two separate entities, and so from the very beginning of my vocation I wanted to dedicate my life to the Church. The Legion of Christ itself and Regnum Christi only make sense in the Church, because the Church is the universal sacrament of salvation, as Vatican II expressed so well.

The apostolic initiatives we undertake are all motivated by our love for the Church. If it were for the glory of our institution, our intentions would be shortsighted and miserly, simply empty and wrong. We seek the Church's good. So to answer your question about the origin of this trait of our spirituality, I would say it springs from our Christ-centeredness, the faith that does not drive a wedge between Christ and the Church.

St. Catherine of Siena, who loved the Church and the Pope so dearly, used to say that to work for the Church, the tender Bride of Christ, is the most useful toil to be found on earth. And in another of her writings she says that everything we do for the good of holy Church is so meritorious in God's eyes that our minds cannot grasp or imagine it.[7] To love the Church passionately is to want to strengthen her with our steadfast fidelity, to work for her day and night to make her grow, to seek her benefit at all times above any other interest, to live trustingly in her bosom despite criticism, persecution, or misunderstanding, and to be utterly loyal to the Church's teaching and Magisterium.

I describe the love we should have for the Church as love that suffers, keeps watch, and senses the heartbeats of our own Mother.

[7]Letter 85, to Nicholas of Osimo.

And this love cannot be indifferent or lethargic. Like every true love, it has to be passionate, to the point of giving our lives for the one we love. This is my idea of a man of the Church, and I have tried to pass this spirit on to everyone I have dealt with.

109. What are the most pressing problems that you see in the Church at this time?

We have already mentioned a number of them in the course of our conversation. We discussed secularism, the postconciliar crisis, the decline of vocations to consecrated life and the priesthood, the loss of faith, theological confusion, the lack of credibility on the part of some of the clergy because of their unworthy behavior, infidelity to Church doctrine, the serious doctrinal and behavioral aberrations in some of the Church's children, including priests and religious, and the many Catholics falling away from religious observance and the Church's moral norms.

The problems that come from outside the Church, when people attack or persecute or plot against it, do cause a lot of harm, but the problems that have always affected the Church most are the internal ones, those that have wounded her unity in faith or charity. That's why Christ prayed for the unity of his Church: "Father . . . may they be one as we are one" (John 17:22). Schisms, separation, and all the different divisions among Christians have caused the most havoc in Christ's Mystical Body. That is why we should do all that it takes to protect our unity of faith, which is threatening to come apart in a number of places — for example, when people refuse to acknowledge the authority of the Church's Magisterium, when they hold different views to what Church doctrine says on issues to do with liturgy, discipline, sexual morality, dogma, and so on. I believe we should all be very alert to achieve the unity that our Lord begged of his disciples the night before he left this world; and I believe this is where the greatest problems and difficulties find their way into the Church.

I don't want to be alarmist in this regard, but I do believe that threats to Church unity are with us in seed form, and they are a danger we must not underestimate. If we truly love the Church passionately, I think the greatest favor we can do her is to be sons who love her as she is, and not as our personal idealizations or speculations would have her be. To fight this virus, to which we are all exposed, it is always effective to stay abreast of the Pope's teaching, reading his writings and discourses, trying to be as united in mind as possible with his Magisterium and with the bishops in communion with him. We should discard any doctrine that strays to a greater or lesser degree from his, since they remove us from unity, which is guaranteed by the one in the Church who is the visible foundation of unity and who presides in charity.

110. It is evident that the postconciliar crisis notably affected both male and female religious life in the Church. Do you think this crisis is irreparable? What do you see as the way to renew religious life at the root?

I would like to begin by calling to mind that religious life in the Church is a gift from the Holy Spirit, who enriches her with his gifts and renews her through the holy life of men and women religious. A glance at Church history shows how men and women religious have adorned her with a holiness that takes the most varied of forms, all of them overflowing with total dedication to Christ and his Church. The Council decree on the renewal of religious life, *Perfectae Caritatis*, contains a beautiful teaching on the essence of religious life, which is to follow Christ by practicing the three evangelical counsels — poverty, chastity, and obedience — at the service of the Church and all people. Religious men and women have always been like beacons guiding people to God. Contemplative religious especially have been a constant conscience-call reminding us that what really matters is the "better part" of which Christ speaks to Martha when she complains that her sister Mary isn't helping with the housework (Luke 12:42), and which consists in listening contemplatively to God's word and dedicating yourself entirely to serving him.

The Council simply wanted to update some nonessential customs in the way religious life was lived, which were no longer useful or applicable; it never intended to change its essence. In the thick of the whole postconciliar crisis, however, the identity of religious life was also brought into question. The crisis affected communities of men as much as those of women, but perhaps the crisis of female religious life has been more glaring, especially in countries like the United States, because the problem of women's identity also came into the picture. Radical feminism depicted female religious life as a type of slavery wherein women could not fully break loose from what they believed to be Church limitations.

Thankfully, the worst seems to be over, but the damage remains and many communities of men and women still search for the identity of religious life.

You ask me for solutions, and I don't think there is only one. At the most I can offer some suggestions. First of all, I don't think we should be afraid to show religious life for what it is: a way to take up the gospel in all its radicalness, which is the same as to say in all its beauty. We mustn't be afraid to show young people what it is to follow Christ: poor, chaste, and obedient, in the ways peculiar to each institute, without coming to an "arrangement" with the spirit of the world. Religious life has always brought with it separation from the world, a break with secular lifestyles that are a far cry from the gospel spirit. No one can serve two masters. No one can be a religious and live a worldly lifestyle. This break is necessary, but it is not the purpose of religious life, which is, as we know, to live in perfect charity towards God and neighbor. It is a response to a call to love more, to love better than in the world; a purer, more perfect, more beautiful love.

The founders of congregations and institutes, the men and women the Holy Spirit inspires with concrete ways to follow Christ — ways approved by the Church — express in their rule, constitutions, and writings the way the members of each religious institute are to follow Christ. So in religious life renewal always comes from a return to its sources in the gospel, but also to the authentic spirit of the founder, called the founding charism, without submitting it to minimalist interpretations that drain it of its content. It is common knowledge that when an institute returns to the spirit of the founder, exactly as the competent ecclesiastical authority approved it, fervor returns to their communities; and to the degree they stray from it, they become less faithful and observant.

In doing vocational outreach to the youth, we have to get over the fear of presenting the gospel life every bit as demanding and radical as it is. I have known young people who tried out religious life in certain institutes with high hopes, but after a few months' experience returned home let down because the lax lifestyle in religious life was not very different from their life in the world before joining. Christ was always clear with his disciples about the demands that come with following him. He spoke of a narrow path, of the need to carry your cross every day, letting go of your life, serving others, dying like a grain of wheat so as to bear fruit. When he met the rich young man, symbolic of all who visit religious communities thinking about their vocation, he didn't lower the requirements to try to attract him; actually, he stated them as clear as could be: "If you wish to be perfect, go and sell what you own and give the money to the poor, and you will have treasure in heaven; then come, follow me" (Matt 19:21). The youth did not accept the terms. He hung his head and went away sad, because he had many riches. At that point Christ didn't say, "Okay, don't worry. We can make a deal. It will be enough to give away half and keep the rest for yourself." Christ wanted all or nothing. A radical choice for the Kingdom of heaven, or a worldly life. We give the impression at times of making worldly compromises in the way we live religious life, and that's what fails to attract. A look around is enough to see which congregations have the most vocations, and they're not exactly the ones that offer a lowered ideal but those offering ways to follow Christ that imply total self-giving, without any trimming down whatsoever.

I am very confident that religious life, as a concept, has already been renewed. What we need is to apply *Perfectae Caritatis*, *Vita Consecrata*, and the other magisterial documents that speak about it. We can expect to see again many young men and women knocking at the doors of communities that live in fervor and discipline, prayer, dedication, and fidelity. At our university in Rome and our schools of the Faith we have established courses for superiors of women's communities and nuns in general, to teach them how to present religious life and help them live it faithfully and out of love. Thanks be to God, this has received a warm welcome, with a growing interest and number of participants each year. This shows that the desire is really there to renew religious life in depth and present it to the world in all its beauty and all its gospel radicalness.

111. We have discussed the laity, religious, and priests. We have yet to speak about the bishops, whose role is essential for the Church's future. Some people complain that they intervene too little and accuse them of a *laissez-faire* approach. Others accuse them of interventionism and meddling in politics, while others say they are showmen, always wanting to be in front of cameras and in the editorials. Still others say that the figure of a bishop has been eclipsed by the all-powerful bishops' conferences. What is your view of bishops on a worldwide scale?

This is a question I sincerely could not respond to with any precision, and I really don't feel qualified to answer it. What I can say is this: being a bishop has always meant much sacrifice and suffering, but much more so in this day and age; the present situation is highly complex and demands from bishops exceptional preparation and wisdom.

Bishops represent Christ the Head in their dioceses. They are the successors of the apostles. The Church entrusts to them the service of authority, governance, preaching the gospel, watching over the purity of her faith, making her holy by administering the sacraments. The bishop is the spiritual guide of his flock, the shepherd who gives his life for his sheep, as Christ did. Because they are the ones who govern, it is very easy to throw every possible criticism and accusation at them, as if they were to blame for whatever isn't working in the Church, as if they were responsible for everything that happens in the diocese, good or bad. Humanly speaking the responsibility that rests on their shoulders is significant, so serious that in antiquity there were priests and deacons who, on learning that they had been chosen for bishop, fled from the city to avoid so heavy a burden.

Over the almost twenty-five years of John Paul II's pontificate, nearly the entire episcopate has been replaced worldwide. The vast majority are faithful, abnegated shepherds who guide their flocks on the paths of the gospel. More than making a judgment on the episcopate of the world, I would invite everyone to pray for them, for each of the men God has entrusted with a portion of the People of God. Theirs is a heavy responsibility, their task is enormous, and the means at their disposal are often meager and insufficient.

I can bear witness that in Latin America many bishops live in real poverty and devote themselves day after day to their pastoral mission with loving dedication, living among their priests and their people like true fathers in the faith. I can say the same of the bishops I know on other continents. Thanks be to God the Church has many good shepherds who defend their sheep from the attacking wolves, even at the expense of their lives. They aren't afraid to declare themselves in favor of the Church's true Magisterium, risking their popularity in the media. They take unpopular decisions to defend the truth of the gospel unambiguously. They govern with a firm hand the flock that Christ entrusted to them. These men are shepherds after God's heart, the kind of men today's Church needs, who bear her up amid the storms that lash against her from every side.

Episcopal conferences were formed to help bishops live their episcopal collegiality more deeply and respond more easily to the pastoral needs of regions or countries. Therefore their purpose is eminently pastoral, since each bishop is still the highest authority in his diocese and does not have to answer to anyone but the Holy See as regards its governance. It's possible that in some cases episcopal conferences may have overstepped, taking away the local bishops' rightful role as leaders in their dioceses. However, their function has been very positive inasmuch as they help all the bishops of a given country become more aware of the overall situation of the faith there, and decide on common pastoral goals and measures. I think we are reaching a level of maturity that makes it easier to balance a bishop's unalienable responsibilities in his own diocese and the mission of the episcopal conference.

I repeat that all of us, beginning with priests and religious, need to support in every way we can the work the bishops do, loving them with true supernatural love, taking their pastoral or doctrinal instructions to heart, and seeing them as fathers in the faith and not as mere religious managers, which is how the media often portray them. Bishops often find themselves somewhat alone, misunderstood by the clergy and the faithful themselves. This brings us back to the theme of unity. All we can do to strengthen the bonds of unity and charity in every sense and in every direction will strengthen the Church and make it grow in holiness and apostolic dynamism.

112. During John Paul II's pontificate, there has been a prolif-eration of canonizations and beatifications. Why do you think the Pope is so interested in highlighting models of holiness?

One of the characteristic notes of Christ's Church is holiness. The Church is holy because she is the Bride of Christ, the Holy One, the Word of God made man. Although we all know that not all the Church's children are holy, since in her bosom there is room for sinners as well — the Church is also Mother — even so the Church is holy. She is holy with Christ's holiness, but also with the holiness of her sons and daughters. I believe that the Pope doesn't want us to forget this. By presenting us with the ex-ample of those who, in very different ways and in the most varied historical and cultural circumstances, have borne witness with their heroic virtues to the fact that it is possible to imitate Christ, he wants to show us that the path to holiness is also open to each and every one of us: if they could, why not us? If they could make grace triumph in their lives in spite of their limitations, in spite of so many obstacles; if they managed to carry the treasure of the faith to the end in those earthen vessels of human nature, then we, too, should strive with all our strength, but trusting in the power of God's strength, to make God's holiness triumph in us.

Vatican II reminded all Christians of their universal call to ho-liness, to perfection in their love for God and neighbor. Holiness is not only a prerogative of clergy or religious. All of us, in our vari-ous states of life, can be holy because all of us can love "to the end" as Christ has loved us.

Perhaps popular imagination has identified saints with wonder-workers, the hearers of special revelations, somewhat distant from society, even a little odd in their behavior. Holiness can entail ex-traordinary phenomena, but this isn't absolutely necessary. You can live a normal life, committed to the responsibilities of family, work, and society, and be a saint. This wasn't exactly a Vatican II discovery, but the Council brought it out more, returning to the origins of Christianity when Christians called each other "saints," as St. Paul did in his letters (2 Cor 1:1; 13:12). The doors of holiness are open to all who are willing to go through them.

In beatifying a servant of God or canonizing the blessed, the Pope shows the whole Church not only the theoretical possibility of reaching holiness, but also a concrete achievement, an example of someone like us who really did it. This encourages us and invites us not to give up our daily effort to imitate Christ, in spite of the rebellion of our flesh, the dishonesty of the world, and the snares of the devil.

I know a number of young people who have taken a vocational decision thanks to the example of one of these models of holiness. The Pope is a great educator and he likes to use symbols. Each saint and blessed is a model, a living symbol of real, achievable, possible holiness. What is marvelous about them is that their paths are all different, although there are elements common to them all. They all chose to make God the passion of their love, and service to their fellowmen their badge. But just as rivers reach the sea by different routes, they all found their own. "There are many rooms," Christ tells us, "in my Father's house" (John 14:2). No one should feel like a stranger in that house, or feel excluded from the Father's love.

The Pope once more spoke of the idea of holiness with a sense of insistence and urgency in his apostolic letter *Novo Millennio Ineunte*, written on the threshold of the third Christian millennium (see n. 30-31). He states that holiness should be the perspective given to every pastoral path in the Church (see n. 31). No one is exempt from this task, because we are all called to be perfect in love.

113. There are many martyrs among those canonized and beatified by the Pope. Martyrdom has blossomed in the twentieth century perhaps as never before in the Church's history since the

first centuries. You yourself witnessed the sacrifice of a number of martyrs in Mexico's Cristero War. According to Tertullian, the blood of martyrs *is* the seed of new Christians. Shouldn't we be seeing more fruits of Christian life as a result of the many martyrs of the twentieth century?

In reality, the fruits of martyrdom are visible to God's eyes; we humans perceive them only partially and not directly. God has his pace and his time. Even so, there's no doubt that the fruit of Christians who have given their lives for the faith or have been confessors of the faith is there for all to see. The springtime of the new evangelization, which we referred to earlier, is intimately related to the blood of the martyrs, as also undoubtedly the emergence of new movements and forms of consecrated life. As I said before, I also think you can draw a line of spiritual continuity between the martyrdom of the Cristeros in Mexico and the birth of the Legion of Christ. But of course only God can see and draw this line. We can see a few traces and make a few deductions and inferences. But he is the one who governs the world and guides the threads of history as it pleases his will. Only he knows, in his infinite wisdom, all the paths, individual and collective, of salvation history.

The blood of the martyrs permits us to hope in a better future for the faith and for the Church, in spite of all the problems and discouraging signs there may be. Martyrdom implies that a man or woman loves to the end, as Christ did, to the point of giving his life for those he loves. These men and women have given their lives, united to Christ's life, for our salvation and our faith. They are our protectors and our advocates. They are signs of God's power in the fragility of our human clay.

Through them we also experience the marvelous dogma of the communion of saints, perhaps a little forgotten. This dogma assures us that the treasures of grace coursing through the veins of the Church are for all of us; they're shared. In a certain sense we have a "right" to them; not a right in the strict sense because we never have a right to grace, which is always an unmerited gift, but in the sense that we have access to them through the Church's treasures of grace.

Anyway, I believe that throughout the twenty-first century and the third millennium in general, we will keep seeing rivers of grace reaching the Church from the supreme sacrifice of all those thousands of men and women who gave their lives for Christ. Tertullian was right: the blood of martyrs is the seed of new Christians. The seed has been sown, the grain of wheat is already cast into the furrow. We are sure that the fruit will come, and in part has already come. We are already harvesting in song what others have sown in tears. But the harvest will be even more abundant: "Look around you, look at the fields; already they are white, ready for harvest!" (John 4:35). The fields are ready. Others have sown, but we have to gather in their fruit: "I sent you to reap a harvest you had not worked for. Others worked for it; and you have come into the rewards of their trouble" (John 4:38). To do this we need apostles, workers willing to go to the Lord's harvest and reap the abundant fruit that awaits us, always amid weariness and tribulation, but with the joy of being able to gather fruits of eternal life.

114. Speaking of vocations, what is in your opinion their future in the Church?

The situation varies a lot from country to country. In Latin America, Africa, and Asia, vocations are on the rise. The problem, as I have mentioned, is the scarcity of formators for priests. In Europe and North America, on the other hand, the situation is more critical, especially in some European countries with long Christian traditions, such as France, Germany, Belgium, and Holland. In Eastern European countries, however, such as Poland, Slovakia, and Lithuania, the situation is more positive.

In reality, as I see it, the vocational issue is intrinsically linked to the faith of a church or a community. Where there's a living faith, vocations happen. Where the faith is withered, vocations dwindle. Other factors come into play as well. An important one is the example that priests set. If the priesthood is presented as a lifestyle that fulfills you, even humanly speaking, when you live it well, young people will feel more attracted to that way of life. If priests live their vocation as a burden — grudgingly, indifferently, apathetically, unenthusiastically, or without conviction — it will be much harder for vocations to happen. I also think it important not to be afraid to offer the priestly vocation as an option to a young man as he chooses his path in life. John Paul II chose this topic for his traditional address to the parish priests of Rome for Lent 2002, telling them that the time had come to present to young men the vocation to priesthood without any qualms. I am convinced that God keeps calling, that the problem is not with him but with us: we're afraid to call in his name, we don't really believe in the priesthood, we don't pray enough. That's why I think the vocational ministry should have wider horizons.

Also, and this is a determining factor, for there to be vocations there have to be believing families who welcome them as a gift. So there also has to be an adequate pastoral ministry to families. There have to be families for whom the faith is something real, daily, enlightening all the aspects of life. It's clear that most vocations to the priesthood and consecrated life come from truly Christian families.

To pastoral ministry to families we should add an intelligent youth ministry that will help young people listen to God's call. We also need priests who are convinced about their priesthood, who are unashamed to guide those called and help them make a wise vocational discernment and a generous, mature decision, based on premises of faith. Therefore, in my opinion, vocational outreach implies the combination of adequate pastoral work with families and youth; the witness of holy, zealous priests; constant prayer asking for vocations on the part of the believing community; and a clear and intelligent proposal of this vocation.

I am also optimistic in this area, even in countries where the situation seems darker. It's a question of laying the groundwork that I discussed above, and the fruits will not fail to come; it may be sooner or later, but they will come. In the meantime we have to follow the Master's command faithfully and perseveringly, praying to the Lord of the harvest to send workers to his harvest (Matt 9:38).

115. We haven't said much yet about women and their role in the Church. Regnum Christi forms many women and even organizes activities on this topic. Do you think that women are more open to the faith than men? What future do you see for women in the Church? Do you think that someday the Catholic Church will allow women priests?

In his Apostolic letter *Mulieris Dignitatem*, John Paul II dedicates beautiful pages to describing Christ's relationship with women, and women's relationship with Christ. Women clearly have a special religious sensitivity, perhaps because they, in God's provident plan, bear in their womb the mystery of life and in a special way are entrusted with life, to protect and foster it. It was women, as we know, who were faithful to Christ unto death, and it was to them that Christ first entrusted the task of spreading the message of his resurrection.

Traditionally, women have been the ones to teach the faith and religious values to their children in the home. Normally it is women who teach their children the Sign of the Cross, the basic prayers; they take them to church to light a candle, whispering in their ears that Jesus is present in the Eucharist as a friend, and so on. Women have something of a sixth sense for sharing the faith naturally and spontaneously.

The various strains of radical feminism, from the Sixties on, presented a completely different image of woman. It's true that the women's liberation movement had its just demands. Women used to be thought of as second-class employees in professional life; many of their rights as workers and even as human beings were not recognized. The point of departure was just, but then entered all the ideological arguments that distorted her image, not only in terms of God's plan, but also from a healthy human, scientific, and philosophical point of view.

In Regnum Christi and in our apostolic initiatives, we give women all the importance they deserve. We believe that women should keep their feminine genius in everything they do, from prayer, family life, and apostolate to professional life. Men love women for what they are, with all the gifts and limitations of their femininity. Today, however, women are presented models of behavior that take them from this ideal and either offer them a false liberation that is merely sexual, or obsess them with professional success.

The problem is culturally very complex and calls for well-conducted study. For this reason we hold congresses, conventions, specific formation courses, et cetera, to study the topic scientifically. We believe that women's issues are vital for the world and the Church, because if women cease to transmit the most essential religious and human values in the family, the whole world will be impoverished in its humanity.

Women are playing more important roles in the Church and will continue to do so. The fact that they don't receive the sacrament of priestly orders does not imply any kind of discrimination against them. The Church must be faithful to her Founder's will, and he conferred holy orders only on men, even though on other issues he went beyond the cultural conditioning of his times. The Church's tradition understood this from very early on, in both the East and West. The Holy Father merely reminded Catholics of what Catholic tradition has constantly taught, clearly stating that the Catholic Church will not change its mind on this issue in the future because it is a definitive doctrine.[8] It is thus not a personal

[8] *Ordinatio Sacerdotalis*, May 24, 1994.

opinion of Karol Wojtyla's, but a doctrine of the Catholic Church defined as such by the supreme and universal Shepherd. Other religious confessions may make other decisions, perhaps on the basis of democratic principles or so-called cultural adjustment. But the Catholic Church will never be able to change its doctrine or discipline based on democratic standards, because the deposit of faith doesn't depend on majority vote, it's a gift that God gave the Church by revelation.

The Pope makes it very clear that this doesn't mean that the Church looks down on the role of women in the Church, any more than Christ looked down on his Mother's role in the apostolic college and the early Church. He simply ordained that there be different functions but one and the same charity and one and the same spirit. In this sense we can say with St. Paul, "There is a variety of gifts but always the same Spirit; there are all sorts of service to be done, but always to the same Lord; working in all sorts of different ways in different people, it is the same God who is working in all of them" (1 Cor 12:4-6).

VII

Personal Experiences

116. Trust and hope are typical of John Paul II's teaching, as shown, among other things, by the title he gave his book *Crossing the Threshold of Hope*. But, are there reasons to hope? Do you yourself hope in a better future for the Church and the world?

I am firmly convinced that the Church, Christ, God's Kingdom, will triumph in history. Revelation clearly tells us so. What we don't know is how we will reach that final point when the power of Christ will submit all things, including death, to the Father. We don't know when that time will come, or what twists and turns the story of the Church and mankind must take before getting there. We know that the weeds will grow alongside the wheat until then (Matt 13:24-30), and in the meantime the life of man will be a constant struggle, as the book of Job says (see 7:1). Precisely because numerous evils would beset our existence, Christ taught us to trust, not to be afraid, to hope against all hope. In times of difficulty in my life as a founder, in order to face the future serenely it has always helped me to read the verse from Psalm 37 that invites us to put all our worries in the Lord's hands and to trust him absolutely: "Commit your fate to Yahweh, trust in him and he will act" (v. 5). The Pope's teaching follows the same vein. Like him, I firmly believe that there are indeed reasons to hope.

Reasons based more on supernatural motives than on an economic, political, or social analysis of the present reality of the world and the Church.

We can hope because redemption has already been accomplished on the Cross and in the Resurrection. If there had been no Cross and if Christ had not risen, our hope would be utterly in vain, totally unfounded. We can hope because the Holy Spirit helps his Church at all times, as Consoler and Advocate, guide to the truth, and Teacher of perfect love. Yes, we can hope, we can and must overcome the fears that prey on us and paralyze us, trying to whisper in our hearts that hope is useless and vain.

I can admit to you as a personal experience that I had many an occasion to exercise hope when I was founding the Legion of Christ. Humanly speaking, many times it seemed as if everything was against its happening; sometimes it looked as if the congregation itself would be suppressed; everything would disappear; it had only been a dream, beautiful but no more than an empty dream. Yet Christian hope, theological hope, beckoned me to discover God's provident plan in every step we took and showed me that if one door was shut, another would open on the spot, revealing new and unimagined horizons. Yes, we can hope; hope is not vain, for as St. Paul says, Christian hope never lets us down (Rom 5:5).

117. Does that mean that Christians should basically be optimists?

Some authors portray Christianity as a repressive religion that systematically denies the joys and pleasures of life; due, according to them, to its negative, Manichaean or Jansenistic view of the human person. This view does not correspond to Christianity as we find it described in the gospel and the Church's teaching.

It is true that Christ didn't hide from his disciples the reality of the Cross, grief, suffering, the narrow path. But he never said that this path would produce unhappy or repressed men and women. Quite the contrary. Let's look at the lives of the saints, the men and women who imitated Christ to perfection. Look at the life of Christ himself. Do we see unhappy, dismal men and women, humanly unfulfilled? No. If anything impresses us, it's the exact opposite: the sense of radiant vigor that shines in their lives, some of which, from a human point of view, would seem weak and fragile.

A person who lives in intimate union with God cannot be sad or pessimistic. St. Teresa of Avila used to say that a sad saint is a bad saint. There's no room for sadness and pessimism because God is the source of joy and happiness. Perhaps all people see from the outside is the tribulation and anguish through which God leads the lives of people of faith. But these trials are nothing compared with the glory that will show forth through them and the joy the world does not know, which God gives as a gift to those who welcome them with faith and love.

118. Do you see any relation between optimism and prayer? If people pray more, are they more optimistic?

When you pray, you listen to God. Prayer is a deeply human act in the sense that you come face-to-face with the truth about yourself and acknowledge that you are God's creature. When you pray, you know that you aren't the final reference point of truth, and there is a standard of truth that is beyond you to which you must adjust. If you lose the sense of prayer, you lose the sense of proportion, the sense of God. For this reason Pope John Paul II says that Christians who do not pray are "Christians at risk" (*Novo Millennio Ineunte*, n. 34). In reality, the same could be said about any person: whoever doesn't pray is at risk of losing the ultimate sense of his existence, which in the final analysis comes from his relation to God.

The man who prays learns to see everything from God's perspective, and reality seen from God takes on a new, deeper, and more radiant meaning. The man who prays is not unaware of the realm of evil that threatens us from the inside as well as from the world around us, but he knows that God is much stronger. So I would say that prayer guarantees not a facile, naïve optimism, but one that is mature, founded on a basic anthropological realism that enables you to understand yourself, others, and the world, with the depth that you acquire when you contemplate all this from the heights of God.

119. Then why do we find it so hard to pray?

Prayer can be hard work because it means committing our whole human person, and above all because it awakens our conscience, through which God sends us messages for our life. Paying attention to our conscience can also be difficult because possibly it is telling us that what God is asking of us at a particular moment conflicts with our preferences and whims. This gives rise to a struggle, like the one that took place between God's angel and Jacob, described in the book of Genesis (see 32:24-32), in which God must be victorious, or better said, man wins to the degree that he yields to God's demands.

In addition to the difficulty in being sincere with God in prayer, it is also a fact that in order to pray we need a strong interior life. People today, on the contrary, tend to be focused on outward things, on what they feel and see, on empirical realities. It taxes them to have to enter into their inner world, into the world of the supernatural.

Great people of prayer like St. Teresa of Avila didn't hesitate to say that one of the greatest temptations the devil ever used on them was to give up praying. Another saint, St. Alphonsus Ligouri, said that those who pray are saved, those who do not pray are condemned. But this vital necessity for anyone who wants to breathe the air of the spirit is exposed to the many distractions of everyday life, even the good things we do, such as when we want to do many things for God, and forget the God we do them for. This activism is another obstacle to prayer that Jesus himself singled out when he fondly praised the attitude of Mary, Lazarus's sister, who attentively listened to his words while Martha was caught up with all the serving: "Martha, Martha, you worry and fret about so many things, and yet few are needed, indeed only one. It is Mary who has chosen the better part; it is not to be taken from her" (Luke 10:41-42). The treasure of God is no easy booty and is given only to those who win it with the arms of prayer. The grave danger would be to give up prayer because of the difficulties we find along the way. We have to persevere, following Christ's command, "You should be awake, and praying not to be put to the test" (Mark 14:38).

120. Do you learn to pray, or does it come naturally? What advice would you give someone who wants to learn how to pray?

For me, prayer is a heart-to-heart conversation with God, so I would venture to say that you learn to pray by praying. To me it's something quite natural. On the one hand, I listen in my heart to what God wants to tell me; I hear it in my conscience. He always speaks to those who have the doors of their soul open. On the other hand, I speak to him very simply, just like I'm speaking to you, about my dreams, hopes, uncertainties, cares, longings, ideals. I ask him for his grace and to protect my faith until death. I listen to him; I ask him for his grace so as to fulfill his will; I thank him for all he gave and gives me. I adore him, I praise him, but it's all natural, without pompous phrases or artificiality. It's simply me being with God and him being with me. The lover delights in the presence of the beloved, and it's not a question of a time-slot during the day, but your whole life. If we love God as the greatest of the commandments tells us — with all our heart, all our soul, and all our strength — it won't be hard or complicated to be in his presence and live in a constant conversation of love with him.

Of course, this implies gradual growth. In prayer you gradually begin to enjoy God's presence; you discover him little by little; he progressively reveals himself to you. In my own case I go over and over the great mysteries of our redemption to contemplate them: the Incarnation of the Word, Christ's Birth, his Passion, Death and Resurrection. Little by little it gets easier and easier to talk to him about interests we share such as the Church, spreading God's Kingdom, those who suffer, saving souls, and so on.

Personally I don't believe there is a "technique" for praying, as there is for reading or learning languages. However, there are some methods that help. For example, it is always recommended that you start by putting yourself in God's presence, exercising the theological virtues. This is all very useful, and it is useful, too, to end your meditation with a resolution. But the important thing is to unite yourself to the Father through Christ, following the Holy Spirit's inspirations. If you want to learn to pray, you need to listen carefully to the Holy Spirit, the gentle guest of the soul: be attentive to all his inspirations, docile to him, sincere, generous, and open to the path of love that he, the Spirit of love, suggests to you.

Nor should we forget the importance for the Church of liturgical prayer, which also has its learning process: living the Eucharist, the Liturgy of the Hours, and the other liturgical and sacramental celebrations in a true spirit of prayer. The entire liturgy is an invitation to pray. That is why in our centers we form our seminarians in the liturgical spirit, according to the Church's mind and norms, so as to help them unite themselves to God by celebrating the liturgy. We spend as much time as is necessary to prepare the liturgy well, choosing and learning appropriate hymns. Gregorian chant especially, of long tradition in the Latin Church, helps you raise your soul to God and live the mystery of Christ in the harmony of its simple melodies, flooding your soul with a deep peace. Also sacred polyphony, and other appropriate and beautiful forms of singing, plus all the rich symbolism present in Catholic liturgy, lead you to immerse yourself in the contemplation of the mysteries of our redemption that the liturgy celebrates and makes present.

121. Everyone faces greater or lesser trials in the course of his life, which God allows to make him holier. You have had your share. What has helped you to persevere amid your trials and not become bitter, especially when your suffering is caused by ill will?

Earlier I referred to a verse from the Book of Job [Job 7:1] — I remember it in the Latin version: *"Militia est vita hominis super terram"* ["The life of man upon earth is a warfare"], which has often helped me remember that man's life on earth is a battle. So the battle hasn't surprised me. I know that you must fight if you want something in life. And by the grace of God I have always wanted my battle to be for Christ and the Church. Surely a true Christian can't expect to go through life without the cross? My battle has had a meaning: Christ crucified. Yes, I think I've suffered because of the trials God has allowed in my life. I don't deny it. But I have seen many other men suffer without meaning, and for me that's the worst thing that could happen to someone. With God's help and by his grace, I have been able to give my battles meaning. And that is why I have always considered myself fortunate, truly blessed, and in the measure of my limitations I have done my best to help those who suffer without knowing why, giving them a reason to live and to suffer. I have tried to give them the reason that kept me going, the one that made me want to live and suffer: friendship with Christ. I haven't always succeeded. I have failed many times. But I believe that God's action goes far beyond the frontiers of the visible, what our eyes can see. I know that God can do wonders in the depths of a soul, and so I have always hoped in the victory of grace.

As for the men who have been the cause of some of my sufferings, I have tried to look on them as a Christian should. Often there was no ill will, they simply thought they were doing what was right. At other times, when there might have been conscious ill will (if there was, only God knows), I have tried to forgive wholeheartedly my brothers who wounded me. I have prayed for them and seen all this as part of God's plan, who always tries to purify us and make our love more perfect. One of the greatest graces God has given me in life is that I never learned to hate, or to harbor rancor, resentment, or desire for revenge in my heart. This has given me a life of abundant peace and happiness in God's service.

Above all, I try to activate my faith in God. Without faith Christian life is very difficult, not to say impossible. But faith reveals to us new horizons of divine goodness, poured out lavishly on our lives, horizons of forgiveness, mercy, and compassion. Faith reveals to us a provident Father who watches over all his children. This is what helps us to trust and to battle and forge always forward, never wasting time wondering if people have said or done negative things against us. Instead, I try to go through this life doing all the good I can and trying to win as many people as possible to Christ's friendship.

122. In your writings you often talk about living with eternity in mind. Where did you get this idea?

No doubt from the Holy Spirit, because it's not something I ever consciously looked for. I mentioned earlier how when I was very young, in my early adolescence, I already found myself on a little hill overlooking Cotija, the town where I was born, contemplating it from up there. I would look at the red-roofed houses, the lofty bell tower rising above the other roofs, my family's house, my friends' houses, the school, the other churches, the cemetery. At twelve or thirteen I was spontaneously faced with questions about the meaning of life, the point of all the hustle and bustle, the people working themselves so hard to survive, and then, what? What was there after this life? The loneliness of the cemetery with the silent tombs of townspeople who in years past had toiled so much to pile up honors or wealth, and now it was all over for them. I looked at the distant hills on the horizon and wondered who lived beyond them. Men and women like the ones in Cotija, fretting about the same things, only to die and disappear too? I would ask myself what was the one thing that would never pass away, because it is eternal, so that I might grab hold of it with all the strength of my being. The one answer I found, and that shed light on my heart, was this: God alone. God alone does not pass away. He alone is eternal, and I told myself that I must anchor my life in the eternal alone. All these thoughts were very simple. Not at all complicated, an adolescent's thoughts. But they left a deep mark in my soul. From then on, I always wanted to live with eternity in mind. It matters everything to me to win eternity and possess God forever. That is what really matters. To lose it is the worst thing that could happen to me.

As I said, I am sure it was no doubt the Holy Spirit somehow guiding my thoughts so as to introduce me into the new stage in my life that was to be the founding of the Legion and Regnum Christi. This longing for eternity, and the short-lived nature of things temporal, have dominated my life ever since. It has driven me to make the most of the lifetime God has given me to win eternity and help others to find it. Anything else in my opinion is wasted time and nonsense.

123. If you were born again, would you choose to be a priest again, and found the Legion of Christ and Regnum Christi?

If I could be born again I would try to follow God's will for my life out of love. You say "choose." Really, a priest "is chosen": "You did not choose me, no, I chose you; and I commissioned you to go out and to bear fruit, fruit that will last" (John 15:16). It wasn't I who chose to be a priest or the founder of a religious congregation and an apostolic movement. In the vocation there is a mystery that precedes us, according to the experience of the prophet Jeremiah: "Before I formed you in the womb I knew you; before you came to birth I consecrated you; I have appointed you as prophet to the nations" (Jer 1:5).

In my life I have always tried to do what God wanted of me, however hard it was for my nature, even if I would personally have preferred easier paths, with fewer complications. However, after eighty-three years of life, sixty-nine of them spent following my vocation, I can say that the path God chose for my life has made me immensely happy. I can't picture greater happiness than serving God, and in this sense, yes, in a hypothetical second life, I would like God to choose me to be a priest. The vocation to priesthood is sublime. Only in heaven will we be able to value it properly. I am not sorry for being a priest, for having followed and continuing to follow Christ by his paths, which for the most part are cross and sacrifice. I can also tell you that I have found great happiness on this path, so much so that one of my greatest sufferings is my inability to make people understand the great happiness they are giving up when they don't follow Christ on the path he has in mind for each of them.

Truly, God's wisdom is infinite, his pedagogy wonderful. He doesn't reveal his plan for us in a flash, but step by step, day by day. Maybe if I had seen all the suffering my vocation has brought me, my human nature would have turned coward and rebelled. So, great teacher and loving Father that he is, God revealed little by little the steps he wanted me to take, and at each step I always found enough grace to keep following his path. God wants us to move at his pace, to live day after day trusting him and not worrying about the future, which doesn't depend on us: "Each day has enough trouble of its own" (Matt 6:34). So if I were born again, I would live my life again with absolute trust that God's will for me is one and the same as my greatest possible happiness and that of my brothers and sisters. That would motivate me to devote myself with all the passion of my being to doing that divine will, accepting his plan for me out of love, whatever it might be.

124. What has hurt you most in life: being criticized, not being understood, infidelity, ingratitude?

All the sufferings you mention are moral ones. Yes, I do think moral pain is much greater and deeper than physical pain, although the latter can at times be very hard as well. I couldn't tell you which of them was worst. I've never dwelt on it; I try instead to offer them to God and pray for those who had a part to play in causing them. I can say that one pain that pierces the heart to its very core is infidelity and betrayal — especially by friends. In this sense I can understand, however remotely, something of what Christ suffered when he was betrayed by one of his own, Judas, whom he really considered his friend. He must have suffered greatly, not so much because of the betrayal itself but rather for Judas, for the drama of his life and death.

I have tried to thank God for the opportunities he gives me to suffer something for his sake, because suffering is also a grace from God. We can learn important lessons from suffering — perhaps the best, the deepest ones. No one likes to suffer, but God's plan for redeeming man includes a phase of suffering and pain. When it touches our lives, our first reaction is to rebel, but then God helps us to learn important lessons of love, humility, trust, and faith. And in hindsight we discover that the painful times in our lives were totally flooded with a special presence of God, even amid the darkness and the suffering.

But if you want to know what has caused me the most suffering, I will tell you without hesitation that my greatest suffering in life is to see the immense needs that people have and the Church has, and not be able to do more to help them. Whether by God's grace or by my upbringing, I have always been very sensitive to others' problems, to their material and spiritual problems. I am especially concerned that each person has the chance to find Christ, and in him eternal salvation. Perhaps it's my practical nature, but when I see these problems, I react by trying to solve what I can, what I can reach, be it little or much. And something that has always made me suffer immensely is my powerlessness to do more to help my brothers and sisters. The only remedy to this kind of suffering is a likewise tremendous trust in God, in his sanctifying Spirit, because I'm sure that countless brothers and sisters of mine receive his interior enlightenment, which pierces to the depths of their souls, revealing to them that God loves them with infinite love, and that each of them is called to live the fullness of this love eternally.

125. What is your attitude in the face of the aggression and slander against your person, and towards the individuals who slander you?

Since I was very young by God's permission I've had to face aggression and slander directed at my person and at the Legion and Regnum Christi. This has been an ever-present mystery in my life. Perhaps at first it surprised me a little, but I quickly understood that a disciple of Christ cannot follow a different path to his Master. My basic attitude has been to try to live Christ's commandment of charity at all times, to its ultimate consequences. Out of love for him I made sure never to give them their own back. Following his example and the advice he gave his followers, I have prayed for those who did this to me, making sure to forgive them with all my heart, without harboring the least grudge or ill will for them in my soul.

Nor have I wished to waste even a minute of my life defending myself from insults, accusations, and slander, because I always wanted, and still do, to use the short time God gives me to carry out his plan for my life, up to my last minute.

126. What is it about Christ that fascinates you most?

Everything about him is fascinating, because he is God himself. I have spent much time meditating on what this verse from John's gospel means to me: "And the Word became flesh and dwelt among us." Every time I meditate on it, I learn something new. I'm enthralled by the God who chose to take our weakness to himself for one reason alone beyond the grasp of our minds: love, merciful love, since the gap between us and him is infinite and could be filled only by mercy. His love wished to lower itself to me, to every man and woman who ever lived, or lives, or will live in history. He chose to live the same life as each one of us, and die the death of the vilest of men.

It always fills my heart to feel Christ's love for me personally; not his love for mankind in general, but for me. To feel loved by him in spite of everything, in spite of suffering, pain, being abandoned, rejected, misunderstood by others; to feel that he keeps on loving us even when we are in sin, even in our littleness, is something that truly moves me. But it's not just a question of feeling, of mere emotion. It moves my will to want to tell my brothers and sisters this good news, this gospel, that God loves us infinitely, that "God loved the world so much that he gave his only Son, so that everyone who believes in him may not be lost but may have eternal life" (John 3:16). To understand and experience his love is a grace Christ is ready to give to everyone who asks him for it humbly, in faith and perseveringly.

127. What has the Blessed Virgin Mary meant to you in your life?

It is hard to find words to express such a deep and heartfelt experience. We all love our earthly mothers, but when we talk about them, when we try to express our love, words seem to fall short. My love for her comes spontaneously and naturally. I learned it at home, especially from my mother. When we were little, my siblings and I used to place flowers before her statue in May, to show her our love. I discovered my vocation in May, the month especially dedicated to her, and I placed my vocation in her arms, as well as my priesthood and the foundation of the Legion and Regnum Christi.

She was at my side during the hard years when the Legion was being founded; I received the sublime gift of priesthood under her mantle, on Tepeyac Hill. I remember a very special grace that I was granted through her intercession on one of my trips to Rome in the Forties, which I mentioned earlier. When I had been refused the approval of our Constitutions, just before I left the Eternal City, I paid a visit to a side altar in St. Peter's Basilica, the one dedicated to the Gregorian Virgin. There in conversation with her I was granted special strength from God to push ahead on the exhausting path of the foundation, and I received a spiritual certainty that the approval I longed for would come through her intercession, as indeed happened. In thanksgiving, I return every year with the community of the Legionaries in Rome to celebrate holy Mass on that altar and again put my life and priesthood in her hands.

I place the whole Legion and Regnum Christi in her hands, as well as each of the projects and institutions that we begin, because where Mary reigns, victory is sure. I am convinced, through personal experience, that when Mary takes hold of a vocation, a community, a project of spiritual perfection, or an apostolic endeavor, it is very difficult, if not impossible, for Christ's enemy to triumph.

My devotion to her is very simple: a son's relationship with his Mother. I bring her my requests quite simply, and leave them in her hands. And especially I try to imitate the virtues that marked her life: her faith, humility, obedience, generosity, spirit of sacrifice, her self-giving to others, her hope, poverty, purity, her love for Christ and the Church. Walking at her side I feel safe. She is at the foot of my cross as she was at her Son's. She never leaves me alone in times of pain, though others may. I make the Holy Father's motto entirely my own: *"Totus tuus, ego sum, Maria."*

It is a tender relationship, but not a sentimental one: It is strong and deep. Mary fashions great souls, sturdy in faith, intrepid in apostolate, people of contemplation and prayer. She is also Mother of the Church and Queen of Apostles. Every day I entrust to her the souls whom God has put on my path so that they will make it to heaven with me. As a sign of gratitude to her, I've made sure that great events and celebrations in the congregation and Regnum Christi are always in the context of Marian feast days. I could say so much more about Mary. St. Bernard used to say, *"De Maria nunquam satis,"* you can never sing her praises enough. I simply invite everyone to experience firsthand the strength and encouragement that come from her presence in our Christian life.

128. In trying to follow a vocation like yours, have you ever been afraid or felt like not continuing?

I think we are all exposed to fear. Fear is an emotion that moves us to flee a future evil we want to avoid. The problem is not feeling fear; it's letting it overcome you. In this sense, I have felt fear when looking at the dimensions of the mission God entrusted to me, just as any man feels the disproportion between what he is and the mission God entrusts to him. The prophet Jeremiah also felt fear before the mission God was giving him, and the Lord comforted him with these words: "Do not say, 'I am a child.' Go now to those to whom I send you and say whatever I command you. Do not be afraid of them, for I am with you to protect you" (Jer 1:7-8). Fear vanishes when we know that God is at our side and is with us, when we know that he never leaves us on our own. His company gives us unknown courage because it comes from him and from the eagerness and strength that appear in a humanly inexplicable way in our struggle to be faithful to our mission.

Occasionally it can also occur to us to give it all up and turn back. In this regard I think God has given me a special grace never to feel the temptation. Once I began I knew that my life was definitively committed to Christ and that there was no room for other options. Yes, I have felt weariness, the weight of "a heavy day's work in all the heat" as we read in the parable of the vineyard workers (Matt 20:12), but I've always known I could never look back if I wanted to be worthy of Christ; to look back is a betrayal, and you can't betray a friend like Christ.

129. According to *The Imitation of Christ,* some people almost never have any temptations, others have them almost their whole life long and feel them very intensely, while others have them only during some special times. If I may be bold enough to ask, which of these categories do you think applies to you?

I would like to answer your question by giving it a twist and making it positive. The point of departure is the fact that God chose to make man fundamentally free since he wanted to have a relationship of love with us. And there's no true love unless the one who loves is free, since love implies choosing the person you love. Since he wanted us to love him freely, he created us free. And that's the way he wants us, just as he created us: free. Our every commitment to him should be made in freedom and never under any kind of duress. Human freedom, however, unlike divine freedom, is exposed to making a wrong choice, the choice of an evil that on the surface seems good. As long as we live, we are free, and our freedom is in a position to choose good or evil. Temptation incites us to make wrong choices, choices that go against God's will. Temptation is so human and it is so intimately a part of man's nature that Christ himself chose to be tempted three times in the desert.

I thank God infinitely for the gift of freedom. I love being free to choose God. I love being able to answer God, not driven by fear or need, but because I truly love him above any other person or thing. I have a habit of renewing my choice for God every day. I tell him that I choose him today, that today I want to love him with all my heart, doing his will for me. Every day I want to begin again, as if it were the first day, as if it were the last day, as if it were the only day of my life. This way we can live our love for God with unsuspected fullness and unspoiled freshness.

Like any man, I have also felt the tug of other choices, of an easier life on more comfortable paths; but God has given me grace so abundant that it has made me understand, as a truth as plain as day, that any path in life without God is the most bitter for man. So with the help of his grace I have been able to choose, within my limitations as a human being, the path of God's will, always threatened by the possibility of other paths but at the same time always fully certain that the path on which God was leading me, which is always a way of the Cross, is the path of true love and the greatest happiness.

I don't know if I've had more temptations or fewer than others, or if I've had more suffering or less in my life than others. I've never troubled to compare myself with others. My concern was and is to be faithful to God's gift, to use my freedom well, to use my life for the good of the Church and Christ's Kingdom. Besides, I don't think it's helpful to compare yourself with others since God has a unique road for each person, with personal paths, very personal graces, and he knows what is best for each of his children.

130. In Toronto the Pope told the youth that he feels young inside, even though he is old outside. Do you feel young too?

There can be young people who are old in spirit, and old people with youthful spirits. The Pope belongs to the second category because what makes young people young is their enthusiasm for great ideals, their desire to give their lives for something greater than they are, to give themselves totally to someone they love. And we all know that John Paul II has kept intact the ideals of his youth, when he chose to give himself totally to God as a priest.

That's why he is young, because there is love in his spirit, and you see it in his eyes and in everything about him.

I was born the same year as the Pope, 1920. My body, like his, feels the weight of the years. By God's grace I find in my soul the same dream of devoting my life to Christ as when I left home at fifteen. Life has its knocks for everyone. Sometimes they might embitter us or fill us with resentment. But I don't think this is Christian. By God's grace I have kept my peace of heart over the years, and I think this inner peace helps us to view the world, ourselves, the Church, time, and eternity in a balanced, serene way.

I no longer have the physical energy of a twenty- or thirty-year-old, but I don't think love has declined in my heart; rather, it has steadily grown stronger and purer over the years. I don't know if I feel young or old. What I want at this stage in my life is what I have always wanted: to be faithful to Christ until death, fulfilling the mission he gave me. Yes, perhaps it's true, I want to see my love ever new and ever young.

131. Staying faithful to Christ until death is an enormous grace, the grace of perseverance. Can you pray for this grace?

Ever since I was very young, I have always prayed to God, through Mary's intercession, for this grace, the grace of graces — to persevere in his service until death. I know that my human freedom, which we were discussing not too long ago, is fragile. I know I can let God down any time, and that I need him like a fish needs water or like our lungs need air.

The grace of persevering is totally undeserved, but we should ask for it every day, humbly and very trustingly, confident that our Lord will give it to us in his infinite mercy. I tell people to make this prayer every day, to persevere until death, to strive to be faithful to God until their dying breath. I am convinced that our Lord hears this prayer, prayed humbly and with the motherly intercession of the Blessed Virgin Mary.

132. Looking back from where you are in life, can you say you are happy with what you have done?

I have to admit that I don't like "looking back," because I think what's urgent is to look at what you can do for the Church right now. What has or hasn't been done is in God's hands. He will judge our actions. I'm very fond of St. Paul's words when he says to the Philippians, "I forget the past and I strain ahead for what is still to come; I am racing for the finish, for the prize to which God calls us upwards to receive in Christ Jesus" (Phil 3:13-14). I am more concerned about the future than the past, because there is still a lot left to do.

Naturally the past helps me to thank God for his loving, provident help and to learn lessons that will be useful in the future. We shouldn't erase from our memories all that the Lord has done for us. We can be allowed to examine how our life has been, much as you do when you examine your conscience, so as to make the very most of the gifts of the present. And when I make this pause in my life so as to see it through God's eyes, I can't help thanking him for using me as an instrument to work with him in his plan to redeem men, through the Legion and Regnum Christi. You asked me if I was satisfied with "what I've done." I have to say that God has been the true "doer" in any good I have done to serve the Church. What really matters is not what Father Maciel may or may not have done; what matters is what God does through each one of us, at times even in spite of us. I have tried not to get in the way, to do the part it was up to me to do, within my limitations, so as to collaborate in his plan in service of the Church. I am satisfied that I said yes to God and fought to be faithful to everything he asked of me.

But this is not a personal satisfaction from a human point of view; it's a spiritual satisfaction that comes from seeing what God has achieved through me, as his instrument. Any satisfaction I feel comes from having loved Christ, souls, the Church; from being an instrument in God's hands to collaborate with him. I would be very foolish to think that the achievements all come from my human capabilities, my human capacity. If someone said to me, "You know, without you none of this would have been possible," I wouldn't believe him. God could have done it a thousand different ways. As electricity travels along a wire, that's how God's grace has gone through me to give light and hope to others. But it's not about personal achievements, either in the past or now. To think of it like that would be a farce. I would be lying to myself.

Thanks be to God I see and feel this very clearly, and it frees me from any possible emotional or intellectual vanity, past or present. I know that everything God has accomplished through the Legion is his doing. I see myself as an instrument, like something different from the Legion. I look at the Legion, I contemplate it, I meditate on it, and I see everything that God has done and is doing through it. But it's him; it's not me.

Yes, it's true that God has done good things through the Legion and Regnum Christi, but, on the other hand, I feel that our contribution is still tiny compared with the Church's needs and what I had dreamed of. When I see all that the Church needs today and how little we are still able to give it, I can't help feeling that there's still much to do, that we can do a lot more. In this sense I can say that I'm not satisfied. I would have wanted to do much more for Christ and the Church.

It is a serene kind of dissatisfaction, though, because I know that others will come and do it; they will give continuity to my work and the work of the present Legionaries and Regnum Christi members. My great dream has always been to serve the Church, and I am convinced that God will keep sending many workers to his harvest, thousands and thousands of apostles to preach the gospel to the world, in the Legion and Regnum Christi, and in many other institutions in the Church.

133. In his apostolic letter *Novo Millennio Ineunte*, John Paul II wrote: "Ours is a time of continual movement which often

leads to restlessness, with the risk of 'doing for the sake of doing.' We must resist this temptation by trying 'to be' before trying 'to do' " (n. 15). You have been a man of action *and* contemplation your whole life: How are you able to combine these two facets of life, which seem so contrary? How can you be Martha and Mary at the same time?

Really, you can't have quick and easy recipes in the life of the spirit. What I have always believed is that if you want to do things for God and the Church, you have to be a person of deep interior life, a real contemplative. The Church's history proves this truth. If you're not a "man of God," you can't work effectively for him. The Holy Father proposes to modern man a return to interiority, to discover the mysterious presence of God in the depths of their souls, and re-evaluate the role of conscience. All of this belongs to the realm of "being" and not necessarily that of "doing." You can get something back for what you do; I do something, and I get paid for it. But being is not always remunerated monetarily. That's why it is much easier to focus on doing than on being. But if we fail to find ourselves, if we fail to be reconciled with our being; if we don't know who we are, where we are going, what we want, what our destiny is, then what we do is directionless, and there comes a time when all the machinery we have assembled can turn against us. It is necessary and urgent to recover our inner life, the life of the spirit, not only because it makes it easier to find God, but because if we do so, we will not lose ourselves.

The gospel passage about Martha and Mary reminds us about all of this. Jesus taught us all a lesson by correcting Martha's attitude. We should remember that Martha as well as Mary and Lazarus were Jesus' friends. Jesus loved them dearly as his friends, and they were very much at ease and open with one another. That's why Martha was bold enough to ask him to reprimand her sister, who was leaving her to do the serving, and with the same openness Jesus gives her an answer that we could classify as "tough": "Martha,

Martha, you worry and fret about so many things, and yet few are needed, indeed only one. It is Mary who has chosen the better part; it is not to be taken from her" (Luke 10:41-42). Martha wanted to serve the Lord, but it was "worried" service; it wasn't backed up by interior life. Jesus is not simply scolding service as such, but her fretting as she serves, her activity-turned-activism. On the other hand, he praises Mary's attitude, the attitude of listening, deeply entering into the mystery of God revealed in Christ.

In reality, I don't think there is a real opposition between authentic contemplation and authentic action. An authentic contemplative is an authentic apostle. In my life I have always found the strength to act by contemplating the mystery of Christ. I think each one has to find the way to balance action and contemplation with the help of God's grace and a good spiritual director. If we want our activity to be effective, we need to be contemplative. Only if we contemplate the mystery of Christ in prayer can we express it to others with conviction. That is why, as the classic saying goes, apostolate is *"contemplata aliis tradere,"* giving others what we have already contemplated ourselves in our personal prayer.

134. On the fiftieth anniversary of his priestly ordination, John Paul II said that for him the Eucharist is the center of his whole day, the axis around which all his activity turns. Is that your experience as a priest, too? How can you explain to people the value of the Eucharist — especially to young people, when many of them get bored at Mass and go more out of duty than conviction?

For every priest the Eucharist is the center of his life, the well where he draws the strength to be faithful to Christ day after day and live in his company all life's great and small events. The Eucharist is what enables priests to live their total consecration to God in celibacy. There they find a remedy for their solitude, the constant renewal of their friendship with Christ, his presence full of passionate love. The Holy Father has reminded priests of this so many times, especially in his letters to us on Holy Thursdays. This is my experience, too. In celebrating holy Mass every day I have been able always to renew my love for Christ and find his love; I've been able to unite myself to him throughout the events of every day; to build the Church by praying for all humanity, for the Pope, for bishops, priests, religious, the men and women consecrated to the Kingdom, the laity, those who suffer, the sick, the imprisoned, everyone; and to unite my poor life to Christ in sacrifice to the Father for the world's redemption.

If you want to understand the Eucharist well and partake of it fruitfully, you have to prepare yourself well. The Mass becomes a meaningless rite if your soul isn't prepared; if you don't first have a prayer life, long to receive Christ, deeply believe in what is being celebrated, desire to unite your life to his, to thank God for all his gifts, to ask forgiveness for your faults. On the contrary, if you have all these dispositions, holy Mass is the climax of your spiritual day because in it we can be united to Christ in the most perfect way possible on this earth. Since many people have lost the kind of interior life we were earlier speaking of, and their ability to read religious language and rites, as well as their appreciation for God's grace, it is harder for them to participate actively in the Eucharist. We need a renewed catechesis on the Eucharist, its meaning, and each of its parts. We need to recognize the fact that the priest celebrating the Mass has a primary role in this. If the faithful perceive his devotion, faith, fervor, and intense participation, they themselves will be moved to live the celebration of the Eucharist more intensely and deeply.

The Eucharist's sanctifying power is extraordinary because the Eucharist contains Christ himself. Through it our soul makes direct contact with the Lord, thanks to the tremendous gift he chose to give us as a memorial of his Passion and Resurrection. If you really want to develop a deep interior life and be a contemplative soul, you must live on the Eucharist, the manna from heaven that God gave us for our pilgrimage through this world. My life is and always has been nurtured by it, and every day as I lift up the consecrated host and offer it to the Father for the salvation of all people, my soul adores in silence the mystery of this new Bethlehem and this new Calvary.

The World of Today and Tomorrow: Looking Toward the Future

135. In his apostolic letter *Novo Millennio Ineunte*, John Paul II often quotes the gospel according to St. Luke about the miraculous catch of fish (Luke 5:1-11), emphasizing especially the point where Christ tells Peter to "put out into the deep" (*duc in altum*). What does it mean to you to "put out into the deep" in the Church and the world today?

The Pope was evoking a special moment in Christ's relationship with his disciples, especially Peter, and applying it to the Church's present situation. I find this scene very beautiful and suggestive. Jesus had begun his apostolic ministry in the region of Galilee. Immediately his preaching and his many miracles among that simple folk draw a great multitude: the sick, the possessed, the paralyzed, the blind, et cetera. They all want to hear Christ's surprising message and receive the grace of his healing power. The crowd was so great that in order to speak in peace and to be better heard, he got into Peter's boat to preach from the water's edge.

Once his preaching was over Jesus tells Peter to "put out into deep water." It's an order: *Duc in altum*. The second part of the phrase is less quoted and often forgotten: "Put out into deep water, and lower your nets for a catch." Jesus' command had a specific purpose: He wanted to teach Peter a lesson on fishing. As we know, Peter was a fisherman and knew the Sea of Galilee like the back of his hand. He had been born on its banks and had spent nights and days on its waters, lowering the nets ever since he was a boy. From those years he learned his trade, possibly inherited from his father. He knew where, when, and how to find the shoals of fish. Peter knew that, from a human point of view, it wasn't the best time to cast his nets, nor was it the best place. That's why he's bold enough to tell the Master: "We have been working all night and have caught nothing." He knew that nighttime was the best for the kind of fish they were looking for in that lake. They had already tried it. They had used all their skill but caught nothing. The nets lay empty on the big planks of the boat, awaiting a better opportunity. Peter gives Christ a valid human reason not to cast his nets, not to obey his order. To human logic it made sense not to repeat something that hadn't worked. But his sentence didn't end there: "But in your name, I will pay out the nets," making it clear to Jesus that he, a professional fisherman, would never have fished there at that time of day, but that his trust in Jesus was greater than the confidence that came from his experience and practice. In a word, he was saying that he trusted Christ more than he trusted himself.

We know how the passage ends. Peter lowers his nets, and they are instantly filled with fish, so many that they needed the help of the other boat. Peter and the other disciples, fishermen like him, are amazed. They throw themselves at Jesus' feet, acknowledging their Master's greatness and their own nothingness and wretchedness. But Jesus lifts Peter up and says, "Do not be afraid. From now on it is men you will catch." Once they reached shore, Peter, with James and John, his partners, leave everything and follow him.

This passage is very rich in imagery and meaning. I believe that's why the Pope chose it for the Church in the new millennium. Humanity has reached this juncture in history, proud of its knowledge, technology, and experience, just like Peter was proud to know a fisherman's trade perfectly. With the words "put out into the deep," Jesus is telling Peter that there are still new experiences to be had, that he doesn't know it all, there are new powers of knowledge outside his world, regions of mystery that he has yet to explore. When the Pope invites the Church and humanity to "put out into the deep," he is telling us to enter into the mystery of God, by faith. This is "to put out into the deep," to believe more strongly, to hope more longingly, to love more passionately.

The path of trust and faith is valid for all humanity and for each person, for the new millennium and for all of history. We can say that human life is about putting out into the deep, accepting afresh the surprise of God, beginning again with renewed ideals each day. This gospel scene shows us that the one who trusts in God like Peter and lowers his nets in the Lord's name, will triumph in life; success in life comes when you absolutely trust in God's wisdom and power despite all appearances to the contrary and any adverse circumstance.

Once tested in his faith and trust, Peter receives a new mission: to be a fisher of men, to share his faith and trust with others. He and the other fishermen leave everything behind and become disciples. They want to learn from Christ how to live in faith and in trust. Christ himself tells them, "Do not be afraid. Do not let fear overcome you, for I am with you." This is the Pope's message to the third millennium, the same message he gave as he began his pontificate, the one he has repeated during his recent trips to Toronto, Mexico, and Poland: "Do not be afraid. Trust." I think he chose this gospel scene to give all of us — the world, the Church, each person and each Christian — a message of trust and faith. It invites us to take the path of the three theological virtues and cast our nets in his name, knowing that he will fill them with an abundant catch.

136. Today much is said about globalization. Communication, too, is being globalized by new forms of media such as the Internet.

Some demonize the "great web" of global communication, while others exalt it as a great cultural revolution. What do you think?

As for globalization, I want to begin by saying that Christianity contains the seed of a globalized world. The Christian faith was called, from the very start, to spread throughout the entire world. Christianity's vocation is universal: "Go out to the whole world; proclaim the Good News to all creation" (Mark 16:15). So globalization is positive, especially regarding information, as in the case of the Internet, because it is a new medium made available by technology that can help us spread Christ's message throughout the whole world, as he told us to in his missionary mandate.

I remember suggesting to some friends in the Vatican Curia, during the Fifties, that they invest more in the media than in building new churches. Not that we shouldn't build new churches; they are necessary, too. What I wanted to highlight was that the media are the new *Areopagi* where we had to preach the gospel. I have always seen the media, and generally all the ways and means that technology makes available, as a wonderful opportunity to share Christ's message.

The world of the Internet you refer to is indeed very complex and not without ambiguity. It is like a worldwide market with all kinds of wares for sale, good and bad. Unfortunately, much of what is offered has to do with activities unadvisable for a Christian or any rightly formed moral conscience. You have to discern which sites can contribute something to your formation and those that are simply a waste of time or corrupt your moral conscience.

From an apostolic point of view, the Internet is an invitation to all Christians to use this great new worldwide marketplace to offer positive, gospel-inspired initiatives. We have to be creative in doing good. Thanks be to God, there are already a good number of sites and services available for Christian formation and Church information that are doing much good, such as the Zenit news agency you direct. There are sites that help people meditate on a

Bible passage, do a spiritual retreat, or choose good books or religious material. The Vatican has a site, a number of episcopal conferences, too, various Catholic groups and associations that offer worthwhile material for study, preaching, catechism, consulting, and so forth. There are also very valuable educational opportunities, and constructive and fruitful chat rooms. In this sense, the Internet has created networks of people around common interests, which is a wonderful opportunity for humanizing and evangelizing all areas of social life.

My opinion about the new technological developments that have revolutionized the world in the twentieth century and will continue to do so in the twenty-first has always been that we should make the most of them for good purposes, make them serve the gospel. The tool itself is morally neutral. It's up to us how we use it to make it an instrument that will spread good or, as unfortunately is often the case, one that serves evil.

Therefore, speaking of the Internet, I think that in the case of those who have not yet developed mature and reliable moral judgment — children and adolescents, for example — parents and educators need to monitor very closely their use of it, so it doesn't become a sheer time-waster or a means of moral corruption. In our schools we make the Internet available to both parents and students, teaching them to use it responsibly and to make the most of all the educational possibilities it offers. We shouldn't be afraid of the Internet; we should learn to use it for the good of the human person and harness it to spread the faith.

137. Another of today's great issues, with a future we can only guess at, is bioethics. In 2001 the Pontifical University *Regina Apostolorum* opened the world's first School of Bioethics. Why this interest in the world of bioethics? What is the future of bioethics?

As the name indicates, bioethics has to do with the ethics of life, and discusses a series of moral issues, both theoretical and practical, that humanity and the various legislative bodies must address: new questions that had never been asked before, such as what to do with frozen embryos created by artificial insemination, or whether it is licit to clone human beings. It's enough to read the daily paper to find new and complex questions of this sort. These are absolutely new situations and questions that beg mankind's moral conscience and the Christian faith for an answer. A few years ago they looked like science fiction, only possible in novels or the movies. Today they are dramatically real and demand an urgent response. To give an answer there first has to be an ethical reflection on human life and, through it, on man, his essence, and his destiny.

That is why we opened the School of Bioethics, in which experts in theology, philosophy, law, medicine, and life-ethics study these issues in an interdisciplinary fashion. They rigorously respect the scientific character of medical and biological topics. The results then become the object of serious ethical reflection, the basis of which is the Christian view of man and his purpose in this world. As well as promoting research on these issues we want to train generations of experts in this specific field, who will provide competent statements and judgments as members of the ethics committees of countries, hospitals, and pharmaceutical companies. They, in turn, can train priests, doctors, high school and university professors, and laypeople engaged in various kinds of work related to the respect for and care of life.

What is at stake in bioethics is not just theoretical questions for the lab, but matters that affect the lives of millions of human lives and humanity as a whole. Discoveries in genetics are wonderful. But the ethical dilemma resurfaces, which we commented on when discussing the Internet: how will we use these discoveries, to what ends, with what view of man?

In this new branch of learning, which we could classify as frontier or vanguard, you have the clash between different concepts of man and ethics. The Church, expert in humanity, has much to say and should indeed say it, since her view of man is enriched with the contribution of the higher light of revelation. Our concern, therefore, like that of other Church institutions, is to make the Church's voice heard, and also to present, in the marketplace of bioethical ideas, the authorized voice of a group of experts seriously committed to scientific research and respect for human life from its conception to its natural end.

138. An obligatory question: after 9/11, will the world be the same?

I believe September 11, 2001, will be a date humanity will long remember. For everyone, and especially for the American people, it was a hard blow, but America has displayed praiseworthy maturity, and faith, in the face of these tragic events.

September 11 left a new sensation of vulnerability, previously unknown, in the consciousness of humanity. Nations and individuals are less trusting in their relationships. The psychological consequences for many, not just for those affected directly, are very deep.

Though I do try to keep abreast of world politics, I am not a political analyst and I make my simple reflection rather as a priest and Christian, in solidarity with all those who suffered unjustly because of the horrendous terrorist attacks, and praying to God insistently that he grant the world the priceless gift of peace, which is so threatened and so fragile. Pope John Paul II, whenever conflicts have menaced humanity during his pontificate, and more specifically when these particular attacks were carried out, has reminded the world that peace is a true gift from God; we have to persevere in praying for it, while at the same time putting into motion all the conditions humanly possible to make peace a reality. Rather than a political analysis, then, I prefer to keep praying and working in the measure of my possibilities, to eradicate the injustices that underlie many conflicts. I pray to God to give men hearts that will not feed on hatred or revenge, but sentiments and attitudes of forgiveness, acceptance, respect, and charity.

139. Some authors predict a now-close apocalyptic finale or a clash of civilizations. What do you think?

Personally I am cautious about making statements on the future, which is in God's hands; he is the Lord of history. We discussed how he leaves humans totally free to act, and in this sense the future depends on man, on us, on the world we want to build for tomorrow. When will this world end? God alone knows. We know, like St. Paul, that "the world as we know it is passing away" (1 Cor 7:31), that we ought to live in this world as travelers headed for eternity, and that Christians are called to be builders of peace, justice, and love. This task might seem like a fantasy, but nevertheless it isn't, inasmuch as each of us, in our particular field of action, can create true oases of justice and love.

What I do think is important, is that each one of us be constantly aware that the last days are near for him, that we live our lives on the edge of eternity and we cannot live as if the eternal realities didn't exist. I don't mean we should live in constant anxiety, but be vigilant, knowing that at any moment the Lord may come and that we should be ready for his coming.

As for a clash of civilizations, here again I will not venture a statement. It is true that there are significant differences between Christianity and Islam. But there are also common elements we should not ignore. I mean, for example, the authentic piety of many Muslims, or their sense of God's transcendence. I think we ought to find between the two religions the basis of dialogue and peaceful coexistence. But this will take time, and the will to avoid the clash of civilizations that several authors speak of. In this sense the position of the Holy See and specifically John Paul II seem to me to set the example: sincere search for dialogue, reciprocal knowledge, and mutual respect. This is the only way to avoid the kind of confrontation that has the potential to turn very dangerous for all of humanity.

140. There are those who blame religions for being an element of division and discord in the past and at present, the cause of many wars and bloody conflicts, and that it is now time to build a society and a culture without a religious element. What is your opinion?

I don't think you can generalize. It is true that religions have been and still are an excuse to fight and wage war. Europe is quite familiar with wars of religion, which bloodied the continent for so many years in centuries past. But here again, you have to keep in mind that the causes of those wars were not merely religious. There were many economic and political interests at stake. An authentically religious person is peaceful and respects others. That is why the devout people of the various religions are peacemakers.

It is true, on the other hand, that in some religions there are shoots of fundamentalism that promote the expansion and defense of their religion through violent means. But we are all aware that fundamentalism does not necessarily reflect religion as such; rather, it is a deformation of religion.

There is growing evidence that religion is on the rise in the world. Contrary to what Marxism-Leninism predicted — the death of religion, opiate of the masses — religion is returning. It brings an element of spirituality into a world dominated by economic and material interests. This proves, yet again, that there is an inherent need for God in man. The heart of modern humanity, too, is anxious. Groping, man seeks paths to give direction to life, and values to give meaning to everything he does. Communism with its utopia and its secular religion attempted to give people this meaning, but it failed utterly because it did not respect human nature, denying its freedom and natural religiosity.

Our current post-communist world is in search of itself. You cannot live on economic and material values alone. Thus, in the most diverse ways — from New Age to attraction to the occult or religions of Asian origin — man seeks to find an existential fulcrum. This is doubtless another wonderful opportunity for the new evangelization, although, on the other hand, the reigning confusion of ideas creates new problems.

By nature man is *homo religiosus*. When this dimension of man is ignored, his personal and family life, and society itself, gets thrown out of balance. Naturally, the different religions have to be examined critically. We acknowledge that they can possess valid elements that the Holy Spirit can use to carry out Christ's saving mission. But accepting and being open to the religious phenomenon in general does not lead us to say all religions are the same. Christ is the only Savior, the only Mediator between God and man, and outside him there is no salvation. The Vatican declaration *Dominus Iesus* was intended to remind all Christians of this fundamental truth of the Christian faith, without which it entirely loses its content.

141. Lately there have been signs in the international news that world peace is under threat. We are all aware that the Holy Father bears in his heart this deep concern, and he has asked Catholics to pray the rosary for this intention especially. Do you think that peace is possible, and under what conditions?

I share the Holy Father's concern for peace, and I believe all people of good will do, too. Peace, as we know, is the result of human effort, but it is even more so the fruit of prayer, because peace is a gift from God. That is why the Pope tells us insistently not to cease praying that the hearts of the leaders of nations will be governed by sentiments and resolutions for peace.

You ask me if peace is possible. A glance at the history of humanity from its remotest origins seems to suggest it isn't, for there have always been wars between nations and conflicts between individuals. As Christians, however, we have the grave obligation to strive for peace, the peace the angels announced at the Savior's birth in Bethlehem: "Glory to God in the highest heaven, and peace to men who enjoy his favor" (Luke 2:14). In recent centuries the Church has grown more acutely conscious of her mission as peacemaker in the world; and despite the accusations and malicious polemics she faces, there is no doubt that the Church is and has been a worldwide point of moral reference for those who fight in favor of peace.

However, as you point out, there are preconditions on which peace is based. The principal one I want to mention is justice: *opus iustitiae, pax*. Every effort towards creating a situation of justice among nations and individuals favors peace. We mustn't forget Paul VI's, and later John Paul II's, call to create the civilization of justice and love. It is impossible for real love not to want justice, nor can we call charity what is owed in justice. I believe we have the moral duty to teach the new generations to appreciate justice and peace, and seek them sincerely. This is a long-term but necessary endeavor, because mankind's future is at stake, given the very powerful tools of destruction now available.

Christ calls blessed "the peacemakers; they shall be called sons of God" (Matt 5:9). Sentiments and actions contrary to peace cannot be from God. It deeply impresses me to see the example of great men and women, who in the midst of serious conflicts have preferred the way of peace and negotiation to violence, even if they had to pay with their life for choosing this difficult path. For example, Yitzhak Rabin, who chose to follow this path for his people when many others urged the contrary. He always believed that they could come to an understanding with the Palestinians and in the end he decided that the best solution to the conflict was that of peace. That is why we honored him publicly at Anáhuac University in Mexico City and named a cultural center after him, dedicating it to "universal friendship between all peoples." There were and are many others like Rabin, Christians and non-Christians, who make a stand for the cause of peace. I believe we should present them as models to the new generations to gradually create a culture of peace and not of violence.

142. You just mentioned the initiatives of a university of Catholic inspiration to honor a member of the Jewish religion. Can we say that this openness is a sign of the times?

I believe so. The Lord is inspiring us to be more and more open to our Jewish brethren and see them as our elder brothers in the faith, as they are and as the Pope calls them. We must all overcome the old prejudices that plagued our mutual relations on both sides. John Paul II has made bold gestures, such as visiting the synagogue of Rome and praying before the Wailing Wall or at the "Memorial to the Martyrs and Heroes of the Holocaust" in Jerusalem. We must love this people, to which Christ, Mary, and the apostles belonged — the people who inherited the promises — removing from our hearts any feeling that does not come from the most sincere charity. By no means does this imply approval of the political decisions of a given state, but our hearts should be open to those who, by God's design, preceded us in our faith in the one God.

We, for example, have found a very positive welcome in various Jewish communities, especially the Jewish community of Mexico. Anáhuac University has made joint agreements with the Hebrew University of Jerusalem, the University of Tel Aviv, and Ben Gurion. The Anáhuac now offers a diploma in "Jews, Christians, and Muslims in the Mediterranean Crescent," in coordination with the Hebrew University of Jerusalem. We published several books on Jewish-Christian dialogue. Anáhuac University itself offers an annual scholarship for excellence to each of the schools in the Jewish community. The university has also established the

Shimon Peres Chair for Peace, in coordination with the University of Tel Aviv. In fact, Mr. Shimon Peres, Nobel Peace Prize winner in 1994, former Prime Minister, and former Foreign Minister for Israel, formally inaugurated his chair on January 11, 2003.

But this openness equally extends to members of other religions, especially the other great monotheistic religion, Islam. Though we haven't had any opportunities to take concrete steps with them, we are open to it, because I believe it is crucial to world peace that there be knowledge, dialogue, and mutual understanding between the members of religions, especially with the members of the Muslim religion.

143. Earlier you recalled a famous speech by Paul VI where he spoke of Satan's penetrating the very Church, but many people, including Catholics, don't believe in him any more. Do you think it's still necessary to believe in the devil and hell? They don't mean much to people anymore. Wouldn't it be better to avoid speaking about them? Do you believe the devil still influences today's world?

The core of the Christian faith is to accept that Jesus of Nazareth is the Son of God who took flesh in the Virgin Mary to save us. At the end of his gospel, St. John declares that he wrote it "that you may believe that Jesus is the Christ, the Son of God, and that believing this you may have life through his name" (John 20:31). All the other dogmas in the Creed derive from this nucleus of faith. The Good News, therefore, is essentially to preach Christ, who reveals to us the Father's love in the Holy Spirit. But around this basic truth there are others, revealed by God and taught by the Church's tradition, such as the existence of the devil. The recent *Catechism of the Catholic Church* reminds us that the devil was originally a good angel, created by God, who later rebelled against him and committed an irrevocable sin. Christ calls him "a murderer from the start" (John 8:44) because from the very beginning he tried, and keeps trying, to bring about man's spiritual ruin. Scripture clearly states, "It was to undo all that the devil has done that the Son of God appeared" (1 John 3:8).

Catholic doctrine tells us that the devil's power is subject to God's. Although as a pure spirit he is a powerful creature, he cannot stop the advance of God's Kingdom, though he can create obstacles. He can cause grave harm and attack our human spirit and even our bodies, but his action is controlled by God's providence, which makes all things turn out for the good of those who love God (Catechism, n. 395).

The Church believes that the devil exists as a personal being. He is not a myth used to explain evil and its action in the world. Yet we have to avoid resorting to diabolical action to explain every kind of event, because man's freedom collaborates as one of the causes of moral evil and sin in our world, although you can't deny a certain indirect influence by the devil.

Christians fight the devil by praying and uniting themselves to God, and by receiving the sacraments. The believer knows that the devil's power is limited and that anyone united to God by grace has nothing to fear. On the contrary, as we see in the gospel itself, it is the devil who fears the outbreak of the Kingdom of heaven that happens when Christ comes, and when men decide to imitate him by living holy lives.

As for hell, the Church, which transmits revealed truth to us, believes that it exists and is eternal (Catechism, n. 1035). Its principal suffering consists in being separated forever from God, in whom man finds the complete happiness for which God created him. Perhaps in the past certain preachers resorted to the quick and easy theme of hell to make an impression on their listeners. But perhaps we have gone now to the other extreme: utterly ignoring this truth. The gospel message is mainly centered on the revelation of God's love. But this same message tells us that it is possible culpably to reject this love, to refuse to accept it freely and voluntarily.

The Church didn't invent the truths about the devil and hell to scare people and chain their consciences. Rather, they are a call to act responsibly, a summons to conversion, to want to keep always lit the lamp of our love for God, which can go out. And therefore we should always live with an attitude of loving watchfulness so as to defend ourselves from the Evil One and in this way keep our love for God from going out completely and even turning into hatred of him, as happens in hell.

144. Someone said that "beauty will save the world." Recently this idea was repeated in the annual Encounter at Rimini (2002). The message to this encounter written by Cardinal Angelo Sodano on behalf of the Holy Father affirms that "beauty has a unique pedagogical ability to draw us effectively into the knowledge of the truth. Ultimately, it leads to Christ, who is the Truth." Why are these topics mentioned so little in the Church? Aren't they more attractive to the new generations than hell and the devil?

As I said before, the gospel's central message couldn't be more positive: It is the revelation of God, who is Love and Mercy. We heard this message again during John Paul II's recent trip to Poland, all of it focused on this theme. But the Church, in preaching the gospel, the Good News, is obliged to propose it whole and entire, just as Christ preached it. The reason is very simple. The Church, following Christ's preaching, offers the world the true Love, not a surrogate or cheap love. Authentic love, which a well-known Protestant theologian [Dietrich Bonhöffer] calls the "costly grace," entails demands that are hard for our human nature. We shouldn't forget that original sin left terrible consequences in man and in the world. The truth of the gospel is not a theoretical truth that fails to commit your life. It is a vital, saving, transforming truth. Thus, Christian doctrine, like human experience itself, is one coin but has two sides to it. It has the positive, truly beautiful side of the gospel, with the feelings of goodness that it entails, and also a side we could call ascetic, demanding, the part that authenticates the true love the Church proposes.

While it's true, as we have said, that the faith tells us that evil, sin, and hell really exist, above all it wants to open our eyes to the wide horizons of beauty, truth, goodness, and love. I believe we have to give young people and adults today the whole gospel, with both its sides; the "bare" gospel, as St. Francis of Assisi put it. It is therefore necessary, very necessary indeed, to teach young people to contemplate the beauty of created things and, through them, come to know their Creator. The youth of every era, but especially our own, are very receptive to these values, perhaps because they seek in them a refuge from our banal, commercialized society. True beauty is far more than mere bodily or physical beauty, though it doesn't exclude it. It is the beauty of a holy soul, in which the Holy Spirit dwells. The beauty of the Christian virtues, of self-donation to others, of a conscience at peace with itself.

On the other hand, we can't hide from young people the other part of life itself and of Christian life: struggle, effort, challenges, personal inclination toward evil. It is the authentic Christ who fascinates and attracts, with his personality that combines seemingly contradictory facets — neither a "candied" Christ nor a Christ who is no more than a judge. The ideal of Christian life is to come to know Christ, who is the Truth, but this knowledge has to be able to integrate, on the higher plane of faith, the gospel paradoxes.

145. Do you think that what people have begun to call the "John Paul II generation" will have a role to play in humanity's future?

It's interesting that "the John Paul II generation" is a name the young people gave themselves. They're the ones who began participating in the first World Youth Days in Rome in 1985, and were between twenty and thirty years old then, and now are between thirty-five and forty-five. They are adults now, but the unforgettable experiences of the World Youth Days with all the graces and personal experiences implied in discovering the faith, the reality of the Church and the extraordinary personality of John Paul II have marked them forever.

During those encounters of youth and faith, they discovered a new face of Christianity. Perhaps for many of them the faith was synonymous with antiquity, churches empty of young people and full of adults who seemed to lack strong and genuine ideals and living a withered, somewhat comfortable Christianity, tailored to the requirements of the times. The encounter with Christ that John Paul II offered them — the fascinating Christ of the gospels, the Christ who could fill a lifetime with meaning, the Christ it was worth living for and dying for, the Christ who opened their eyes to the broad horizons of the Church and the wonderful adventure of working to extend his Kingdom in the world — changed the course of their lives once and for all. The people of "the John Paul II generation" are bishops, priests, men and women religious, contemplative monks and nuns, consecrated laypeople, committed laypeople, catechists, housewives, businessmen, workers, farmers, et cetera. What they have in common is a new understanding of what it means to be a Christian, a healthy pride in showing their faith, an awareness that they have a vocation and mission, a joy in suffering for their deepest convictions, a happiness in sharing the wealth of their Christian interior with others, the ability to live their faith in Christ free of complexes in an often hostile world that often subtly persecutes whatever is religious, specifically what is Christian.

Yes, I think this "generation" or now "generations" of John Paul II will play a determining role in the Church's future. I also believe that we can call them "the Vatican II generation." They are also fruit of this great Council that renewed the Church and that unfortunately, as we have already discussed, was misinterpreted by many in the ensuing years. But this council contained in seed form the elements of renewal necessary to rejuvenate the Church. With the undoubtedly charismatic figure of John Paul II, we have been able to see and feel the fruits. They can and will be much more abundant still. But this generation is out there, working and acting in the silence of everyday life, beautifying the face of the Church in many countries of the world with the holiness of their lives and the joy of their faith.

146. Do you think Christianity will go back into the catacombs?

Only God knows. He is the Lord of history. It will depend a lot from country to country. We can't really compare the situation of Christianity in countries like Saudi Arabia, for example, where public Christian worship is prohibited as contrary to Koranic law, interpreted strictly, or in China where there is still open persecution, with periods of greater or lesser openness to Catholicism, or the situation in Western Europe or in Latin America.

Without necessarily calling it "Catacomb Christianity," in my opinion the faith blossoms favorably in relatively small groups or communities where people know and appreciate each other for who they are and where they can freely express their faith. I see how much it helps Regnum Christi members to live their Christian faith when they know they can count on the prayer and moral — and if necessary, material — support of their team members. In a more and more anonymous society, people look for groups that personalize, and the same happens with the faith. That's why more and more Christians want to express their faith in associations where each person is recognized and accepted.

Parish communities are still as valuable as ever, but it is very important for them to create space where Christians can express their religious faith and their desire to share it with others. In this sense, parishes can learn a lot from movements, just as movements can learn from parishes the meaning of catholicity, how to welcome everyone who approaches them, avoiding the ghettos that some associations of the faithful can become, even with good intentions. We have always reminded Regnum Christi members to support their parishes in all they can, to go to Sunday Mass as a family at their parish, to help out in parish activities, to contribute the Regnum Christi spirituality as an enrichment itself to parish life, along with whatever other associations and movements there might be in the parish, and to develop parish-based apostolates. The Church is structured territorially, organized into dioceses and parishes, and we can't disregard this. At the same time, the Holy Spirit has raised up other movements throughout history, movements we could call "transversal," that beautify the Church, within already existing structures, with a great variety of charisms. There can be tensions and differences between the two. That is natural and human. To overcome them we should turn to dialogue, charity, and obedience to those who have pastoral responsibility in the Church.

Returning to the core of your question, it may well be that the Church will return to the catacombs in some countries or be actually living there already, as in China and in some Islamic countries. In the countries of the West, Christianity is becoming a minority in a secularized society and small groups of Christian life are once again forming, where the flame of faith is easier to fan and where charity and fraternal welcome, practiced in an atmosphere of prayer, help the members to strengthen their faith in Christ and live radically their commitment to him and his Church. I think the situations vary greatly from country to country and continent to continent, and in each place Christianity may evolve differently in unforeseeable ways, since the Holy Spirit's action is so powerful that it can turn what we thought arid steppes into fertile soil.

147. Earlier we addressed the divergence between "being" and "doing." Now I would like to do the same with "being" and

"having." Our world today fluctuates between these two poles, although it often seems to favor the latter. On the one hand, there is a deep desire for authenticity and a sincere quest for values. On the other, we have the unrestrained craving for a comfortable life, wealth, pleasure, and power. The conflict between being and having also takes place at an individual level in each person's conscience. Which of the two do you think will prosper in the world? Are we moving towards a world of values (being) or a world of mere craving for possession, pleasure, or power (having)?

The battle between being and having is as old as mankind itself. The temptation to look for fulfillment in things outside ourselves — possessions, pleasures, control over others — has been ongoing throughout the history of humanity. As you say, the same confrontation takes place in each person. Each person is faced with a series of decisions, determined by an earlier and more fundamental option, between being and having. Sooner or later everyone must face a question like this: What do I want in life, to "be" more or to "have" more; do I want to grow in my values, in wisdom and grace, or will I hoard up material goods, run frantically after pleasure, greater wealth, and a higher social position?

There can be moments in life when the showdown between being and having becomes dramatic. Such was the case of St. Thomas More. If he had followed the capricious commands of his king, he would have kept and even improved his position in the kingdom as chancellor and personal friend of the king. But his conscience obliged him to be faithful to it, his Catholic faith, and the Pope. As he weighed his difficult decision in one pan of the scales, he could see piling up all the reasons that pulled him towards a decision in favor of "having" — the visible, material things, those that brought fame, money, or ease. In the other lay the values of fidelity to God, his conscience, and his Catholic faith. The choice was strictly personal. He could have tilted the scale to one side or the other. The ultimate decision depended on his conscience. He chose to be true to his values, to "be" more, to be faithful, at the price of his life, at the price of losing all material things. But as he himself rightly admitted, there are times in life when you can lose everything, even your life, but what you must not lose are your reasons to live. He preferred losing his life over losing the reasons that gave his existence meaning.

In life, the decisions are not always as tragic as in St. Thomas More's case, but sooner or later the time must come to choose once and for all. Will the world lean towards being or having? I don't know. I think some will decide to have more, to heap up goods, wealth upon wealth, pleasures upon pleasures, more and more power and honors. But there will always be others who choose to "be" more, to be better, to be better parents, to be more affectionate towards their spouse and children, to be more kind and obliging to others, to be better brothers and sisters to their fellow human beings, more responsible about their role in society, more committed to their faith in Christ, more faithful to their consciences. It's in each person's hands to choose one or the other. The world will be what each of us does with our freedom. If we want a better world, we have to begin by being better ourselves. We mustn't wait for others to start. If a person counts more for what he is than what he has, then clearly the right decision is to "be" more. I think each of us should ask God for the grace to choose being over having. Only on this foundation can a truly human and Christian world be built.

148. What can we do so that, in these early years of the millennium, the lives of Christians will not be pinned down by "a life of mediocrity, marked by a minimalist ethic and a shallow religiosity" (Novo Millennio Ineunte, n. 31)?

The mediocrity of Christians has always been one of the great blemishes of Christianity throughout history. Tepidity and mediocrity are a constant threat to the human spirit. Sacred Scripture reproaches this attitude in the harshest of terms. The Lord commanded these words to be written to the Church in Laodicea: "I know all about you: how you are neither cold nor hot. I wish you were one or the other, but since you are neither, but only lukewarm, I will spit you out of my mouth" (Rev 3:15-16). God doesn't want hearts that half love him or love him indifferently. He created us for love and doesn't want love to degenerate into mediocrity. The gospel spurs our conscience on to greater perfection and greater love. On any of its pages we find words we can't be indifferent to, that prod our heart and pierce it like the double-edged sword described in the Letter to the Hebrews (Heb 4:11).

The Holy Father is on target when he warns Christians about the danger of mediocrity, ethics that settle for the indispensable minimum required to keep our consciences more or less at peace, and a shallow religiosity that makes us satisfied with certain rites or certain expressions of devotion but fails to transform our human hearts. The underlying temptation is to live a "bourgeois" ethics and religion that leave you free of complication, without any great distress to suffer or major decisions to make, not having to boldly cast in your lot with Christ and the gospel.

Today's society, so hedonistic and materialistic in so many ways, labels as "dreamers," "madmen," "bigots," and "fanatics" those who take the struggle against mediocrity seriously and are on fire for the cause of the gospel. But how can you live for the cause of Christ and his Church without passion? How can true love possibly not be passionate? I don't mean it should be blind or irrational, but when you truly love, you don't give just a part of yourself, you give yourself whole and entire to the person you love.

The Pope proposes to us the radical path of the gospel, belonging totally to God, loving him with all our hearts, not being mediocre, and overcoming our free and easy compromising with the world.

Love, as I mentioned, is the only way I can see to live this attitude and overcome mediocrity. When you love, you want the best for your beloved; you try to give the best of yourself. This can lead to large demands; it shakes us out of our indolence, sets us on our feet, on a constant journey, on a constant search for the best, most perfect, noblest, holiest things. This is the path of authentic love that helps us overcome minimalism and shallow religion, because true love, in both its horizontal and vertical dimensions, is always pointed towards the logic of the greatest, most perfect gift of self.

149. The Pope has repeatedly invited all Christians to participate in what he calls the "new evangelization," which isn't so much about preaching a new gospel as about presenting the gospel with new ardor and new methods. Do you think it possible to evangelize a world that seems to be drifting further and further away from Christ?

It's true that the world seems to be walking away from God in many aspects. But on the other hand, we witness its desperate search for the transcendent. You cannot stifle the thirst for the infinite that exists in the human heart. Money, sex, or technology cannot totally satisfy a spirit made to possess God. The famous phrase from St. Augustine, at the beginning of his *Confessions*, is forever valid: "You made us for yourself, Lord, and our hearts are restless until they rest in you."[9]

Going on sociological appearances, the program for the new evangelization seems doomed to failure, but in reality it is not so. This is because Christians don't go only by sociological indicators. Their guide is their faith in Jesus Christ. It didn't look very reassuring either to have to evangelize the world in the first century of our era when Christ told his disciples to go to the whole world and preach the gospel. But Christ didn't put his trust in human measures alone, but in the power of God. In this same trust John

[9]*Confessions*, 1, 1, 1: *PL*, 32, 660-661.

Christ Is My Life

Paul II throws down the gauntlet of the new evangelization, because the gospel is urgent for the world, which needs this saving message today more than ever. Those who believe in it look like madmen or fools in the world's eyes, and nonetheless they are true visionaries and prophets. I think the new evangelization, beyond the results it may achieve, is a necessity, a binding duty for all Christians. If the world is full of materialistic and consumeristic concerns, if it is obsessed with sex, pleasure, and power, it needs the gospel. The weeds can never be pulled up completely. They will grow alongside the wheat. Our duty is to sow wheat. If there are weeds, there they will remain. We have to fight so the wheat will grow, so that the world is not deprived of the seed of the gospel, so that anyone of goodwill who wants to hear the message can do so.

When the Pope invites us to tackle the great challenge of the new evangelization, he is very much aware of the obstacles that exist, especially in the West. However, when Christ sent out his apostles to evangelize the whole world, the situation was much worse, humanly speaking. On the other hand, the estrangement from Christ you refer to is very relative. It is true that a secularized mentality has deeply penetrated all of Western society, but it is also very true that the seeds of the gospel are still present and their fruits are evident. The Christian values that shaped Europe's soul are there, even now inspiring millions of people, shedding light on society and the political consciousness of many states. Today the young and less young continue to look for God in ways that could be called desperate, in some cases.

It is precisely because the world is in decline and dying for lack of Christ that we have to evangelize it. This is when we have to cry out like St. Paul, "Woe to me if I should not preach the gospel" (1 Cor 9:16). Every Christian should make St. Paul's cry his own. Announcing the gospel is not a privilege of priests; it is the task, the honor of all the baptized. It is not fanaticism or proselytism. In a society like ours, assaulted by all sorts of propaganda, especially commercial, but also ideological and political, why should the gospel proposal be singled out as "proselytizing"? We must not be afraid to proclaim the gospel in the new *Areopagus* of culture and the media. Some would be happy if the Church's voice were no longer heard in the squares, but the Church must speak; she has to preach Christ; she cannot be silenced because her mission is to be light of the world and salt of the earth.

Preaching the gospel has always entailed a grave risk. Today is no exception. To be an apostle means endangering your reputation and status, and even your life; it means leaving your comfort zone and not fearing to be labeled as crazy or a dreamer. This doesn't unsettle a true apostle. He knows he is running a risk, but he is sure of what he is reaping. As St. Paul said, "I know who it is that I have put my trust in" (2 Tim 1:12). An apostle's worry is to be faithful to Christ, faithful to his command to announce the gospel. Christ today is looking for apostles, workers for his vineyard, missionaries, volunteers for the gospel. We need lips to announce him and feet to reach the ends of the earth so that no one is left without hearing the Good News; hearts burning with the flame of love for Christ; souls in love and willing to give everything for him, even life itself; men and women of the spiritual stature of St. Paul, who make themselves all things to all people to save some for the cause of the gospel (see 1 Cor 9:22). When the world seems to walk away from Christ is when he walks toward it, and he will do so through the apostles of the new evangelization.

John Paul II's call to everyone to participate in the new evangelization also implies the renewal of the pastoral methods we have been using, to see if we can improve them in relation to the new circumstances. I believe that this renewal of pastoral methods is already afoot in the Church, but it is also true that much remains to be done. We have to realize that we can't confine ourselves to our sacristies or churches, waiting for the people to come.

We have to go and look for people where they are, casting aside any fear or timidity. Christ's "Be not afraid," so often recalled by the Pope, is applicable here as well. We must not be afraid to invent new ways of bringing the gospel to mankind that is craving for it. But this can only happen if we have apostles in whose hearts the love of Christ burns strong.

150. *Novo Millennio Ineunte* tells us to place all pastoral planning for the new millennium under the "primacy of grace." What does this expression mean on a practical level?

We all run the risk of being a little "Pelagian," believing that with our action, our work, or our ideas we can change the world, change people's hearts, and save people. John Paul II reminds us of a gospel maxim: "Cut off from me you can do nothing" (John 15:5). We can put together any number of pastoral plans, be always on the go, run initiatives that mobilize thousands or hundreds of thousands of people; but if God's grace is not at work in the hearts of people, and if we rely on our strength alone and not on God's, we are headed for failure. Without Christ's grace we can do nothing. Grace holds absolute primacy in the spiritual life.

This doesn't rule out the need for human cooperation. Man also has to do his part. God does nothing if a person resists his grace, but grace precedes whatever human work that is going to give results in terms of salvation.

This principle, emphasized by the Pope in *Novo Millennio Ineunte*, is easily forgotten in a society like ours, which trusts blindly in human endeavor. An apostle should never forget that God is always the one to take the first step, that his power and wisdom are infinite, and that man depends on him in every respect. When you look on it with faith, this principle is obvious. However, using human reason alone, disconnected from faith, it can be a scandal to those who trust more in their own strength than in the power of God. John Paul II, once again, wants to help us keep in mind what is truly essential in Christian life.

151. In the future, will the world still believe in love? Paraphrasing a famous book by Hans Urs von Balthazar, is love worthy of faith? Do you believe in love?

Love is not a forgotten theme. Man cannot forget it if he wants to find himself deeply. In *Redemptor Hominis*, the Pope wrote, "Man cannot live without love" (n. 10). But love is a gift, and as such a revelation. Man can hope for it, beg for it, ask for it, but he cannot obtain it on his own strength alone because love ultimately comes from God, and is actually one and the same with him, for he is Love.

Love is what defines man. If a person loves, he finds complete fulfillment. If he does not, he has absolutely failed. We could even say that heaven will be the possibility to develop without limit all man's capacities for love, while hell is the absolute and eternal resistance to love.

Since man was created to love, to give himself totally to the one he loves, love holds such an attraction for the human person. The crucial point is to find and live not just any kind of love, but authentic love. Many today would separate love and truth, but in reality they are inseparable. If you live in the truth, you must necessarily live in love. To build love independently of truth, therefore, is to live in falsehood and not to love. You cannot love when you voluntarily live a lie. In Christ we find both truth and love revealed. He is the gospel, the Good News for each one of us. To believe in Christ is to believe in love, in the Father's true love for each one of us.

Because I believe in Christ, and he is the revelation of love, I do indeed believe in love: in love revealed, in love's ability to save and redeem. I believe that love is worthy of faith. I believe in its power to save the world. But any true love is a crucified love, one that has to pass through the Cross to reach the splendor of the Resurrection. Love, at least in this world, includes pain. This is the part we find hard to accept. Oftentimes we seek a romanticized love where everything is nice, a love with no times of Calvary. The love Christ has revealed to us is the love that gives its life for those it loves: "A man can have no greater love than to lay down his life for his friends" (John 15:13). Yes, love — the crucified love of Christ — saves the world, and united to his love, ours.

152. "We are certainly not seduced by the naïve expectation that, faced with the great challenges of our time, we shall find some magic formula. No, we shall not be saved by a formula but by a Person, and the assurance which he gives us: *I am with you!*" (*Novo Millennio Ineunte*, n. 29). These words of the Pope inspire us to hope. But in a history so full of calamity, suffering, war, and injustice, how is it possible to perceive the "I am with you" that Christ assures us of?

The Church does not only propose a "doctrine," but a "Person" to believe in and to love: Jesus Christ. The atheist philosophers of the twentieth century came up with "magic formulas" to establish a new world. Each had his own formula, and they all failed because formulas can't save. Christ saves us, the Son of God, made man to save us from sin and death. To turn our eyes to Christ, the way, truth and life, at this juncture in history is what the Holy Father asks us to do and what the Church asks us to do. Return to Christ, our Redeemer, our friend, our brother. Rediscover Christ, this is the great challenge for Christians, for each one of us. Know him truly, follow him, love him. There is no other name under heaven by which we can be saved (Acts 4:2).

I am firmly convinced that the great evil of today's world is its ignorance of Christ; his teaching that is love, mercy, and for-giveness; his person, true God and true man. Many Christians do not know Christ. For many of them he is a distant and merely historical figure who fails to touch their lives and consciences. But when Christ enters the soul of a person who opens up to his love, when Christ becomes the center of a person's life, when in faith you experience his love, then life can never be the same: it has to be divided into a before-Christ and an after-Christ. Not only the history of mankind, but also the story of individual people is deeply affected by the wonderful fact that the Word became man, taking on a human nature.

To meet Christ is to meet the revelation of love. To meet Christ is to meet the radiance of beauty. To meet Christ is happiness. How right St. Francis of Assisi was when he walked the streets of his native city exclaiming in tears: "Love is not loved!" The world needs Christ. Only in him will it find what it seeks. This was the initial intuition of John Paul II's pontificate when he asked all people, and especially Christians, to "throw wide the doors of your hearts to Christ; open to him the vast fields of politics, economics, and culture. Do not be afraid." Fear of the great and grave threats of the future, fear of ourselves, fear of great failures, fear of death: only absolute trust in Christ's redeeming power can overcome them all.

He said "I will be with you always, until the end of the world," and he is faithful to his promise. He will not fail us. He is with us, with each one of us in the depths of our soul, in the Eucharist of our churches, in our streets and squares, in our great cities, in our slums, in the great belts of poverty and destitution in the Third World, in the most inhuman suffering, in the deepest loneliness, in every human situation, in the countenance of our brother, in the sacraments, in the words of the Pope and the bishops in communion with him, in the gospel, in all the truth, goodness, and beauty scattered among the weeds of falsehood and evil throughout this world. A world that is a vale of tears, yes, but also the theater of divine action where we can discover the eyes of God-with-us and feel his friendly hand that squeezes ours and invites us, as Jesus invited Peter: "Put out into deep water. Walk. Do not be afraid. I am with you."

Biographical Note

Interviewer Jesús Colina, born in Miranda de Ebro, Spain, in 1968, is the founder and director of ZENIT News Agency, now with editions in Spanish, French, English, German, and Portuguese. He is the Roman correspondent for the weekly supplement *"Alpha y Omega,"* distributed by the Spanish daily newspaper, *ABC*. He has worked in Rome since 1991 as a correspondent for a number of French, U.S., and Latin American publications. He and his wife, Gisele, have three children.

Index

The numbers in these index entries refer to question numbers in the book, not to page numbers.

Sophia Institute Press®

Sophia Institute® is a nonprofit institution that seeks to restore man's knowledge of eternal truth, including man's knowledge of his own nature, his relation to other persons, and his relation to God. Sophia Institute Press® serves this end in numerous ways: it publishes translations of foreign works to make them accessible to English-speaking readers; it brings out-of-print books back into print; and it publishes important new books that fulfill the ideals of Sophia Institute®. These books afford readers a rich source of the enduring wisdom of mankind.

Sophia Institute Press® makes these high-quality books available to the general public by using advanced technology and by soliciting donations to subsidize its general publishing costs. Your generosity can help Sophia Institute Press® to provide the public with editions of works containing the enduring wisdom of the ages. Please send your tax-deductible contribution to the address below.

For your free catalog, call:
Toll-free: 1-800-888-9344

Sophia Institute Press® • Box 5284 • Manchester, NH 03108
www.sophiainstitute.com

Sophia Institute® is a tax-exempt institution as defined by the Internal Revenue Code, Section 501(c)(3). Tax I.D. 22-2548708.